Other Popular Titles Available in Hardcover from Scarecrow Press

Smile When the Raindrops Fall: The Story of Charley Chase by Brian Anthony and Andy Edmonds-Carruth.

The White Brothers: Jack, Jules, and Sam White interviewed by David N. Bruskin.

Company of Heroes: My Life as an Actor in the John Ford Stock Company by Harry Carey, Jr.

Wife of the Life of the Party by Lita Grey Chaplin, with Jeffrey Vance.

Once Upon a Time: The Films of Sergio Leone by Robert C. Cumbow.

Featured Player: An Oral Autobiography of Mae Clarke edited by James Curtis.

Planks of Reason: Essays on the Horror Film edited by Barry Keith Grant.

Charlie Chaplin: Intimate Close-Ups by Georgia Hale, edited by Heather Kiernan.

The Films of Oliver Stone edited by Don Kunz.

Written Out of Television: The Encyclopedia of Cast Changes and Character Replacements, 1945-1994 by Steven Lance.

A History of Horrors: The Rise and Fall of the House of Hammer by Denis Meikle.

Charles Dickens on the Screen by Michael Pointer.

That's Enough Folks: Black Images in Animated Cartoons, 1900-1960 by Henry T. Sampson.

Memoirs of a Professional Cad by George Sanders, with Tony Thomas.

Handbook of Old-Time Radio: A Comprehensive Guide to Golden Age Radio Listening and Collecting by Jon D. Schwartz and Robert C. Reinehr.

The Films of Mack Sennett, compiled by Warren M. Sherk.

The New Historical Dictionary of the American Film Industry by Anthony Slide.

The Silent Feminists: America's First Women Directors by Anthony Slide.

Dance on Camera: A Guide to Dance Films and Videos edited by Louise Spain.

September Song: An Intimate Biograph
Weld.

Larry Parks pantomimes to "My Mammy"
in The Jolson Story.

Blackface to Blacklist

Al Jolson, Larry Parks, and "The Jolson Story"

Doug McClelland

The Scarecrow Press, Inc.
Lanham, Maryland, and London
1998

for Sarah Alpern

SCARECROW PRESS, INC.

Published in the United States of America
by Scarecrow Press, Inc.
4720 Boston Way
Lanham, Maryland 20706

4 Pleydell Gardens, Folkestone
Kent CT20 2DN, England

First paperback printing 1998

British Library Cataloguing in Publication Information Available

The hardback edition of this book was previously catalogued by the Library of Congress as follows:

McClelland, Doug.
Blackface to blacklist.
Bibliography: p.
"Film credits": p.
1. Jolson story. 2. Jolson, Al, d. 1950. 3. Parks, Larry, 1914-1975. 4. Entertainers--United States--Biography. I. Title.
PN1997.J5583M33 1987 791.43'72 86-29797

ISBN 0-8108-3530-4 (pbk: alk. paper)

™ The paper used in this publication meets the minimum requirements of American National Standard for Information Sciences—Permanence of Paper for Printed Library Materials, ANSI Z39.48–1984.
Manufactured in the United States of America.

▪ CONTENTS ▪

Preface v

1. "The Jolson Story": A Close-Up 1
2. "Jolson Sings Again": A Close-Up 17
3. "Let's Get It Moving!" 30
4. Encore 83
5. Critics' Choice 93
6. The Parks Story 101
7. Jolson's Movie Wives 127
8. The Jolson "Characters" 145
9. Asa Loves Ann 158
10. There She Is, Miss Stoned America 165
11. Green and Levin: The Quiet Men 171
12. Writers to the Left and Right 180
13. Looking for a Bluebird and List'ning for His Song 195
14. The Invisible Stars 217
15. Larry and Jolie Were Not Sweethearts 229
16. Accuracy, Smacuracy! 241
17. Such a Tsimmes! 253
18. Jolson As Jolson At Last 264

Epilogue 271

Film Credits 277

Bibliography 279

About the Author 284

▪ PREFACE ▪

Just about everything a motion picture could have against it, *The Jolson Story* had.

It depicted the life of the self-absorbed Al Jolson, another generation's lusty-voiced premier entertainer who, if not exactly washed up, was proving no competition for Bing Crosby and Frank Sinatra, the reigning crooners of euphoric, post-war 1946. The songs used in the film were *old* old. The producer was a man who had never produced a movie before. The director was past his prime. The cameraman had never photographed a color film before. There were no big-name stars (when the Hollywood star system was at its peak). On top of all this, it was a musical in which the four music-making principals did not do their own singing, and, furthermore, were sometimes doubled in the dancing department as well.

Moreover, there was much competition at the movies in 1946, which has been called the screen's last golden year. "Every night," said *Variety*, "was Saturday night."

Among the films moviegoers saw that year:

Anna and the King of Siam, *The Best Years of Our Lives*, *The Big Sleep*, *The Blue Dahlia*, *Blue Skies*, *Brief Encounter*, *Caesar and Cleopatra*, *Canyon Passage*, *Centennial Summer*, *Cluny Brown*, *The Dark Corner*, *The Dark Mirror*, *Deadline at Dawn*, *Devotion*, *Dragonwyck*, *Dressed to Kill*, *Duel in the Sun*, *Easy to Wed*, *Gilda*, *The Green Years*, *Guest in the House*, *The Harvey Girls*, *Henry V*, *Humoresque*, *It's a Wonderful Life*, *The Kid from Brooklyn*, *The Killers*, *Lady in the Lake* and *Love Laughs at Andy Hardy*.

Also, *Margie*, *Monsieur Beaucaire*, *My Darling Clementine*, *My Reputation*, *Night and Day*, *Night in Paradise*, *Notorious*,

Of Human Bondage, The Postman Always Rings Twice, The Razor's Edge, Road to Utopia, Saratoga Trunk, Scarlet Street, The Searching Wind, Sentimental Journey, The Seventh Veil, Sister Kenny, Smoky, Song of the South, The Spiral Staircase, A Stolen Life, The Strange Love of Martha Ivers, The Stranger, Three Little Girls in Blue, Three Strangers, Till the Clouds Roll By, The Time, the Place and the Girl, To Each His Own, Tomorrow Is Forever, Undercurrent, The Verdict, The Yearling, and Ziegfeld Follies.

The Jolson Story still created a sensation, entrancing not only the oldsters but, it sometimes seemed, particularly the youngsters, and brought the legendary Jolson, then somewhere in his sixties, one of the great comebacks in show business history. The film became Columbia Pictures' all-time money-making attraction up to that date--according to trade reports, only three prior films had grossed more: The Birth of a Nation (1915), Gone with the Wind (1939) and This is the Army (1943). One theater manager, whose neighborhood movie house in Staten Island, New York, was practically deserted every evening in the 1960s, recalled then that when he played The Jolson Story twenty years before he had to stand on a chair in the lobby to direct the hordes of customers in and out for the whole week. He said the film set an attendance record at his theater that was never broken.

It was equally popular overseas, particularly in England. Lancashire's Leslie Halliwell, author of The Filmgoer's Companion series, discussed the phenomenon in his recent memoir, Seats in All Parts, about a youth spent in movie palaces escaping dreary industrial surroundings. He wrote:

> I adored The Jolson Story. I had not been expecting too much.... But I pottered along to the Rialto and slipped into my seat about twenty minutes from the end of the first house, just as Larry Parks and Evelyn Keyes were singing and dancing "Around a Quarter of Nine." I immediately liked the low-key style, the discreet sentiment, and the off-beat ending, and by the time I had seen it through again, and listened to Jolson's voice singing thirty-odd songs, it was already among my favorite films despite the show business clichés.... I was not alone: word-of-mouth made it an enormous hit, and it was held over for a second week, during which of course

I went again.... Over the next couple of years I saw it six or seven more times.... And in every case I had to queue to get in.

Al Jolson himself handed out buttons that asked, "How many times have you seen The Jolson Story?" The critics liked it but the public could not seem to get enough of it.

At dances, parties and park concerts ... in school talent shows and movie theater aisles ... on streetcorners in front of malt shops--wherever young people congregated, teenagers got down on one knee, Jolson style, to mimic the venerable entertainer's "soul-stirring adenoidal tremolo,"[1] his "innate rabbinical wail,"[2] and sing "My Mammy" or "Rock-a-Bye Your Baby with a Dixie Melody" or "Swanee" or "April Showers." I know, because, just entering my teens when the film came out, I had a scraped right knee myself (until, a while later, I saw Ronald Colman portray Othello in A Double Life and converted to upright Shakespeare).

For all of these reasons, plus the simple fact that I loved--love--the movie, I have written this book centering on the tempestuous making of The Jolson Story plus its entertaining if less startling sequel, Jolson Sings Again. The two films brought great success to most of those involved in their production, but tragedy was waiting in the wings.

• • •

The fact that The Jolson Story has little reputation among contemporary film enthusiasts is an injustice. It is also a mystery to many.

Perhaps it's the times: today, there is not the nostalgia for Jolson's era that existed when the film was released, both for those who still remembered it and those who were discovering it. In addition, leads Larry Parks and Evelyn Keyes never attained the generations-spanning superstardom of the Garbos, Gables, Davises, Tracys, Hepburns, Bogarts, Garlands, Crawfords, Astaires and Cagneys whose films are revived to this day. The sweet portrait of Jewish family life in The Jolson Story, something of a breakthrough in 1946, may look bland next to the more recent stinging characterizations in Goodbye, Columbus, Portnoy's Complaint, Annie Hall, and My Favorite Year. The blackface portions have clearly offended some raised consciousnesses as well.

Perhaps it's because the name of Al Jolson itself has faded a bit: many people in their thirties today were not even alive when he died in 1950. Still, young people of other generations were educated, or were interested enough, to know about the outstanding figures from previous epochs, in and out of show business. This does not seem to be true now, especially in the area of popular music, where culturally narrow striplings--despite increased resources unavailable to their forebears--don't want to know about anything predating Elvis Presley. A few years ago, when I first got the idea for this book, I discussed it with a twenty-five-year-old editor at a major book publishing company, who asked, "Al *who?*" End of discussion.

• • •

Preparing *Blackface to Blacklist*, I talked to dozens of people close to both *The Jolson Story* and *Jolson Sings Again*. Never in my professional or personal life have I encountered so many contradictory versions of an event or events. Jolson was charming; Jolson was an egomaniac ... Jolson was on the set of *The Jolson Story* all the time; Jolson was never on the set ... Jolson and the actor who portrayed him, Larry Parks, became inseparable; Jolson and Larry Parks were distant ... Evelyn Keyes was the only actress considered for the role of Jolson's "first" wife; dozens of actresses were considered for the role of Jolson's "first" wife ... *The Jolson Story* was expensive to make; *The Jolson Story* was inexpensive to make ... Producer Sidney Skolsky deserves all the credit for the success of *The Jolson Story*; producer Sidney Skolsky deserves little or no credit for the success of *The Jolson Story*.

"The palest ink is better than the most retentive memory," said a sage named S.G. Champion. He was so right.

With the kind cooperation of many, however, the true story behind the two Jolson stories eventually came into focus. Making this possible were interviews and correspondence with the following primary sources, herewith thanked warmly (though, sadly, in several cases posthumously): Dede Allen, Janet Blair, Lee Bowman, Clay Campbell, Dane Clark, Milton Delugg, Lucille and William Demarest, Jo-Carroll Dennison, George Dunning, Marshall A. Green, Barbara Hale, Darryl Hickman, H. Bruce ("Lucky") Humberstone, Helen Hunt, Fred Karger, Truck Krone, Henry Levin, Joseph H. Lewis, John Livadary,

Stephen Longstreet, Jean Louis, Ethel Martin, Miriam Nelson Meyers, Mary Ann Nyberg, Leo Pillot, Virginia Rees, Tamara Shayne, Mollie Silverman, Phil Silvers, Sidney Skolsky, Andrew Solt, Morris Stoloff, Joseph Walker, Marjorie Walker, and Rudy Wissler.

Also helping to make my long-time dream a reality, and to whom I am much obliged, are:

Sarah Alpern, The Bradley Beach (New Jersey) Public Library, Marguerite Chapman, John Cocchi, Kirk Crivello, Gary L. Doctor, Elinor Donahue, Charlie Earle, Eddie Brandt's Saturday Matinée (North Hollywood, California), Samuel A. Gill, Lester Glassner, Lee Graham, Jay Harnick, Herbert Hartig, Josephine Hutchinson, The International Al Jolson Society, Inc., Kenneth G. Lawrence's Movie Memorabilia Shop of Hollywood, Mark Kineavy, Miles Kreuger, Su Lesser of Columbia Pictures (Burbank, California), Beverly Linet, Otis R. Lowe, The Memory Shop (New York City), Jim Meyer, The Motion Picture Academy of Arts and Sciences: National Film Information Service (Beverly Hills, California), Movie Poster Service (Canton, Oklahoma), Movie Star News (New York City), The Newark (New Jersey) Public Library, The Original International Al Jolson Society, Eleanor O'Sullivan, Hildy Parks, Bea Smith, Jerry Stone, Dorothy L. Swerdlove and staff of The New York Public Library Performing Arts Research Center, Lou Valentino, and Gwen Verdon.

Special thanks for numerous generosities go to Betty Garrett, widow of the actor who gave Al Jolson new life in his film biographies, and to that extraordinary man himself, the embattled Larry Parks.

Columbia Pictures, of course, rates hearty thanks for making The Jolson Story and Jolson Sings Again in the first place.

Finally, there is the incalculable gratitude due the late Al Jolson, who lived up to a rousing on-stage promise that became a familar part of our language and lore. First heard from a makeshift stage in one of the temporary theaters that sprang up in San Francisco after the great 1906 earthquake, it was Jolson's trademark exultation for more than forty years. And it was no exaggeration. Jolson's signature cry was probably never more outrageously employed than one evening during a post-World War I veterans benefit at the Metropolitan Opera House. Enrico Caruso, opera's foremost tenor, had just sung "Vesti la giubba," inspiring bravos amid thunderous applause. Before the hubbub had a chance to subside, minstrel man-cum-Broadway star Al Jolson pranced onto the hollowed Met stage and exclaimed,

"You ain't heard nothin' yet!"

Doug McClelland
Spring, 1986

References

1. _Life_ magazine.
2. _The Village Voice_.

■ BLACKFACE TO BLACKLIST ■

■ "THE JOLSON STORY": A CLOSE-UP ■

> Joe Gillis: You used to be in silent pictures. You used to be big.
>
> Norma Desmond: I am big--it's the pictures that got small.
>
> From "Sunset Blvd."

The Jolson Story retains its melodic charm and brio today, but its impact on 1946 audiences--unless one was there--can only be imagined.

There had been film biographies of musical personalities before--fading legend Al Jolson even had supporting roles in a couple of them: Swanee River (1939), in which Don Ameche portrayed Stephen Foster; and Rhapsody in Blue (1945), introducing Robert Alda as George Gershwin. In vitality, popularity and general know-how, however, probably only Yankee Doodle Dandy (1942), starring James Cagney in his Academy Award-winning performance as George M. Cohan, could be compared to the Jolson celluloid saga at the time.

Everything just seemed to work. The songs, of course, were a major factor. To moviegoers just coming out of several war years, when most of the popular tunes of the day seemed to reflect saying so long to loved ones or passing the ammunition, the vintage Jolson numbers (written by a myriad of composers--some, like "Avalon," in collaboration with the entertainer himself) had a refreshing vigor and nostalgic appeal. Many of them, while hits in their time, had not been heard for years, and while their sentiments were sometimes sticky (when not downright maudlin) or simple-mindedly good-timey, their jaunty innocence and infectious melodies captivated audiences. It was an interesting phenomenon that young viewers, who perhaps had never heard many of the songs before, were in some ways the most exhilarated.

Then there was Larry Parks, the little-known young "B" movie actor catapulted to stardom in one of the choice roles (and performances) of the decade. Although required by the screenplay to be considerably more naïve, not to say nicer, than Jolson was reputed to be in actuality (and considerably less married), as well as minus a notable physical resemblance, Parks masterfully conveyed the compelling exuberance and charisma of the man. Parks was no singer, nor indeed was he said to have had much natural musical instinct at all, yet it would be almost impossible to think of anyone else in the part. Jolson imitations had been a glut on the market for years, and Parks' supple, uncanny job was not mere mimicry. Something magical (and perhaps not even explainable) happened when the person of Larry Parks and the uncredited soundtrack voice of Al Jolson got together--this, despite the fact that off-screen the two men were not especially compatible. On-screen, it was a better wedding than most of Jolson's marriages. Parks' emphatic strutting/prancing/mugging/eye-rolling/lip-curling coalesced into a stunning whole; his representation of Jolson, with its amazingly accurate synchronization of the songs, was probably more effective than Jolson himself had ever been on the screen.

Withal, many credited the film's astonishing success to Jolson's own dynamic voice. Sometimes harsh, and unmistakably the well-used instrument of an individual past youth, it was still vital, unique, and irresistible. It boomed from the freshly recorded soundtrack with such unbridled enthusiasm that audiences, conditioned by the more restrained crooning style of the day, were both startled and captivated. Those who had been around for a while opined that Al Jolson, although in his sixties, was singing better than ever, and those who saw The Jolson Story were not of a mind to dispute them.

Jolie was back!

• • •

The opening credits for The Jolson Story are revealed with the turning of an old-fashioned recording cylinder while Jolson's ebullient soundtrack voice performs "Let Me Sing and I'm Happy," indicating immediately that we will shortly be in that jubilant state of mind ourselves.

The Jolson Story: Vaudevillian Steve Martin (William Demarest) tells the audience to "sing out or ya get out!"

The story begins in Washington, D.C., around the turn of the century. At Kernan's burlesque theater, comic cellist Steve Martin (William Demarest) does his acrobatic turn to "On the Banks of the Wabash," then asks the audience to sing along. The response is tepid, so Steve announces, "You either sing out or ya get out!" The sweet young warbling of an adolescent lad (Scotty Beckett) rises above the others. At the finish, Steve asks his name; it's "Asa Yoelson." Suddenly remembering that he is supposed to be singing with his cantor father (Ludwig Donath) at the synagogue, Asa and girl-next-door Ann Murray (Ann Todd) bolt the theater.

Steve visits the Yoelsons to request that young Asa be allowed to join his act. "Asa will sing," his father advises, "but where his people have always sung." Asa wants to join Steve, running away to be with him. He is apprehended and taken to a Catholic home for boys where his parents arrive to find him singing "Ave Maria."

"Singing without his cap on," frowns Papa Yoelson.

To which the priest in charge (Ernest Cossart) responds, "It's not so much what's on the head as what's in the heart, is it, Cantor?"

The Jolson Story: Young Asa Yoelson (Scotty Beckett) sings at the synagogue with his father, Cantor Yoelson (Ludwig Donath).

Asa vows he'll keep running away unless he is permitted to work with Steve. He is next seen in a theater balcony singing "When You Were Sweet Sixteen," at last a part of Steve Martin's act.

[An unsung hero of this early portion of The Jolson Story is youthful actor-singer Rudy Wissler, who, uncredited, dubs the vocals for Scotty Beckett. His pure, mellifluous high baritone on the soundtrack does much to distinguish this part of the film.]

In quick succession, the balcony-riveted young "stooge" also renders "After the Ball" and "By the Light of the Silv'ry Moon," and is soon observed to assert his own personality more and more in the act. "I could sing much better on the stage," Asa implores his partner, "because then I could sing right to 'em instead of the backs of their heads and see their faces."

Meanwhile, postcards arrive regularly at the Yoelson home in Washington from the towns in which they troup. When Mama Yoelson (Tamara Shayne) reads that Asa is in "Dubookay" (Dubuque), Papa corrects her: "That's pronounced Dybbuk, Mama." After receiving a card from the state of Washington, Papa comments, "Walla Walla--this town they liked so much they named it twice!"

During a performance of "Goodbye My Bluebell," Asa's voice breaks: it is changing. He finishes the number whistling. "That's showmanship!" exclaims Steve proudly.

The next postcard the Yoelsons receive is signed, "Your loving son, Al Jolson." His mother cries, "Papa, Asa isn't Asa anymore!"

While his voice is also changing, Al only whistles in the act. Then Larry Parks and the singing voice of Al Jolson take over the role with an a cappella rendition of "When You Were Sweet Sixteen."

There follows the film's explanation of how Al Jolson began to perform in burnt cork. When featured blackface singer Tom Baron (Bill Goodwin) gets drunk and passes out backstage, Jolson blacks up, then sneaks on in his place. He sings "Ma Blushin' Rosie," in his nervousness forgetting the words at first but rallying to strut through the routine with many of the familiar Jolson mannerisms on display. (Even when "Parks" hums, it is Jolson's voice.) Impresario Lew Dockstader (John Alexander) offers to hire him for his minstrel show--without Steve. At first Jolson refuses, but finally he gives in. With the Dockstader men's singing group, he performs (in blackface) "I Want a Girl," after a while pleading in vain for a solo. When he also asks to use some of the new jazz music he has heard in New Orleans, the intractable Dockstader suggests he might be happier elsewhere; Jolson agrees.

He returns home, sees his now grown-up boyhood girlfriend, the pretty Ann (Jo-Carroll Dennison), and nearly chokes on his mother's spicy horseradish. He says he's been working with writers, trying to create songs out of the music he heard in New Orleans.

At Steve Martin's secret urging, Tom Baron phones Jolson to tell him that he's now managing the new Winter Garden Theater on Broadway where there is a spot in the show for Al. On opening night, the production runs long and his bosses want to cut Jolson's number. Before they can, he bounds on stage blacked up and tells the audience to "Settle back, you ain't heard nothin' yet!" Against the red Winter Garden curtain, he sings "My Mammy," while a visibly moved Steve Martin watches. He receives a standing ovation.

A trade paper calls him a "surprise smash." When Mama Yoelson reads this, she asks, "Asa smashed something?"

Jolson's star ascends, while Steve Martin frequently finds himself "at liberty." When Jolson lands a starring role on Broadway, he convinces Steve to be his manager. He opens in The Honeymoon Express and, once again, in front of that Winter Garden curtain, sings "I'm Sitting on Top of the World."

The Jolson Story: Al Jolson (Larry Parks), second from left in quartet, sings "I Want a Girl" with Lew Dockstader's Minstrels. Below: Jolson (Larry Parks), visiting with childhood sweetheart Ann Murray (Jo-Carroll Dennison), eats Mama's "very strong" horseradish.

In another overlong show, Jolson, this time as star, stops the action, asks the cast to sit down on stage and explains how the plot comes out. Then he orders the house lights turned up; "If I'm gonna sing to you, I'm gonna see you." With a huge shot of his blackened face superimposed over the audience's smiling countenances, Jolson rips into "You Made Me Love You," done entirely in close-up.

Jolson to Tom Baron: "I want to get close to the audience. I want a runway."

A runway is built, and in a long shot the real Al Jolson briefly replaces actor Larry Parks to sing, dance, and whistle "Swanee."

Jolson tours the United States. "Toot, Toot, Tootsie! (Goo'bye)" is heard on the soundtrack as Mama Yoelson flips through pages from her scrapbook on Jolson, and Steve entreats his workaholic charge to take some time off and enjoy life.

In the production number "The Spaniard Who Blighted My Life," Jolson (with a curl in his forehead) sings, clowns, mugs and camps through the comic piece--"I'll raise a bunion / On his Spanish onion." Afterwards, childhood sweetheart Ann Murray introduces her fiancé (Jimmy Lloyd) to a stunned Jolson. He quickly goes into another show.

At a Sunday concert for show people, a now grey-templed Jolson announces that he is leaving the next day for Hollywood and talking pictures. Sitting in the audience with producer Florenz Ziegfeld (Edward Kane) is young musical comedy performer Julie Benson (Evelyn Keyes), star of Ziegfeld's next production, Show Girl. A flirtatious Jolson asks what song she'd like to hear. She tells him "April Showers." He sits on the runway and sings directly to her, finishing the number on his feet with an "r"-rolling, dramatic flourish--"whenever Ape-par-rrril showers come a-lo-o-ong." Then he does "California, Here I Come," which, down on one knee in

---

The Jolson Story: Jolson (Larry Parks) sings "The Spaniard Who Blighted My Life." Below: Julie Benson (Evelyn Keyes), new Ziegfeld star, meets Jolson (Larry Parks) at a concert and requests "April Showers."

the Jolson manner,[1] Julie mimics at a party later. Jolson arrives as she is doing it, falling in love with her that same night.

They talk on his balcony till dawn, and she confides that what she really wants is a quiet family life. "It [show business] was in your blood when you were born, but I'm just a pretty good hoofer and I got a lucky break," she continues.

In Hollywood, Jolson stars in The Jazz Singer, the film that would start the talking pictures revolution. Back in New York, he attends Julie's opening in Show Girl during which, while dancing down a staircase during the "Liza" production number, she gets a dizzying attack of stage fright. Jolson stands up in the audience and belts out the song, giving her the courage to go on. They marry in Connecticut. When she visits his parents, Mama Yoelson serves the bride her hot horseradish which causes Julie's face to flush (thanks to a red spotlight) and her eyes to bulge out.

The whole family goes to the theater to see Jolson in The Jazz Singer. As the movie's Jolson sings "Rainbow 'Round My Shoulder" off camera, the audience's Jolson sings along. Behind him a man (Will Wright) leans over to complain, "That's Jolson singing, mister. He's doing all right."

The film is a hit, and Jolson--despite his initial difficulties with film techniques--returns to Hollywood for another. When her show closes in New York, Julie joins him there and Jolson convinces her to do films, too. She is shown rehearsing to the strains of "The Lullaby of Broadway" and "42nd Street," then sings and dances in a production number of "She's a Latin from Manhattan." She is a hit; there are more rehearsals, more films. Jolson is heard singing "Avalon" off-camera at a Hollywood party.

The Jolson Story: Julie (Evelyn Keyes) imitates Jolson (Larry Parks) singing "California, Here I Come" at his farewell party before leaving for Hollywood. Below: Papa (Ludwig Donath), Jolson (Larry Parks), Julie (Evelyn Keyes), Steve (William Demarest), Mama (Tamara Shayne), Dick Glenn (William Forrest), Tom Baron (Bill Goodwin) attend the première of The Jazz Singer.

Julie is shown starring in the films Gold Diggers and Flirtation Walk, clearly indicating that Julie Benson is actually meant to be Jolson's ex-wife, Ruby Keeler, who appeared in films with those titles but refused to allow her name to be used in The Jolson Story.[2] Then Jolson and Julie co-star in Go Into Your Dance, with Jolson in top hat singing "Around a Quarter of Nine" while dancing with a diaphanously gowned Julie.

Julie still yearns for the quiet life but for a while defers to her husband's compulsion to perform. Eventually, he tells her that if it will save their marriage, he'll give up show business. "Al, you can't make me a gift of your whole life," she answers. But they buy a house in the Southern California countryside and Jolson retires.

As a surprise for Jolson, his parents fly out to celebrate their wedding anniversary with their son. Another arrival is Tom Baron, who says he has a new show that would be right for the restless but still inactive Jolson. At the Yoelsons' wedding anniversary dinner on Jolson's patio, Papa hums the melody of "Anniversary Song"--"Remember that, Asa?" He coaxes the musically abstaining Jolson to sing with him, then Papa dances with Mama while a vivified Jolson completes the song.

The gathering then moves on to a nightclub where the master of ceremonies, calling Jolson "the greatest entertainer of them all," asks him to "give us a song." He does "Waiting for the Robert E. Lee" while Julie watches with a sad smile. When the audience cries "More! More!," Jolson calls the floor show's cast out to sit down and exclaims, "You ain't heard nothin' yet!" He sings "Rock-a-Bye Your Baby with a Dixie Melody."

At their table, Julie says, "You see, what he didn't have at home, Mama, was an audience--live faces." In the throes of song, Jolson's visage is superimposed over those of the transfixed spectators. Next, he does "April Showers." Julie quietly leaves, telling Steve Martin, "Look. When did you last see him as happy as that?" As he finishes the song, the camera slowly pulls up and away as "The End" flashes on the screen.

• • •

The Jolson Story: Jolson (Larry Parks) and Julie (Evelyn Keyes) perform "Around a Quarter of Nine" in Hollywood.

The Jolson Story: As Julie (Evelyn Keyes) prepares to walk out of his life, Jolson (Larry Parks) sings "Rock-a-Bye Your Baby with a Dixie Melody."

Under the caring scrutiny and guidance of Columbia Pictures President Harry Cohn, executive producer Sidney Buchman, producer Sidney Skolsky and director Alfred E. Green, The Jolson Story was filmed with exceptional flair. Even the occasional clichés seemed fresh. Small moments from the film loom large in the memory, too. Such as the imaginative way certain scenes changed: The young Jolson, pleading in a priest's office to be allowed to become a singer, makes a gesture that, as the scene dissolves, is duplicated by the gesture for the song that he is immediately seen performing in a theater balcony ... a train departs screen left taking the older Jolson away from friend Steve Martin while he cries "Steve! Steve!," the scene quickly segueing into Jolson and seven other blackface singers strutting on to a stage from that same screen left singing "I Want a Girl."

The many sets by Stephen Goosson and Walter Holscher are attractive, atmospheric, tasteful, and believable. In particular, the various theater production numbers (choreography credited to Jack Cole, production numbers directed by Joseph H. Lewis) actually look like they are taking place behind a proscenium arch--something frequently not true with other movie musicals in those still sky's-the-limit, Busby Berkeley-influenced days.

Joseph Walker's Technicolor photography has a rich, deep, almost golden cast whereby even the details and hues of paintings behind the players are sharp. It is especially flattering to willowy, reddish blonde Evelyn Keyes, who fairly glows. At home in drama or comedy, the talented actress never looked as lovely on the screen before or since, no small thanks, also, to the graceful outfits designed by Jean Louis. Performance-wise, by virtue of her personal charm, sensitivity and an occasional flash of wry humor she manages to make appealing a character who can't help coming off intrinsically selfish and unreasonable (as delineated in the screenplay, for which Stephen Longstreet receives on-screen credit). Perhaps the highlight of her appearance as the pseudonymous Ruby Keeler is her spirited party impression of Jolson singing "California, Here I Come," replete with Jolson lip curl. It is not Keyes' fault that her entrance into the story brings a slowing-down of the film's pace. The romantic problems of the now more sedentary, mature Jolson simply are not as conducive to lively footage as the earlier section detailing his rise to fame.

As Jolson's hometown girl, little is demanded of former Miss America Jo-Carroll Dennison, but her fresh-faced beauty likewise was never seen to better advantage in films than in The Jolson Story.

Playing Jolson's gentle, unworldly Jewish parents, Ludwig Donath and Tamara Shayne are delightful. They create warm human beings who are also amusing--without sacrificing dignity, thanks to the delicacy of their artistry. In those days, the movies were geared strictly for the majority and avoided portraying minority ethnicity, except occasionally to present hearty Irish cops and emotional Italians. Although Jewish family life had been dramatized on the screen before (notably in Jolson's own The Jazz Singer), rarely did the characters discuss their Jewishness and rarer still did they get to a synagogue. Today, the Jewish people of The Jolson Story may look like stereotypes to some, but in 1946 they were a real breakthrough for understanding and tolerance--and in a musical, yet.

Affable Bill Goodwin makes the most of his footage as a Jolson associate, while young but seasoned Scotty Beckett leaves probably the strongest impression of his career as the eager, adolescent Asa, expertly mouthing the lyrics to Rudy Wissler's crystalline vocals on the soundtrack. Child actor Beckett was growing so fast, however, that he was forced to play some of his scenes seated so as not to tower over his adult colleagues.

Stealing many scenes is the flinty veteran William Demarest, who, if he had not been up against the Jolson soundtrack and the Parks bravura, might have dominated the whole show. His brambly but devoted, wise old trouper (actually drawn from several real-life characters) is by turns funny and touching. It is a role of far more range than was his usual lot, and the brilliant Demarest missed no nuance, bringing more to it, even, than could have been expected by any of the creators.

Although there was some criticism of The Jolson Story as being highly fictionalized, and a few rabid Jolson buffs carped that too little attention was given the entertainer's comedy talents, the average filmgoer had scant excuse for complaint. The one and only Al Jolson singing at the top of his form, an inspired, synchronization-perfect Larry Parks, tuneful, nostalgic songs beautifully arranged and orchestrated --these were the things that really mattered in one of the great musical movies ever to come from the film capital.

"Look for it only in books, for it is no more than a dream remembered," read the foreword to the 1939 film classic Gone with the Wind, referring to the Old South. It could also be applied to the Old Hollywood that once produced joyous entertainments such as The Jolson Story. In a film era now dedicated to sleaze, violence, and juvenilia, that Hollywood is only a memory--but a shimmering one.

References

1. Jolson's mannerism of getting down on one knee came about early in his career when he knelt on stage to relieve the pain from an ingrown toenail. The response was so enthusiastic that he kept it in the act permanently.

2. Before he married nineteen-year-old Broadway dancer Ruby Keeler in 1928, Jolson had been wed to two show girls, Henrietta Keller (from 1907-1919) and Ethel Delmar (from 1922-1926), who are not depicted in The Jolson Story. Like Julie/ Ruby, both women had wanted to settle down to a quiet life. Some have claimed that Jolson and Keeler actually met at Texas Guinan's New York nighclub where Keeler was in the chorus. Keeler herself insists they were introduced in Los Angeles, when Jolson met friend Fanny Brice's train on which Keeler also had come West to work. In the thirties, Keeler became a Warner Bros. star in such musicals as 42nd Street, Gold Diggers of 1933, Footlight Parade, Dames, Flirtation Walk, Go Into Your Dance, and Ready, Willing and Able, the best of them with dance direction by Busby Berkeley. In 1935 she and Jolson adopted a son, Al, Jr. They were divorced in 1940, Keeler charging that he humiliated her in public and called her "stupid." Over the years, other reasons for their parting have been given: his possessiveness and jealousy of her most frequent leading man, Dick Powell; his own roving eye; and Keeler's large family, which Jolson said was "always under foot" in the couple's home. In 1941 Keeler married industrial builder John Lowe, who adopted Al, Jr. (renamed Peter). The Lowes had four natural children. In 1969, Lowe died. Keeler made a Broadway comeback in the 1971 musical revival, No, No, Nanette.

■ "JOLSON SINGS AGAIN": A CLOSE-UP ■

> Kings are like stars--they rise and set, they have the worship of the world, but no repose.
>
> Percy Bysshe Shelley

Like most sequels, Jolson Sings Again, which arrived three years after The Jolson Story, falls short of its progenitor. The followup is more sedate, conversational, and contemplative--perhaps as befits a focal character in, as Al Jolson is here, later life, especially when said character is portrayed as not in very good health. If Jolson Sings Again lacks the elements of surprise and razzle-dazzle showmanship of the earlier film, it is still a thoroughly respectable, entertaining close to the Jolson story. Had both Jolson pictures been joined to comprise one feature, the result would have run just about the length of Gone with the Wind. And even with that masterwork, nearly everyone agrees that the second half is inferior to the first.

Henry Levin, who had been working in films only a few years, directed Jolson Sings Again. His was even less potent a cinema signature than that of Alfred E. Green, the journeyman veteran at the helm of The Jolson Story. Many wondered why such important enterprises did not attract mightier contemporary directorial names. True, even though The Jolson Story dealt with one of the best-known figures of the twentieth century's early decades, Jolson's recent career calm had given "sleeper" status to the first film story. But after its sensational reception, top directors must have been open to directing the sequel. One can only assume that the almost pre-sold nature of Jolson Sings Again caused Harry Cohn to feel an expensive "name" director was unnecessary.

Considering the great success of the previous film, surprising, too, is the budget on Jolson Sings Again which looks, at best, half that of The Jolson Story, with virtually no new production numbers. Of course, by 1949, movie musicals in general had become more modest, or restrained, due to two factors: 1) a growing "sophistication" among moviegoers and especially critics who, now impressed by European "neo-realism" and socially significant themes, looked down on the spectacular Busby Berkeley-type production numbers as tasteless and fantastic Stone Age relics--they eventually would capitulate; and 2) a pervasive tightening of film studio pursestrings necessitated by increasing loss of audience to television.

Regardless, the frugality and lack of "musical" trappings in Jolson Sings Again are certainly extreme for a production of its import. Staged by Audrene Brier, most of the film's song numbers are set in Army camps or against plain stage curtains, with a heavy stress on close-ups evidently designed to minimize awareness of production paucity and to emphasize Larry Parks' dubbing virtuosity.

Fortunately, there are still plenty of Jolson vocals on the soundtrack (and a couple of times he even outdoes himself in depth of emotion), plus several reprises from the first film (frequently actual film clips from same). There is also a re-doing of the scene in which a gentile guest of Jolson's does a "choke take" on hot horseradish in the kosher kitchen of Mama Yoelson (Tamara Shayne); this time it's his white-haired manager, Steve Martin (William Demarest), who at this late date should have known what to expect. Once more we hear Jolson's cantor father, Papa Yoelson (Ludwig Donath), chanting in the synagogue. And once more a Jolson story begins with the credits vertically rolling on, as if on an old-fashioned recording cylinder. Only this time, instead of "with" billing they read "Starring" Larry Parks (and Barbara Hale), while instrumental strains of "Rock-a-Bye Your Baby with a Dixie Melody" resonate from the soundtrack.

Jolson Sings Again: Jolson (Larry Parks) embraces Mama (Tamara Shayne) when he learns Julie has left him, observed by Tom (Bill Goodwin), Papa (Ludwig Donath), Henry (Eric Wilton) and Steve (William Demarest). Below: Jolson (Larry Parks) sings "Is It True What They Say About Dixie?" on Broadway.

A written foreword brings viewers up to date on the plot. The first scene is comprised of final moments from The Jolson Story, with Jolson now seen completing the song "Rock-a-Bye Your Baby with a Dixie Melody" in the nightclub setting right after first wife Julie Benson (Evelyn Keyes),[1] realizing she will always place second to his love for show business, has walked out on him. Disillusioned, he notes that at least his audience has always been loyal to him. "She said all I ever wanted was a cheering mob. I'll say this about that cheering mob. That was love, brother. For twenty years nobody ever walked out on me," he boasts.

He rushes into a Broadway show called You Ain't Heard Nothin' Yet!, sings "Is It True What They Say About Dixie?" and "For Me and My Gal" in the hit. Now divorced from Julie, Jolson decides he's long overdue a fling. Giving up music ("The kick's gone"), he travels around the world pursuing fighters, horses, and women. At home his parents continue to fill their scrapbooks on him--Papa: "Monte Carlo. Before they take your money away, they make you dress up, yet." Meanwhile, a new crooner named Bing Crosby has beguiled the public. He is heard, prophetically, singing "Learn to Croon." "And the name Bing," scoffs Jolson's mother. "Go explain people."

As World War II begins, Mama Yoelson dies while her son is cruising in the Caribbean. (In real life, his mother died as he approached adolescence.) Jolson, after a rebuke from his father, becomes "one of the early ones" to entertain American troops overseas. Opening at an Aleutians Army base, he is introduced by Col. Ralph Bryant (Myron McCormick) as "the world's greatest entertainer" but tells his youthful audience, "I sing. If you don't believe me, write and ask your grandmothers." He socks across "Back in Your Own Back Yard." Col. Bryant, a Jolson fan from high school days in Duluth, Minnesota, is also a Hollywood producer and afterward advises the star, "If you're ever in Hollywood...."

Jolson Sings Again: After Mama dies, Jolson (Larry Parks) returns from a cruise to visit Papa (Ludwig Donath). Below: Entertaining troops in Italy, Jolson (Larry Parks) collapses from "a fever" while singing "I'm Just Wild About Harry."

Jolson entertains our forces in battle zones around the globe, singing "I'm Looking Over a Four-Leaf Clover," "When the Red Red Robin Comes Bob Bob Bobbin' Along," "Give My Regards to Broadway," "I'm Just Wild About Harry." On a swingy "Chinatown, My Chinatown," he is accompanied by accordionist Milton Delugg.

During a performance in a bombed-out Italian city, he collapses from "a fever" (malaria) and wakes up in a stateside hospital tended by attractive brunette nurse Ellen Clark (Barbara Hale). Weakly, he warbles a few bars of "Baby face, you've got the cutest little...." Ellen informs the doctor, "I'd say he was gonna be just fine."

Recuperating, he becomes captivated by the teasingly no-nonsense manner, Arkansas drawl and, of course, that pretty baby face of the young nurse who has never heard Al Jolson sing. Trying to get her patient to relax, she relates that back home the pigs never rush around, except maybe when they see a plane or a hawk. When he assents, she exclaims, "My, we'll soon be as smart as pigs!" Papa Yoelson promotes the blossoming relationship, explaining to Ellen, "The only thing--he never learned how to live." (These six words were also once recorded as rival Hollywood mogul Samuel Goldwyn's exact comment about Columbia's boss and life-long Jolson devotee Harry Cohn. Coincidentally?)

Ellen is transferred to an Arkansas Army hospital where Jolson, now entertaining injured servicemen around the country, confronts her with a rendition of "Baby Face." Although apprehensive about the difference in their ages, he is marriage-minded and Ellen encourages him: "I don't see what difference years make. I knew a couple once, same age. Whew--it was terrible."

He continues the hospital tour, but following a perform-

Jolson Sings Again: Jolson (Larry Parks) recovers with the help of nurse Ellen Clark (Barbara Hale), Papa (Ludwig Donath) and Steve (William Demarest), who quips "What gets me is how they tell a fever from his normal condition." Below: Papa (Ludwig Donath) tells Ellen (Barbara Hale) "A waltz is my specialty. Of course, mine is not exactly a cheek-to-cheek style."

ance of "After You're Gone," collapses again and has a "bad spot" removed from his lung. [In an interview once, Jolson called it "an abscess." Why has Hollywood always been so reluctant to come out and name diseases in question? Surely doing so could not be construed as free plugs! For instance, near the end of The King and I royal wife Terry Saunders told royal schoolteacher Deborah Kerr that king Yul Brynner was dying. When Kerr asked what was wrong with him, she replied--typically: "Who can say what it is that makes a man die?" In one of her television spoofs of old movies, Carol Burnett diagnosed one such perennially mysterious ailment as "the movie disease."]

Jolson and Ellen marry, moving, at her suggestion, into the California home he once shared with Julie.[2] "I just didn't want any ghosts around," she explains to her husband. "I wanted you to wrestle with 'em right here. So you knew where you stood about the past." Papa Yoelson joins them.

• • •

Although Jolson's lung has healed, he refuses to sing again, in actuality fearing that because the crooners have taken over no one will want him anymore. Unlike Julie, Ellen is willing to share him with show business and tries in vain to get him to perform at a Community Chest benefit. "All I know, it can't be good when the natural part of a man is moldin' away," she remarks to Steve. One quiet evening at home, Jolson begins to sing along with the radio--"I Only Have Eyes for You" --and agrees to do the benefit.

Steve has to convince the benefit producer (Robert Emmett Keane) who thinks Jolson is washed up, to use him. He finally accedes, but Jolson does not even get billing. The evening is a long one; many people in the audience have left by the time Jolson, the last act, appears. "Hey, where is everybody?", he asks coming on stage. His song is "Sonny Boy," and among the quickly enthralled remaining spectators is old Aleutians colonel-fan-producer Ralph Bryant, now a civilian who tells his wife (Virginia Mullen), "His voice is better now than it ever was. Warmer, more heart." He mentions that "a certain newspaper columnist" recently brought him an idea for a movie about Jolson.

When Bryant asks the entertainer if he would be inter-

Jolson Sings Again: Helped by trick photography, Hollywood producer Ralph Bryant (Myron McCormick) introduces Jolson (Larry Parks) to the actor who will portray him in The Jolson Story, Larry Parks (himself).

ested in having a movie made about his life, Jolson muses that he would be too old to play himself--but, if there were to be a film, he would have to do the actual singing. However, he feels his voice is no longer up to recording all the songs anew for such a project. At the studio, he is convinced otherwise when the playback of his recording of "Toot, Toot, Tootsie! (Goo'bye)" elicits applause from the musicians and conductor Morris Stoloff, the music director of both Jolson films cast here as himself.

Later, cueing the sequel's most original, commented-upon sequence, Bryant and a rhythmically swaying Jolson look at the screen test of a young actor performing "Tootsie!" to Jolson's recording. The projection room lights go on; Jolson exclaims "Wonderful! Who was that?" and is introduced to "a young fellow named Larry Parks." Trick split-screen photography permits the grey actor Parks (as Jolson) to shake hands with the more youthful actor Parks. After all this, who could deny Larry Parks the role of Al Jolson in The Jolson Story?

Shortly, we see Jolson and Parks rehearsing "California, Here I Come" before a large mirror; then the filming of Parks singing, in blackface, "You Made Me Love You" while Jolson, rapt on the sidelines, can't help miming some of the motions. [Interestingly, perhaps because of consciousnesses raised by Hollywood's then-current vogue for films with intolerance themes, only this one short scene of Larry Parks/Al Jolson in blackface was filmed for Jolson Sings Again.]

At last we see the print of The Jolson Story on the way to its first preview in Santa Barbara. In the theater, the anxious, restive Jolson and Larry Parks nod to each other. The Jolson Story credits roll on again, and we hear the Jolson voice exhorting, "Let Me Sing and I'm Happy." The film's most curious sequence, especially for 1949, ensues. Suggesting (from all reports, erroneously) a personal problem that looks like material for a third film biography, Jolson, while his picture unreels, nervously repairs to the lobby. There he proceeds to get high on pills, presumably tranquilizers.

Numerous other musical excerpts from the earlier picture are then shown in the movie-within-the-movie: "Ma Blushin' Rosie," "My Mammy," "Swanee" (a quick runway long-shot of the real Al Jolson), "The Spaniard Who Blighted My Life," "California, Here I Come," "Around a Quarter of Nine" (a glimpse of Parks dancing with Evelyn Keyes, whose back is to the camera), "Anniversary Song," "Waiting for the Robert E. Lee" and the first film's concluding "April Showers." This fragmentary but exciting segment of old footage emphasizes a certain lack of vitality in the newer production's staging. (Some felt that the extensive Jolson Story footage used in Jolson Sings Again was meant not only to entertain but to advertise the planned forthcoming reissue of The Jolson Story.)

The film biography is a smash, bringing Al Jolson a whole new popularity and career. He is heard singing "Pretty Baby" on the radio, then seen at a broadcast selling "Carolina in the Morning" over the shrieks of bobbysoxers. A Community Chest benefit performance (this time Jolson is billed) of "Rock-a-Bye Your Baby with a Dixie Melody" ends Jolson Sings Again, perhaps a shade too benignly.

Larry Parks is still outstanding as Jolson. More sober, less animated than in the first film, he is merely following the requirements of the script--and his character's marching years. Most of the musical numbers are in close-up, and his dubbing to the Jolson recordings remains, with The Jolson Story, probably the screen's supreme example of that peculiar art. The Jolson mannerisms are still clearly evidenced, yet somehow more subtly conveyed by Parks the second time around, allowing the actor to dramatize some of the more mellow songs with a sensitivity even deeper, perhaps, than in the first film. "Back in Your Own Back Yard," for instance, co-authored by Jolson but scarcely one of Tin Pan Alley's more heart-rending ditties ("The bird with feathers of blue / Is waiting for you," etc.), gets its most moving interpretation ever by an expressive Parks in tandem with a throbbingly full-voiced, unhurried Jolson during a war front tour. Jolson's thrilling, once-in-a-lifetime instrument--"warmer, more heart," to use Myron McCormick's/Ralph Bryant's accurate assessment in this final story--was, of course, the raison d'être for both pictures.

Barbara Hale has one of her best screen roles as the quietly influential second (actually No. 4) Mrs. Jolson, a somewhat more reasonable and understanding helpmate than the "No. 1" portrayed in The Jolson Story. Raven-tressed, with dark blue eyes and a peaches-and-cream complexion under vivid Technicolor scrutiny, she further parlays a charmingly bogus Arkansas drawl and a pertly smiling, down-home common sense attitude into a winning contribution. Her blithe presence does much to buoy both the mood and the characters of Jolson Sings Again. A potentially serious nightclub scene, for example, is brightened when Hale's Ellen Clark, asked by the enchanted Papa Yoelson to dance, has to reach under the table first: "Just gettin' back into my shoes."

Never satisfactorily explained, however, was why the powers behind Jolson Sings Again chose not to use the real name of Jolson's wife, Erle Galbraith. Ruby Keeler refused permission for her name to be used in The Jolson Story, but she was divorced from Jolson. Surely his current wife, Erle, couldn't have objected to having her name used in the story of her romance and ongoing marriage.

Ludwig Donath appealingly continues his endearing, surprisingly liberal Orthodox Papa Yoelson who can also be witty. After Papa and the Jolson butler (Eric Wilton) trade compliments on how well they are each looking, Papa remarks, "What a comfort we are to each other." Tamara Shayne, as the loyal, loving Mama, disappears too early from the proceedings, however. So does Bill Goodwin, another holdover as Jolson crony-producer Tom Baron, and less explicitly dispatched than Shayne. William Demarest pops up throughout as Jolson's long-time mentor-manager, but, like Shayne and Goodwin, without the range of opportunities afforded him in The Jolson Story. Still, his gruffly concerned presence is always welcome.

In the only other role of consequence as the Hollywood producer, capable Myron McCormick is an unblushing composite of Columbia Studios President Harry Cohn, Sidney Buchman (born in Duluth, like McCormick's character, and credited with producing and writing Jolson Sings Again) and columnist Sidney Skolsky (who brought the original idea for The Jolson Story to Columbia and is credited as producer of that film but who is absent from the credits of Jolson Sings Again).

Jolson Sings Again is not up to the dynamic appeal of The Jolson Story. A propensity for static groupings on the parts of director Henry Levin and/or producer-scenarist Sidney Buchman takes its toll. So, while one may already have experienced three years earlier what Al Jolson promised with his trademark cry of "You ain't heard nothin' yet!," the second and thus far final Jolson film story is still vastly superior to most sequels.

The melody lingers on very pleasantly in Jolson Sings Again.

References

1. In Jolson Sings Again, Evelyn Keyes appears only in a newspaper portrait accompanying the story of "Julie Benson's" divorce from Al Jolson and, later, from the back in a brief production number excerpt from The Jolson Story. Julie Benson's voice is ostensibly heard on the soundtrack at one point, but it is not Keyes. More likely, it is starlet Randy Stuart who was doing similar anonymous voice-only work at the time in such films as A Letter to Three Wives.

2. Wife "Ellen Clark" was really Erle Galbraith, a pretty X-ray technician Jolson met following a World War II hospital performance in Hot Springs, Arkansas. They married in 1945, when Jolson was sixtyish and Erle twenty-two. As with just about everything concerning Al Jolson, there are (at least) two versions of the story of their meeting. One is that she asked him for an autograph. The other is that she didn't: this one has Jolson spying her near a crowd of fans and, when he asked her if she wanted his autograph, being told no. In Hollywood, he sent for her and got her a few bits in Columbia films, including A Thousand and One Nights (1945), featuring Evelyn Keyes and directed by Alfred E. Green, both of whom would soon be at work on The Jolson Story. Galbraith's heavy drawl was said to have foredoomed a movie career. Similar accents have proved no handicap to many top actresses, so it is probable that the egotistical Jolson just did not want another competitive wife. Ruby Keeler once said, "He was a possessive man [who also] wanted me with him when he was working somewhere." Fourteen months after Jolson's death, Erle married stage and screen writer-producer Norman Krasna, who died in 1984.

▪ "LET'S GET IT MOVING!" ▪

> Passion is like a mountain stream; it admits of no impediment; it cannot go backward; it must go forward.
>
> C.N. Bovee

Actually, Al Jolson got the brainstorm first.

By the early months of World War II, Jolson was pretty much--as a song from palmier days phrased it--"just a flower from an old bouquet." He got an occasional radio spot, but he was showing his age, had not had a starring film in years and his one recent Broadway appearance, 1940's Hold on to Your Hats, closed prematurely when he contracted pneumonia. The only group that now really seemed to want Al Jolson was the captive audience known as our overseas troops, whom Jolson regularly flew out to entertain. Fortunately, he was, as he liked to brag, a wealthy man.

During the spring and summer of '42 he was in New York for meetings with CBS about a radio show scheduled for the fall that would star him. While there, he paid $25,000 for the first ticket to the May war bond première at the Hollywood Theater of Warner Brothers' Yankee Doodle Dandy, the biography of song-and-dance man George M. Cohan, with James Cagney in a dynamic tour-de-force characterization.

"The picture left me on the ropes!," Jolson enthused later. Here was Cohan, an Irish contemporary of his, being glorified in a flag-waving, well-timed film that was sure to win star Cagney an Academy Award nomination and become a classic. A half-hour into the film, Jolson thought to himself, "My story would be just as interesting, just as tuneful, just as American as this. I have a loving family, too." He thought again. "Scratch that last part." For one thing, he probably remembered that, to avoid embarrassment to his name, he had made a verbal deal in 1934 to pay his meagerly talented brother Harry $150 a week to stay out of show business and that after a few years when the money was no longer sent, Harry sued him and lost.

"This is not material for Jolie's life story," he could be imagined musing. (Jolson often referred to himself in the third person, "as if he were a noted historical figure like George Washington," Maurice Zolotow once wrote.)

Then there were the three ex-wives, the estrangement from "Sonny Boy," the child he and Ruby Keeler had adopted, and the then unchic Jewish roots.[1] He finally brushed aside the idea of a Jolson film biography as "daffy" (a word he claimed to have coined years before) and put it out of his mind for the nonce.

Later that year, the same idea would occur to pint-sized (five feet four inches) columnist Sidney Skolsky. Known for his syndicated Hollywood "tintypes" in which he liked to ask interview subjects what they wore to bed (Marilyn Monroe supplied the definitive answer: Chanel No. 5), his tagline was always "But don't get me wrong--I love Hollywood."

Sammy Davis, Jr., claims to have been present when Skolsky got his inspiration. On the Mike Douglas TV show in 1977, Davis recalled:

> Early in my career I played on the same bill as Jolson. It was a benefit at the Shrine Auditorium in Hollywood, a huge place. I was a standby act, in case one of the biggies didn't show. Jack Benny had been on, so had Eddie Cantor. Everybody. Then Jolson came on. Immediately he got rid of the mike, and sent the forty-piece orchestra home, keeping only his pianist, Harry Akst. "Jolie's here," he said. "It's been a long show, so Jolie's only gonna sing a couple of tunes." He was on forty minutes--they wouldn't let him go. Sidney Skolsky, the columnist, was in the audience that night and got the idea for the picture about Jolson's life.

This is how Skolsky remembered it shortly before his

death at seventy-eight in 1983 from acute Parkinson's Disease:

> I was a Broadway columnist but became a Hollywood one when I moved there in 1933 with my wife and small daughter. The incessant sun immediately gave me an allergy and Louella Parsons called me a Communist (which she later retracted).
>
> Besides turning out my columns, I became a script reader at various studios, then assistant to producer Mark Hellinger at Warner Bros. By 1942 I'd decided I wanted to be a producer myself, and one night in bed after I'd been to a Community Chest benefit where Jolson had wowed 'em, I got the idea to do a movie about his life. He was always my favorite star, even though he'd once threatened to punch me in the nose because of a knock he mistakenly thought he'd read in my column. I guess I was spurred on by the fact that Warners was racking up record grosses with Yankee Doodle Dandy, starring James Cagney as George M. Cohan.
>
> When I asked studio chief Jack Warner if I could produce the Jolson movie there, he looked at me as if I'd gone crazy, exclaiming, "Jolson is an old has-been! Besides, we've already done the life of Al Jolson--in The Jazz Singer."

There was some truth to Warner's latter claim, too. In 1927, when Jolson's film of The Jazz Singer kicked off the talking picture revolution, the entertainer told an interviewer, "Is The Jazz Singer the story of my own life? Well, the feller that wrote it claims it was based on an interview I gave him in my dressing room years ago."

The "feller" was Samson Raphaelson, whose work had first appeared as a short story called The Day of Atonement. Later, he adapted it for the Broadway stage as The Jazz Singer, one of the 1925-26 season's great successes. George Jessel enjoyed a personal triumph in the lead, but when Warner Bros. decided to film it two years later, they selected his friend Al Jolson for the lead because Jolson, according to Jessel, put up $180,000 in cash to get the film off the ground. Refuting this, Jack L. Warner said it was Jessel's haggling over salary that cost him the starring role in the film. Whatever the truth, Jessel never got over missing the part that

Tamara Shayne and Ludwig Donath film make-up tests for The Jolson Story under director H. Bruce Humberstone, who soon left the production.

could have insured him show biz immortality, and although he and Jolson continued to socialize over the years Jessel never missed a chance to excoriate him to others.

The film of The Jazz Singer did indeed bear more than a passing resemblance to The Jolson Story--as it did, in fact, to the real-life stories of many Jewish entertainers of the day from orthodox families. The leading character, Jakie Rabinowitz (Jolson), began as an adolescent who preferred singing ragtime in saloons to singing in the synagogue, enraging his cantor father. Following a beating, the boy ran away from home and worked his way toward Broadway where, on opening night, he was needed at home to sing "Kol Nidre" as his father lay dying. More a "singie" than a "talkie," The Jazz Singer featured several Jolson vocals but only one real talking scene: when Jolson, after years away from home, returned to sing "Blue Skies" for his adoring mother and tease her about taking her to Coney Island.

[By 1986 at the Academy Awards ceremony in Hollywood, the line between the two films had become even more blurred--Debbie Reynolds referred to The Jazz Singer as "The Jazz Story."]

Jack Warner may also have remembered that aspects of Jolson's life were said to have been dramatized in Broadway Through a Keyhole (1933). This was one of the first releases of the new 20th Century Pictures formed by Joe Schenck and Darryl F. Zanuck, who had recently resigned as head of production at Warner Bros. where he supervised the making of The Jazz Singer. (The audible singing in The Jazz Singer was the idea of Sam Warner, who died the day before it opened, and the talking in the film was the suggestion of Zanuck.) Columnist Walter Winchell wrote the story of Keyhole which focused on the romantic triangle of a gangster (Paul Kelly), a singer (Constance Cummings) and a crooner (Russ Columbo). Many thought Winchell's inspiration had been the gossip that Jolson had taken Ruby Keeler away from a New York gangster known as Johnny ("Irish") Costello. In spite of Winchell's denials that the Jolson episode had been his source, that year at a prizefight the feisty Jolson punched Winchell. The scribe was compensated by a $10,000 bonus from Zanuck for the publicity he had helped the film to engender.

But Sidney Skolsky persevered with his idea for a movie about Jolson, continuing his proposal to Jack Warner:

> I explained to Warner my idea that Jolson would be played by a young actor modern audiences could identify with, but that Jolson's own voice would sing the songs on the soundtrack. Now Warner was *sure* I was nuts and fired me.
>
> I tried to sell the idea all over town, with no luck. Finally, one night while gathering column tidbits at my favorite hangout, Schwab's drugstore (which many stars frequented and where the Schwab brothers later gave me my own office), Harry Cohn rushed in to buy some condoms. I told him my idea for the Jolson movie, and he grunted, "I'll sleep on it." Four months later he phoned me.
>
> "Get your ass to the studio," he commanded. "We're doing the Jolson movie." I got an office there and began outlining the picture.
>
> At this point there was only one little problem: we hadn't contacted Jolson. I'd been afraid he'd bollix the project. When I finally told Cohn that Jolson didn't know yet, he cursed me out good.
>
> Eventually, Cohn's brother Jack, who managed Columbia's affairs in New York, told Jolson about my

idea; he was intrigued. On the train West, Jolson ran into Jack Warner, whose studio was preparing to film Rhapsody in Blue, the life of George Gershwin. Jack asked Jolson to play a cameo as himself in it, and Jolson--a major stockholder in Warner Bros.--said yes. Then he told Warner that Columbia wanted to film his own life story. Warner saw the opportunity to put one over on his old mogul adversary, Harry Cohn, and before they got off the train he had offered Jolson $250,000 for the picture to be done at Warners--after Warner had told me I was crazy to suggest it!

This was more money than Columbia could offer, but Cohn, an old fan of Jolson's who furthermore was galled at the thought of the detested Jack Warner getting the best of him, only grew more interested. He reminded Jolson that Columbia was famous for putting out one film every year that cleaned up at the box office, and promised that his biography would be the big one for its year. He even talked about the possibility that Jolson might produce some pictures for Columbia, which especially appealed to Jolson because his long-time rival George Jessel was joining 20th Century-Fox to produce The Dolly Sisters, starring Betty Grable and June Haver, and a number of other major musical biographies (Jolson never did produce). At my suggestion, Cohn also offered him half of the film's profits, in lieu of money up front.

That did it.

Jolson agreed. His one stipulation was that he be paid $25,000 for recording the songs--his pride demanded that he receive something for his work. Cohn agreed. And I was more agreeable than either of them!

I was a producer!

That was May, 1943.

Difficulties with The Jolson Story, however, had only just begun.

• • •

For one thing, Jolson was not well. He had come down with pneumonia while doing Hold on to Your Hats in 1940, and in October, 1943, he contracted it again after returning from

Al Jolson and Erle Galbraith, whom he married in 1945.

North Africa and Sicily, where he had also been stricken with malaria while entertaining our troops.

Comedian Phil Silvers, a friend of both Jolson and Harry Cohn, and whose wife, Jo-Carroll Dennison [see chapter 10] was to be in the film, remembered that "Harry Cohn was leery of Jolson's health: could he hold up to the rigors of making the picture? True, he was not going to be in it, but there were many recordings to be made. Cohn and Ben Kahane, his Vice President, went to visit Jolson at the hospital. When Jolson was told of their impending visit, he called his special doctor and got a massive shot of some kind. So when Cohn visited him in his hospital room, Jolson pranced up and down, joking and singing snatches of songs, and was a bundle of energy.

"I was told that when Cohn left Jolson's room, he said to Kahane, 'He's still the greatest. Let's get it moving!'

"Ten minutes after their departure, Jolson collapsed. However, he had made his point."

For a while, though, Jolson continued to have health problems. In December, 1944, he was incapacitated for a time with a recurrence of malaria. And in January, 1945, ten months before The Jolson Story was to start shooting, he was hospitalized in Hollywood for the removal of an abscess on his lung. The Associated Press sent its subscribers a full biographical obituary of Jolson.

Jolson wanted desperately to have a movie made about his life. One reason was that he had a new girlfriend, an attractive young X-ray technician named Erle Galbraith whom he would soon marry, and he wanted to be "great again" for her. "I'll have a whole new audience. I won't have to tell kids to ask their parents if they remember me anymore, and wonder if they still do," he confided to Skolsky. But there was one thing he wanted almost as much as that movie: to play himself in it.

"Who can play Jolie as well as Jolie himself?," he would ask anyone who would listen, including Harry Cohn. But Cohn was adamant: "Columbia has the best make-up department in Hollywood, but we can't make a sixty-year-old look twenty-one. We're going to show you as a young kid in the picture. There'll be romance. The audience will want a young guy. Isn't it enough you'll be doing all the goddam singing?"

But where, persisted Jolson, would they find someone who could recreate his unique performing style?

To which Cohn rejoined, "Eleven different actors have

played Jesus. A Negro played God. We'll find someone to play Jolson!"

While The Jolson Story was still being cast, Harry Cohn had a birthday party at his house where composers Sammy Cahn and Jule Styne presented their specially written musical parody, A Day (and Night) in the Life of Harry Cohn. Appearing in this living room production were Frank Sinatra, Gene Kelly, Peter Lawford, José Iturbi and Jolson, all playing themselves. Phil Silvers was cast as Harry Cohn, while Judy Garland portrayed contract actress Janet Blair, who was then suing Cohn, and Jule Styne played both Jule Styne and Sidney Skolsky.

All Jolson was given was one word of dialogue and one chorus of "My Mammy." As the parody began, Silvers called Styne into his office, demanding to know whether he had found someone to play Jolson in the film biography he was preparing. "I got this fella outside," said Styne, bringing in the real Jolson.

"This guy couldn't play Jolson's father," scoffed Silvers. "I'll kill you for this."

Jolson then surpassed himself with his rendition of "My Mammy." "All those talented people were awestruck," Sammy Cahn has said, "because what Jolson was doing was auditioning."

When Jolson's standing ovation subsided, Silvers said, "Thanks a lot. Don't call us. We'll call you." After Jolson walked off, Silvers shouted for his secretary to "Get me 20th Century-Fox.... Twentieth? Let me speak to Georgie Jessel. Hello, Jessel? You've got to dub this picture."

Always afraid to show weakness, Cohn once told Skolsky that when he was a song-plugger in his youth and tried to interest the great Jolson in one of his tunes, Jolson would sometimes throw him out without even listening to the number. "So when you came to me with the idea for the movie," Cohn went on, "I said yes so that I could be that son of a bitch's boss."

The truth of the matter, according to Bob Thomas in his biography of the Columbia mogul, King Cohn, was that

"Al Jolson was the only man Harry Cohn ever idolized. When Cohn was in the music business, every song-plugger dreamed of placing a tune with Jolson. Cohn's opinion of Jolson as an entertainer never altered.... [At Columbia] Jolson was the only person within memory who could be admitted to Cohn's office automatically."

Jolson's opinion of Cohn was more flexible. Before the contract was signed to film his life story at Columbia, Jolson usually had derogatory things to say about Cohn. "To hell with that crappy Cohn and his crappy studio," he would say. Afterward, there was only praise. When asked about this by Virginia Van Upp (who co-wrote the studio's Cover Girl and produced Gilda), Jolson answered, "Whose bread I eat, his song I sing." Cohn later began using the expression.

As a man, Jolson had many detractors. "It became almost fashionable to knock him personally," noted Phil Silvers. "I know a story that illustrates this. A second-rate vaudevillian who was down on his luck and needed money for his wife's operation went to see Eddie Cantor to try and borrow some money. Cantor was full of sympathy--'Gosh, what a shame. You and your wife did such a great act. Gosh, I wish I could help you.' The man then went to see Jolson, who in essence said, 'Sure your wife is sick. You're both sick. What the hell you are doing in show business I don't know.' During this tirade Jolson went to his desk and wrote the guy a check for $5,000. Sometime after his wife's recovery, the vaudevillian was heard to say, 'What a nice guy Eddie Cantor is, but what a prick that Jolson is.'

"Both Cohn and Jolson were on the surface self-opinionated bastards, but I miss them. They were at least openly savage and if it suited them, rude. But I preferred them to the likes of Jack Warner, Sam Goldwyn and Louis B. Mayer who were real bastards, hiding it behind a so-called religious Jewish background."

George Jessel, a scarcely unbiased observer, said (and said), "As in the truthful portrayal of his life story on the screen, Jolson was only content while singing and acknowledging applause. The rest of the time he was chafing at the bit while getting ready to go on; if he was not 'on,' he was disconsolate and miserable to be around."

In a 1981 article in The Village Voice, J. Hoberman wrote,

> In his streetwise apprehension of American popular culture, his fantastic vitality and his gangsterish monomania to get ahead, Jolson was cut from the same cloth as the so-called movie moguls--the itinerant peddlers, junk dealers and sweatshop entrepreneurs who had parlayed their slum-located, storefront peepshows into America's fourth largest industry.

• • •

Born on New York's upper East Side on July 21, 1891, to a German-Jewish tailor father and a Russian-Jewish mother, Harry Cohn had three brothers and one sister. For a while he was by turn a singer, pool hustler, trolley conductor, and song-plugger. Then he joined with his older brother Jack Cohn and Joe Brandt to form C.B.C. Films in New York, where they produced short subjects called Screen Snapshots. In 1920 Harry moved to Hollywood to oversee production there, settling in the film business' low-rent district nicknamed Poverty Row where the company was soon churning out features. In 1924 when the triumvirate decided that C.B.C. was no longer suitable (it meant Cohn-Brandt-Cohn but many deciphered it as Corned Beef and Cabbage), Columbia Pictures was born. Harry continued as chief of production and in 1932 became President, too.

Although Columbia's base of operations stayed on Poverty Row, as success came it swallowed up more and more of the area, finally occupying most of the long block between Sunset Boulevard and Fountain Avenue and between Gower Street and Beachwood Drive. By major studio standards, it was still physically very compact--Cohn believed in putting any available money into film production, not into such things as better working conditions for his employees. But the close quarters did give workers a spirit of togetherness and also permitted Harry Cohn to wander around and check up on things. Sidney Skolsky liked to say that "Cohn ran his small studio as if it were the Gaiety Delicatessen. He knew every customer coming in and every sandwich going out."

Brawny, if usually overweight, with twinkling blue eyes, the firm-jawed Cohn would have been an imposing presence

Harry Cohn, President and head of production at Columbia Pictures, in 1946, the year The Jolson Story was released.

even without a movie studio behind him. Though married, he was an inveterate ladies man, and there is a persistent story that Cohn had a passageway built from his office to a starlet's dressing room so he could visit on the sly.

In 1935, the studio bought the first forty acres of a subsequent eighty-acre ranch for outdoor filming in nearby Burbank, the city to which Columbia would move decades later.[2]

Columbia's early prosperity was due in no small measure to the achievements of a short, Sicilian-born director named Frank Capra, whose entertaining yet socially aware films of the 1930s brought both prestige and financial gain to the studio.

"[Harry Cohn] was one of the film giants," appraised Capra in his autobiography, The Name Above the Title, "with an enormous helping of what all film giants have in common--guts, imagination and a passionate love of films. In some ways he topped them all. He was the only one to grab a fly-by-night, Poverty Row outfit by the scruff of the neck and lift it to the most continually successful major studio in Hollywood. He forced entrenched moguls to shelve their precious 'committee' system and adopt maverick Cohn's 'one man, one film' method of producing films. Producer-directors all around the world owe a megaphonic salute to Harry Cohn."

Capra went on to say that he had been at Columbia a week or two before he had his first confrontation with Cohn. He said he had heard him every day, storming through the halls, bawling out employees for leaving on lights, smoking and/or drinking coffee. Screenwriter Dorothy Howell told Capra that Cohn barked but seldom bit. Nevertheless, Capra said that in later years he was to see "many a sensitive artist walk out of Columbia as if chewed up by a grizzly. Obviously, Columbia was not a place for the weak or the meek. Here they measured you not by what you could do, but by how you did it under Cohn's bullying."

Not everyone was intimidated by Cohn, though. In the book People Will Talk, by John Kobal, Columbia choreographer Jack Cole recalled, "He was marvelous to work for. I always had a marvelous time with Harry Cohn because I had a very sharp tongue and would use absolutely foul, colorful language, more than he did.... If you were alone, you could say anything to him.... And when he'd get into an argument with you, when you thought you were having a really bad time, he would suddenly say, 'I just want to see if you're going to like what you do. Go ahead.'"

Cohn's boast that he had a foolproof way of determining whether a movie was good or bad has become the stuff of legends. "If my fanny squirms, it's bad," he explained. "If my fanny doesn't squirm, it's good." When he told this to screenwriter Herman J. Mankiewicz, the latter remarked, "Imagine--the whole world wired to Harry Cohn's ass!"

Harry Cohn, whom producer Everett Riskin called "the last of the pirates," suffered a fatal heart attack on February 27, 1958. Lined up in his office at the time were forty-five Academy Oscars won by Columbia Pictures. Advised that two thousand people had turned out for Cohn's funeral, the largest number in Hollywood history for such an occasion, comedian Red Skelton quipped, "Well, it only proves what they always say--give the public something they want to see, and they'll come out for it."

• • •

With the Jolson film biography now "moving," the first order of the day was to get a screenplay. Several writers were hired to handle the project, most of them conferring with Jolson at the Beverly Hills Hotel, his residence when in town from his Miami Beach, Florida, home. "Minstrel Boy," "Rainbow 'Round My Shoulder" and "April Showers" were early title prospects, but the name eventually tacked on the work-in-progress was _Jolson_, patterned after Darryl F. Zanuck's much-touted, costly film biography of the late President Woodrow Wilson entitled _Wilson_ that was soon to complete production at 20th Century-Fox Studios.

Just before _Wilson_ opened in late 1944, Zanuck announced, "If this picture flops, I'll never make another movie without Betty Grable." It flopped.

To avoid comparison with a failure, the similar single-word title of _Jolson_ was quickly jettisoned in favor of _The Al Jolson Story_ and then _The Story of Jolson_, which remained its appellation until just before release of the film, when Harry Cohn, with his usual economy, decreed that _The Jolson Story_ "gets to the point quicker."

Well into production, as expenses were mounting, he also swore to Phil Silvers, "If this picture flops, I'll never make another movie without Rita Hayworth."

One of the early dilemmas facing the writers was how to deal with Jolson's three ex-wives in the story. Since Jolson was looking over his Boswells' shoulders, a sympathetic portrait of him was obviously planned; but these three connubial failures stacked side by side could certainly mitigate against the credibility of their compulsive but otherwise wartless, family-oriented hero. Jolson, always blithely unconcerned with facts and never fond of sharing the spotlight, shrugged, "Leave 'em out." Hadn't Yankee Doodle Dandy omitted George M. Cohan's first wife? Cohn, on the other hand, said, "You gotta have a broad for movie audiences, or they'll get up and walk out of the theater." Since Cohn was providing their bread, the writers sang his song.

Ruby Keeler, because she was the most recent of Jolson's wives, the best known and a star in her own right, was soon selected to be the leading feminine character, the love interest, though a younger actress of the day would portray her. (Jolson was not about to open old wounds by asking her to play herself.) Keeler had married again, though, retiring to a remote section of the San Fernando Valley where she was enjoying anonymity and raising a large family. Sidney Skolsky was elected to go out and see her and get permission for her to be dramatized in the film.

Keeler's immediate response was "I do not want my name mentioned in that picture."

"Why?," asked Skolsky.

"I don't like the man," she replied. "I don't want my children to grow up someday and maybe see the picture and know I was married to a man like that. Hear 'Ruby Keeler' from the screen and Jolson singing love songs to her. Making love speeches to her. Saying, 'Baby, everything you want you'll have. This is Jolie talking to you.' I want none of that."

"Suppose we give your character a different name?," answered a quick-thinking Skolsky.

"That would be all right," said Keeler, who then, just as quickly, demanded $25,000 for the nonuse of her name in The Jolson Story--one didn't live with Al Jolson for almost a dozen years and not have some of him rub off.

Ruby Keeler and Al Jolson, who were married in 1928 and divorced in 1940, at the half-way mark in the 1930s.

Cohn thought it over. Word of her fee got back to the even more budget-conscious New York office, where sales and accounting were handled and which was presided over by Cohn's equally combative brother Jack. The latter never missed a chance to harass his brother about West Coast expenses, and vehemently protested paying Keeler $25,000. That was all Harry Cohn needed: he sent her a check for the amount she requested.

Three decades later, Keeler informed Hollywood Studio Magazine columnist Lee Graham that she still hadn't seen The Jolson Story. Around the same time, however, she told Films in Review writer Ronald L. Bowers that the first Jolson film biography "had nothing to do with our lives."

The authors of the screenplay were encouraged to make

H. Bruce Humberstone, the original director of The Jolson Story, is pictured under the camera on the 1936 film Charlie Chan at the Opera, with, at right, William Demarest and Warner Oland.

the story work first, then (if at all) worry about whether the material was totally factual. Jolson was, after all, well past his salad days, so, reasoned the entertainer and cohorts Cohn and Skolsky, who would remember if certain things depicted had really happened or not?

Final screenplay credit on The Jolson Story went mainly to novelist-painter-critic Stephen Longstreet [see chapter 12].

A director was next on the agenda. In retrospect, the obvious choice would seem to have been contract director Charles Vidor, the favorite of Columbia's musical queen, Rita Hayworth. But in the beginning, The Jolson Story--despite Cohn's extravagant promises to Jolson when he wanted to keep Warners from getting the rights to his life story--probably was not deemed important enough for this top director. Cohn was, if nothing else, a realist; and while in his own gruff way he was very fond of Jolson personally, he was aware that just about everybody else thought the "Mammy singer" was pretty old-hat, notably New York which had opposed the project from day one. (When Ruby Keeler insisted her name be changed in the film, Jack Cohn suggested they give Jolson "a different moniker, too"! Harry Cohn's expletives rent the air.) Vidor, anyway, was then involved with various stages of work on no less than three major productions on the lot, A Song to Remember (1945), Over 21 (1945), and Gilda (1946).

Cohn thought of H. Bruce ("Lucky") Humberstone. A Buffalo native who had moved to Los Angeles in his teens, the scrappy veteran started as a prop boy and assistant cameraman at Universal. He directed his first film in 1932, over the years toiling mostly for 20th Century-Fox where he guided several Charlie Chan films, the well-remembered mystery I Wake Up Screaming (1941) and a number of popular musicals, among them Sun Valley Serenade (1941), with Sonja Henie; Hello, Frisco, Hello (1943), with Alice Faye; and Pin Up Girl (1944), with Betty Grable. At the time that Columbia was looking for a Jolson Story director, the grapevine was spreading good word about Humberstone's as-yet-unreleased quasi-musical for Samuel Goldwyn, Wonder Man (1945), starring the recently imported sensation from Broadway, Danny Kaye.

"If he can handle Kaye," Cohn remarked to Skolsky, "he should be able to handle Jolson. Let's get him before his price goes up." "Lucky" Humberstone was hired to direct The Jolson Story.

Most important of all, however, would be the selection of the actor to portray Al Jolson.

The New York office wanted Cohn to initiate a country-wide search for his screen Jolson like the one Gone with the Wind producer David O. Selznick had reaped torrents of publicity with when he beat the bushes looking for his Scarlett O'Hara. Cohn and Skolsky conferred and opted against it, feeling that the millions who had read Gone with the Wind as a novel had preconceived notions about how Scarlett should look, whereas most people did not even know what Al Jolson looked like--he had, after all, spent much of his performing life on the stage in blackface and, latterly, on the radio.

As soon as it leaked out that Columbia was seeking an actor to play Jolson, a besieged Cohn, reported writer Louis Berg, "was afraid to leave his office for fear of being waylaid by hordes of aspirants who would roll their eyes, stick out their underlips and wail 'I'm-a-coming; hope and pray I'm not too late.'"

Jolson proposed James Cagney, who had recently ended a twelve-year association with Warner Bros. Having seen what the vivid Cagney had just done for the rather passé George M. Cohan in Yankee Doodle Dandy, Jolson felt Cagney could do the same for him. Cohn shot this suggestion down immediately. With characteristic needling candor, he said, "Cagney is one of the biggest, most recognizable stars in the business. What makes you think he'd want to open his mouth and have your singing voice come out? Or that anyone would believe it? Besides, his asking price now is too high. Forget it."

They looked over Columbia's roster of male stars. The all-American William Holden was in the Army, boyish Glenn Ford lacked the essential show biz flash and mustachioed Lee Bowman was too dignified.

"One day when I went to the races with Harry Cohn," recalled Bowman, "he suddenly asked me if I'd like to play Jolson. I said sure, but I secretly thought he was crazy: I was doing straight dramatic roles. He must have got to thinking the same thing, because that was the first and last time the subject ever came up. Coincidentally, a couple of years later I played a singer in Smash-Up, The Story of a Woman--voice dubbed."

The dashing Cornel Wilde, the new bobbysoxers delight, was briefly considered, but he was already set for three expensive Technicolor productions there: A Song to Remember (1945), A Thousand and One Nights (1945), and The Bandit of Sherwood Forest (1946). Cary Grant had had some of his best vehicles at Columbia, but even Al Jolson's outsize ego could not conceive of that most attractive and debonair of British-born stars speaking and singing with Jolson's sometimes 'Rastus-inspired dialect.

Danny Thomas, a singing comedian then making a hit in supper clubs doing some of Jolson's numbers, was under scrutiny for a while. Thomas has said that Cohn told him he could have the part of Jolson "if you'll have that big Lebanese nose bobbed." Retorted Thomas, "This nose has been in my family for generations and I'm not going to change it now." Thomas went on to essay the Jolson role in the Warner Bros. 1953 remake of The Jazz Singer--profile intact. Another young comedian, Sid Caesar, whom Columbia had set to appear in Tars and Spars (1946), was tested for The Jolson Story. Recalled director Bruce Humberstone years later, "Sid came off closer to Danny Kaye than Jolson."

José Ferrer, who had just played Iago to Paul Robeson's Othello on Broadway and was becoming a prestigious (if homely) young actor, had been doing Jolson imitations at parties for years. A Columbia employee saw one of these impromptu performances and passed the word along to Harry Cohn, who spoke with Ferrer in Jolson's presence about the part. Afterward, an insulted Jolson grumbled to Cohn, "Jolie may not exactly be an oil painting, but my punim ["face" in Yiddish] doesn't look that bad!" Ferrer went on to do his imitation of Jolson in the 1954 M-G-M film Deep in My Heart, in which he portrayed the composer Sigmund Romberg.

Dane Clark was thought of next. A brash young New York actor from the Group Theater's touring production of Golden Boy, he had recently become a featured player at Warner Bros. where his work had caused the country's motion picture exhibitors to place him at No. 1 on their list of "Top Ten Stars of Tomorrow." With his acting acumen and energetic, forceful personality, Clark might have been the best Jolson of all. He relates what happened:

> Sidney Skolsky was a friend of mine. I used to see him all the time at Schwab's, where he'd tell me of the progress of the film and that he wanted me to play Jolson. I believe he mentioned it to Harry Cohn who did not object. However, I was in something of a hassle with my boss Jack Warner at the time over a number of things, mostly money, and he wasn't in the mood to do me any favors. What's more, if I'm not mistaken, Warner had recently just missed out on acquiring the rights to Jolson's life story.
>
> When Columbia asked to borrow me for The Jolson Story, Warner said, "No, he can't do it. We're going to star him in a remake of The Jazz Singer, and the stories are too similar." But The Jazz Singer never

> happened--at least not for me. Then, a while later, I refused to sign a new contract with Warners--the worst mistake of my life--and had to go to Europe to work for several years. Sometime after I left Warners they did The Jazz Singer with Danny Thomas.
>
> Naturally, I had wanted to do The Jolson Story. But I don't know if I could have done as well as Larry Parks. He was wonderful.

Clark went on to star in such films as Deep Valley and Moonrise (both 1948) plus many television shows to this day.

Ross Hunter, a good-looking Columbia contract juvenile who had been a child vaudevillian and was now working opposite hillbilly comedienne Judy Canova in the "B" pictures Louisiana Hayride (1944) and Hit the Hay (1945), was under observation, too. At last, though, everyone thought the ex-schoolteacher "too bland." Hunter went on to produce some of Hollywood's most successful films, including Pillow Talk (1959) and Airport (1970).

Dancer Gene Kelly, who was then still new in Hollywood, and whose father, James Patrick Kelly, was once Jolson's road manager, was thought a possibility for the Jolson role as well. Borrowed from M-G-M, he was on the Columbia lot to star with Rita Hayworth in Cover Girl (1944) when he ran into Jolson one day. The older man asked him if he'd be interested in playing him on the screen. The idea appealed to Kelly. He had, after all, earned his greatest acclaim thus far playing self-absorbed entertainers in the Broadway musical Pal Joey and, in his 1942 screen debut, For Me and My Gal. However, he said he wanted to see a completed script before he approached M-G-M about loaning him out again. But when the release of Cover Girl made Kelly a major movie star, his home lot never again let him work for another studio. Moreover, Kelly was in the Navy when The Jolson Story finally went before the cameras.

For a while, the strongest contender of all was Richard Conte. Born in Jersey City, New Jersey, of Italian parents, he had worked at the Group Theater in the 1930s when Larry Parks [see chapter 6] was also there. Ironically, the rising, capable Conte had come to Hollywood to test for the George Gershwin role in Rhapsody in Blue (1945), which went to Robert Alda. He signed with 20th Century-Fox, where he

Columbia Executive Producer Sidney Buchman and Larry Parks on the set of The Jolson Story.

had been noticed favorably in Guadalcanal Diary (1943), The Purple Heart (1944) and A Walk in the Sun (1945) evincing an aggressive, street-smart quality that most of those in charge thought would be appropriate to a portrayal of Jolson.

The fly in Conte's ointment was Larry Parks.

"Larry was the first to test for the part," asserts Parks' widow, actress Betty Garrett, "and the last one to test of about fifty actors ranging from Jolson imitators on the nightclub circuit to film actors like Richard Conte. They finally realized Larry's tests were the best."

Under contract to Columbia since 1941, Parks was appearing primarily in "B" films for the studio when the Jolson film came up. But, besides competence, Parks also had at least one other thing fellow would-be Jolsons didn't have: a close friend at court. This was Sidney Buchman.

Although Harry Cohn's irascibility caused a steady ebb and flow of studio personnel, Buchman's talent and taste made him Columbia's one irreplaceable executive. Born in Duluth, Minnesota, in 1902, Buchman was educated at Columbia and Oxford universities and started as a playwright on Broadway. He and many other dramatists were brought West at the advent of talking pictures. One of the organizers of the Screen Writers Guild, by the early forties he was Harry Cohn's right-hand-man, a leading writer-producer and for three years Vice President in Charge of Production at Columbia Pictures.

In 1951, during House Un-American Activities Committee investigations of alleged Communist subversion in show business, Buchman confessed to his inquisitors that he was a former Communist. However, he refused to name other Party members. In 1953 he was found guilty of contempt of Congress, fined $150 and blacklisted in the United States. Seven years later 20th Century-Fox hired him as a writer-producer to work in Europe. Buchman died in 1975 in Cannes, France, where he had lived for a decade.

He had produced and/or written or co-written the screenplays for The Sign of the Cross, If I Had a Million, Theodora Goes Wild, The Awful Truth, Holiday, Lost Horizon, Mr. Smith Goes to Washington, Here Comes Mr. Jordan, The Talk of the Town, A Song to Remember, To the Ends of the Earth, The Mark, Elizabeth Taylor's Cleopatra, and The Group. In his 1972 book The Hollywood Screenwriters, Richard Corliss listed Buchman as uncredited co-author of The Jolson Story.

Parks and Buchman became friends through propinquity and their mutual political philosophies. A believer in Parks' talent as well, Buchman wanted to help the young actor pull himself out of the "B" movie mire which was trapping many talented performers, and thought that the Jolson film might be the picture to do it. He arranged for Parks to meet with Cohn, Jolson and Skolsky to talk about The Jolson Story. After the introductions, Cohn, who rarely bothered to see any of the studio's hefty output of low-budget films (more than two dozen of which had employed Parks),[3] asked the actor, "Do you work here?"

Much later, Jolson divulged, "Larry was the only candidate who didn't come around and say that he could do a perfect imitation of me, so of course this caught our attention.

I was impressed by his modesty and seriousness, plus the ability I saw when we had a couple of his unreleased pictures screened."

A test was approved, and Parks performed "Swanee" in blackface for the camera to a playback of Jolson's recording of the song.

Parks once admitted, "I had never seen Jolson nor heard him sing when the picture was first mentioned to me." To prepare for the test, he listened to a few old Jolson recordings he was able to obtain, talked to those who had seen Jolson work and observed the man's attitude around the lot. Despite his casual outward manner, Parks wanted the role desperately. Betty Garrett and he had just married; he had to think of the future. "But I never thought I'd get the part," he said.

Months went by after Parks' first test until finally he was called to "sing" again as Jolson. In actuality, Jolson, still smarting because he couldn't play himself, had severely criticized the tests of all the actors (including Parks) who aspired to portray him. "That one looked like a penguin," he'd say, storming out of the projection room. Or, "He'd make a better Jessel." He did not have the final say on who would be cast, but he did have an important vote. The time had come, though, for a decision to be made if he ever wanted to see his life story on the screen. After Parks' second test was screened for the top echelon, Jolson grudgingly threw his vote in with the others for Larry Parks. Cohn called Parks to his office and recognized him this time. He gave him the part.

Physically, Parks was no double for the man he would portray, although, like Jolson, he was dark and not too tall. But that was where the actual physical similarity ended. However, with painstaking dedication he was able to give the impression, as John Springer wrote in his book <u>All Talking! All Singing! All Dancing!</u>, that "Al practically seemed to take possession of the body of Larry Parks for one of the most accurate and enjoyable reincarnations to have shown up on film." Early on, even Jolson confessed his admiration: "My lower lip protrudes when I'm serious, especially when I've been laughing just a minute before. And then, when I talk to people--I've discovered from watching Larry--I switch my face to one side, meanwhile keeping my eyes on them. This makes the whites of my eyes a conspicuous part of my face. All of these things, Larry has down pat." While these external mimicries were vital to a believable characterization of Jolson, what really sold Columbia on Parks was his facility at conveying Jolson's peculiar, almost orgasmic euphoria at being in the spotlight.

A grueling work schedule such as few Hollywood actors have known lay ahead for Larry Parks, who, except for a few forgettable turns in "B" movies, was a musical comedy novice.

Supervised by studio music director Morris Stoloff, who also conducted the orchestra, Jolson worked hard, too, recording dozens of songs for the soundtrack to which Parks would later pantomime [see chapter 13]. The indefatigable, sixtyish Jolson's achievement was made all the more remarkable when one realized that he recently had had a serious lung operation.

Such extensive dubbing of one player with a different, known voice had never been attempted before, although the previous year in Paramount's Out of This World, a satire of the crooner craze, milquetoast comedian Eddie Bracken played a messenger boy who became a bobbysoxers idol when he sang with Bing Crosby's voice. Crosby, then Paramount's biggest star, recorded several numbers for Bracken to mime, and a credit frame at the beginning read, "Mr. Bracken's songs are sung for him by an old friend of his--and yours."[4]

[After The Jolson Story, a number of films tried this method, the most momentous being the 20th Century-Fox With a Song in My Heart, starring Susan Hayward in one of her most beloved performances. In this 1952 release, she enacted the life of crippled songstress Jane Froman with Froman's own soundtrack voice providing the vocals. Much less effective was Jolson Story producer Sidney Skolsky's own The Eddie Cantor Story in 1953. Cantor's voice was used on the soundtrack, but the Warner Bros. film was foredoomed by lead Keefe Brasselle's ludicrously distracting, eye-rolling impersonation of the bug-eyed singer-comedian. More recently, in Tri-Star's 1985 biography Sweet Dreams actress Jessica Lange scored as late country singer Patsy Cline, mouthing the words to Cline's old recordings emanating from the soundtrack.]

Casting the role of Julie Benson, Jolson's love interest, was the next hurdle. Since the character was a dancer, Skolsky (who, notwithstanding his diminutiveness, believed, like Jolson, in "thinking big") originally suggested the studio's terpsichorean "love goddess," Rita Hayworth. "No!" snapped Cohn, reasoning that he was building Hayworth into a top star, that the way the script was being written the girl wouldn't come into the story for almost an hour and would be overshadowed by Jolson anyway. No matter how well the film did, Cohn felt, such a secondary role would mark a come-down for a goddess.

Years afterward, Skolsky, who developed a crush on the bright Columbia actress Evelyn Keyes and even wrote an article for a 1947 Photoplay magazine called "My Romance with Evelyn Keyes," would claim that she was the only girl ever considered for Julie Benson [see chapter 7]. The reedy Keyes, blonde and comely but no sexpot, and also the object of Cohn's roving eye, has provided details to the contrary. Anxious for the role, Keyes said she reminded the boss of her recent praised teaming with Larry Parks in Columbia's Technicolor Western, Renegades (1946). As for the musical comedy aspects of Julie Benson, she pleaded that she had been a dancer before coming to Hollywood as a teenager in 1937, and knew she could carry off the numbers required of her in the film. But Cohn, who knew her professionally just as a skillful actress with a comic flair, merely said, "We'll see."

Meanwhile, vowed Keyes, one girl after another was tested, and she had the "dubious pleasure" of watching them all in Cohn's home projection room.

Actresses seen for the role included blonde Marjorie Reynolds, late of Paramount and Holiday Inn (1941) in which Bing Crosby had sung "White Christmas" to her and Fred Astaire had danced with her to "Be Careful, It's My Heart." A child actress in the twenties who had gone on to do dozens of films, by the mid-1940s she was adjudged a bit "past it" for Julie, and was consoled with a lead in a Columbia "B" musical entitled Meet Me on Broadway (1946).

Among the others mentioned for Julie was Janet Blair, a contract player who proficiently sang and danced in several Columbia musicals during the 1940s. Blair writes me:

> I really have no idea why I wasn't chosen for The Jolson Story. I knew they were considering me seriously for the part of Ruby Keeler, but I was never tested. Just a lot of talk. But very soon the word was out that Evelyn Keyes got it. I was a bit confused and surprised, because I knew she certainly was not a musical comedy lady or a singer-dancer. But she was an excellent actress. Perhaps I should have really fought for that role--but I didn't. I have always felt, and still do, that if the good Lord wanted me to do it, I would have.
>
> I never, never begged for a part, nor would I indulge in any romances or affairs with directors, producers, etc. In fact, the truth is you could honestly have called me the only virgin in Hollywood. I succeeded my own way. Perhaps I could have been more famous and successful if I had played "the Hollywood game," but I couldn't and wouldn't--and still won't.
>
> I forget who produced The Jolson Story, but word was out that he adored Evelyn Keyes. As they say, "You can't fight the bedroom." Amen.

While looking at one of the Julie tests at Cohn's house one evening, Keyes once again begged her still noncommittal employer for the part. Whereupon Cohn's wife, the former actress Joan Perry (possibly aware of her husband's more than businesslike interest in Keyes), spoke up, "Jungle Red" nails bared: "Don't be silly, Evelyn. You can't play that role. You know you aren't pretty enough."

Keyes then accelerated her campaign, sending Cohn telegrams every day, phoning him several times a day, beseeching him to allow her to be Julie Benson.

It was Jolson himself, to believe publicity for the film, who turned the tide for Keyes. Watching her dance in a test for the part early in 1945, he noted, "She has a cameo face. Just what we've been looking for to suggest those good old days." Allegedly, Jolson was unmovable in ruling out the other applicants because he said they looked too modern. It is unlikely that he got any arguments from Skolsky or Cohn.

Keyes began to train and rehearse for her numbers with Jack Cole, the studio's head choreographer in charge of the dances for The Jolson Story, and a Columbia dance director named Audrene Brier, who also worked closely with Larry Parks [see chapter 13].

Now that Keyes had come aboard, Cohn, who had been attracted to her for some time, was doubly bent on elevating the status of the production. Glamour specialist Jean Louis, at the studio for a couple of years, was set to design the women's clothes [see chapter 16].

Always aware of the importance of screen camera work (Columbia had been the first Hollywood studio to install its own film laboratory), Cohn then assigned the distinguished Joseph Walker as cinematographer. With his unique flair for photographing pretty women and pithy comedies, Walker was one of Columbia's strongest assets throughout a long and illustrious career that culminated with a special 1982 Academy Award for his "outstanding technical contributions for the advancement of the motion picture industry."

Born in Denver, Colorado, in 1892, he started as a pioneer in wireless operations, shooting his first feature in 1919, *Back to God's Country*. He went on to photograph almost all of director Frank Capra's vintage successes, such as *It Happened One Night* (1934), *Mr. Smith Goes to Washington* (1939), and *You Can't Take It with You* (1938), for which Walker received the first of three Academy Award nominations. His second nomination was for *Here Comes Mr. Jordan* (1941) and his third was for *The Jolson Story*, his first and last film in color. He shared credit with Joseph Biroc on Capra's (and star James Stewart's) own favorite among his films, *It's a Wonderful Life* (1946).

Walker was Rosalind Russell's pet cameraman, too, working with the foremost career gal of forties cinema on many of her best vehicles, including *His Girl Friday* (1940), *My Sister Eileen* (1942), and *Roughly Speaking* (1945). Irene Dunne was also among the many glamorous actresses who sought his services; he photographed her in *Theodora Goes Wild* (1936) and *The Awful Truth* (1937), plus others.

During preparations for *The Jolson Story*, Harry Cohn remembered another Columbia musical, *One Night of Love* (1934), in which Walker had done wonders photographing the heavy prima donna Grace Moore, whom her previous studio labeled "unphotographable." With carefully planned lighting

Cinematographer Joseph Walker photographed The Jolson Story, his first and last film in color.

and other effects, Walker helped star Moore to look attractive, and the film was a hit. Joan Cohn's catty (and unjust) denigration of Evelyn Keyes' appearance aside, the twenty-six-year-old actress needed no extraordinary measures to look good on the screen at this point. But, as Harry Cohn told a nodding Sidney Skolsky when he brought Joseph Walker to the project, "It couldn't hurt."

In addition, Walker was a renowned inventor of motion picture-related materials, preeminently an early version of the zoom lens. Not long after he photographed Judy Holliday in Born Yesterday (1950) and The Marrying Kind (1951), Walker left films to devote full time to his burgeoning zoom lens business. He had been at Columbia Pictures for twenty-five years--almost as long as Harry Cohn.

The principal supporting roles in The Jolson Story were of less concern to the powers-that-were, so their casting was generally much easier than the two leads had been [see chapter 8]. William Demarest, Jolson's buddy in The Jazz Singer almost twenty years before, was signed to play his vaudevillian mentor and later manager Steve Martin. The character was actually a composite of several parties, especially banjo player Al Reeves, who had inspired Jolson to go on the stage; popular vaudevillian Eddie Leonard, the man responsible for Jolson's first performance in a theater when he had the boy soprano sing from the balcony of a Washington, D.C., theater; A.C. Olson, a vaudevillian who climbed to stardom with Jolson; and Louis ("Eppy") Epstein, Jolson's old friend and manager.

For the part of Cantor Yoelson, Sidney Buchman brought up the name of the Academy Award-winning star who during the previous decade at Warner Bros. had been billed as "Mister Paul Muni." But a disgruntled Muni had recently been talked into playing the secondary role of Chopin's teacher in Buchman's production of A Song to Remember, and was criticized for compensatory overacting, so no one had the temerity to ask him to play fourth or fifth fiddle this time.

Ludwig Donath, a Columbia contract player, and Tamara Shayne then slipped quietly into the company as Cantor and Mrs. Yoelson, as did Bill Goodwin as another Jolson chum. Jo-Carroll Dennison checked in as Jolson's grown-up boyhood sweetheart, Ann Murray, while Ann Todd, as Ann the child, likewise joined the troupe minus fuss [see chapter 9].

It was a little more problematical finding an acceptable young Al Jolson--and ripples relating to this role did not end with the final casting.

The young Asa Yoelson (Scotty Beckett) sings "When You Were Sweet Sixteen" in The Jolson Story.

Understandably, the part of the adolescent Al, which in essence would carry the first quarter of the film, was a matter of considerable import to Cohn and the others. Several boys were tested, and for a while it looked like the gifted, rather working-class young actor Darryl Hickman would be the choice. Hickman, then being seen as lyricist Ira Gershwin as a child in Rhapsody in Blue, in which Jolson had played himself briefly, recalls that he tested at Columbia "and from the initial reaction of everybody, it appeared that I had the part. Suddenly, I was told they had decided I didn't look enough like Larry Parks, then set for the lead."

In June, 1945, Jolson attended a screening at 20th Century-Fox of the Peggy Ann Garner vehicle, Junior Miss, and became quite taken with the wavy-haired, coltishly appealing Scotty Beckett, cast as a teenage Lothario. "That's the kid to play me," he thought, and following a test the fifteen-year-old Beckett became the young Jolson [see chapter 9].

Although Darryl Hickman lost the Jolson role to Scotty

Beckett, in an odd turn of events a few years later Hickman got the role of Clark Gable's son in M-G-M's Any Number Can Play (1949) that was originally intended for Beckett, who was fired just as filming was to begin when, informed Movie Story magazine, he was "picked up on an intoxication charge." It was apparent that the switch took place at the last minute, because, although Gable played scene after scene with "son" Hickman, it was still Beckett's photo as a small child that "The King" gazed at on his fireplace mantle.

Jolson's recording of the songs went on over a period of several months prior to the starting of the film. Cohn allowed him to record only when he felt particularly fit and in good voice, while some of the top musicians in Hollywood agreed to be on a moment's call to be able to work with Al Jolson. Although Skolsky thought it would be good for Larry Parks to observe the man he was going to portray at work, Jolson would not allow Parks into the recording studio.

When Skolsky asked why, Jolson replied, "Recording songs is not me really working. I'm not performing. I don't want him. He makes me nervous. I won't be able to do it."

Skolsky said that every so often he'd sneak Parks in while he was recording, but Jolson always resented it. The columnist-turned-producer sized up the situation: "Jolson's ego was such that he had no need for an alter ego, especially one that had been forced on him. He had never gotten over not being allowed to play himself."

Jolson felt the recording studio visits were unnecessary, because, he revealed later, "I made a moving picture of all the songs, in sound and motion. I stood up against a studio wall in a sweater and overalls, in a small space, and sang them all." Jolson said that Parks studied the 16mm film of this in his dressing room.

• • •

Despite an approaching start date, a satisfactory script for The Jolson Story had not been written.

According to director "Lucky" Humberstone (whose nickname, in this case, would prove to be a misnomer), after he had been active in preparations for the film for several weeks there were still only about ten pages of screenplay. In a 1975 interview with Hollywood columnist James Bacon, Humberstone said he then went to Cohn and asked who was producing the movie. "I am. Nobody else but me produces pictures here," answered Cohn. Humberstone asserted that Cohn told him he was paying Skolsky for the original idea only with a producer's credit on the film, and that Jolson was going to take care of Skolsky if and when profits came.

"Great," said Humberstone. "Here I am working my tail off on the recording stage with Jolson and testing actors and nobody is developing a script. Get me a working producer or I don't start." Humberstone suggested Sidney Buchman.

Cohn then disclosed that Jolson owned fifty per cent of the film, and he owned the other half. He suggested Humberstone meet with Jolson, tell him that he was worried about the lack of script progress and that he wanted Buchman as producer. "Ask him," counseled Cohn, "if he will give up ten per cent of his piece if you can get me to give up ten per cent of mine. That way we can offer Buchman twenty percent to produce the movie."

When they met, Jolson knew immediately that Cohn had put Humberstone up to the proposal, but agreed, saying, "I like your spunk, kid. And I'll go Harry one better. I'll give you five per cent of my remaining forty."

Humberstone continued pre-production work on the film.

In 1978 William Demarest said that "There was a completed script by the time filming of The Jolson Story began, but there were many changes before the picture was finished."

Shooting commenced early in October, 1945. As a token of his good wishes, Jolson gifted Larry Parks with the "lucky" make-up case he had used since The Jazz Singer--the fact that the period of the case's use had seen Jolson's career decline, his divorce from Ruby Keeler, and the onset of poor health dawned on no one, except maybe Al Jolson. A family scene involving Ludwig Donath, Tamara Shayne, and Scotty Beckett was filmed first, followed by a dramatic scene involving Parks and his pantomime to "Ma Blushin' Rosie."

Suddenly, the production was shut down.

In 1984, only months before his death from pneumonia at eighty-two, Humberstone gave me additional details:

> This is the way it was. We were in the throes of the Communist situation in Hollywood in the forties. I didn't know it, but Sidney Buchman was head of the Communist producers, and when I got him on the picture he brought in John Howard Lawson [see chapter 12] to work on the screenplay and Larry Parks to play Jolson, both of whom were Communists, too. It was a squeeze, but I wasn't aware of this at the time or I'd have gone in and whupped them all.
>
> Then, a week or so after we'd started the picture, Buchman came to me and said he would be delivering the script three pages at a time each day. It would be written with him in charge as we went along and would I want to work this way. "What I really need is a rubber stamp director," he said, in effect, to me.
>
> I told him to *get* a rubber stamp director and walked.
>
> He eventually got a director who was on his ass and needed the money. I had cast William Demarest, who was an old friend, and afterwards he told me that Buchman sat on the set through the whole thing, supervising everything while their so-called director stood around twiddling his thumbs. Although he kept his producer's credit, Sidney Skolsky had as much to do with *The Jolson Story* as you did.
>
> I was on the picture for fifteen weeks. I tested several boys for the Jolson role. The only one I remember is Richard Conte, who was awfully good. I think I would have gone with Conte. I recorded all of Jolson's songs. He was the greatest.

Humberstone left the lot immediately.

Harry Cohn had no intention of abandoning the film, though. On the contrary, after absorbing how well the Jolson voice was holding up, and how expertly Larry Parks was impersonating him, he had decided to convert his modest black-and-white program feature into a large-scale Technicolor extravaganza. Bigger sets were ordered (eventually totaling one hundred and seventeen in number), more songs were readied for interpolation. The budget was raised from $1,500,000 to, finally, $2,800,000. Jack Cohn in the New York office continuously registered his complaints, but his brother the President overrode them all. Harry Cohn was more determined than ever to prove the East wrong and the West right, and that Al Jolson remained the star of stars.

They still needed a director, however.

Enter Joseph H. Lewis.

The New York-born Lewis, who today has a cult reputation for his direction of low-budget but stylish film noir melodramas, started as a camera boy at M-G-M. Later, at Republic, he was in charge of film editing and then became director of second units. He began directing features in 1937, going on during the forties and fifties to helm My Name is Julia Ross, So Dark the Night, The Swordsman, The Return of October, Undercover Man, Gun Crazy, A Lady Without Passport, Desperate Search, The Big Combo, and A Lawless Street. But it was the nostalgic Minstrel Man (1944),[5] made on the cheap for the lowly Producers Releasing Corporation but garnering a couple of unheard-of, for PRC, Oscar nominations that brought him to the attention of Harry Cohn. He hired Lewis as a director, and when a replacement was needed fast to re-start and guide through the film life of "minstrel man" Al Jolson, Cohn naturally enough thought of Lewis.

"I came on The Jolson Story after it had been in production about five days," recalls Lewis. "Harry Cohn called me into his office. His executive producer Sidney Buchman was present, too. Harry said, 'Joe, we'd like you to direct the Jolson biography.' Now I was preparing to direct a small movie that I dearly loved, So Dark the Night, so I told him, 'I can't just jump into a picture like that without going over the script and everything. And there wouldn't be time for that.' Harry replied, 'Well, would you like to direct the musical numbers?' And that's what we did."

Continuing his discussion of the film which began shooting all over again on October 24, 1945, Lewis says, "I had many meetings with Harry Cohn and Al Jolson on the numbers. Everything went smoothly. We had a terrific dance director, Jack Cole. He rehearsed the dances and we just sailed through. I worked well with the director they finally hired, Alfred E. Green [see chapter 11], who had just done A Thousand and One Nights for Columbia.

Joseph H. Lewis, who directed the production numbers in The Jolson Story, talks to leading lady Angela Lansbury on the set of the 1955 film A Lawless Street, entirely directed by Lewis.

"Larry Parks was delightful--as an actor. Whatever personal problems that developed between us don't matter. (The next year I directed The Swordsman, starring Larry.) As for Jolson, he did have a tendency to hang around a bit too much, so I had to insist he go to the races."

As Jolson remembered it, "I came on the set of The Jolson Story once, after the 'Rosie' number, to congratulate Larry Parks. I saw that he was nervous, so I stayed away after that."

In reality, Jolson was around a bit more than that. Larry Parks once admitted that it was "very unnerving having

Evelyn Keyes, Larry Parks and Bill Goodwin take time for lunch during filming of The Jolson Story.

Jolson right there in the flesh, looking on with a critical eye, especially when you were representing him in something like a love scene." Parks went on:

> I kissed Evelyn Keyes one day, and I didn't think I had been especially oafish. I knew the scene was coming up, and I had hoped that Jolson wouldn't be around. I was afraid he might be sensitive, because Evelyn was playing the big romance in his life. But he was there, all right, and not missing a thing. As I said, I thought I had done all right.
>
> But just as I feared, Jolson stepped up with a criticism. For once the Jolson confidence, with which he generally bristles, wasn't there, and he seemed a little shy--if you can imagine Al being shy. "No, Larry, that won't do at all," he said, and I thought to myself, "Curses on the male ego--especially when it comes to making love."

> Jolson had me on the spot, because I knew I couldn't top that scene. I had put everything I had into it. It was as close as I'll ever come to Valentino.
>
> "You know, kid," Al went on, "there have been times in my life when I've been inclined to muff a line. It was on such occasions as this. In other words, you were just too, too smooth for me."
>
> At his request, I put in a couple of verbal stumbles.

When Jolson saw the rushes of Parks doing the "Swanee" number, he was again critical of his performance. He went to Cohn and implored him to be allowed to do the number himself. "The song's in blackface, and if you keep the camera from coming too close to me no one will know the difference," he argued--successfully. Despite the effective precautions taken by cinematographer Joseph Walker to insure that moviegoers didn't recognize the substitution, when Jolson did publicity for the film afterward he couldn't help spilling the beans by bragging that he had had to step in when his impersonator failed. "Larry Parks was great in everything," he explained, "but he couldn't move his feet like I do. There's one step I insist on doing no matter what I'm in [it was known as the "little bum" dance step]. I wanted to show my wife I was a movie actor. They gave me one long-shot--about two hundred miles away!"

The year before he died in 1985, cameraman Walker informed me, "Harry Cohn rarely visited the set, but he was very much in evidence when Jolson did his one number for the film, 'Swanee.' He stood to one side beaming as his one-time idol once again captivated an audience."

In the middle of Jolson's performance, Walker cried out, "Cut!"

"How dare you interrupt Al Jolson while he's singing?!," roared Cohn.

Walker explained that a flickering arc light had ruined the scene, but Cohn continued to rail. He stopped when Walker reminded him that the three-strip Technicolor film being used was costing fifty cents a second.

Contract director Henry Levin [see chapter 11], who

Larry Parks is photographed in the "Waiting for the Robert E. Lee" number from The Jolson Story.

would direct the sequel, Jolson Sings Again, witnessed another memorable Jolson appearance on the set of the first film biography. His testimony:

> I vividly recall visiting the set when they were

> filming the Winter Garden sequence where Jolson (Parks) was to sing "California, Here I Come" prior to leaving for Hollywood. It took about two-and-a-half hours to light this huge set filled with several hundred beautifully dressed extras. These extras were mostly old-timers, many of whom had come from New York over the years, and some of whom had actually worked in Jolson shows previously. Well, Jolie wouldn't let an audience like that be bored for hours--besides, he couldn't resist an audience, ever. So while the technicians were busy, Jolie sang and sang and told stories and jokes and sang and sang. And I'm sure he never had a more appreciative audience than those extras. They smiled, they laughed, they cried, they applauded and they cheered. And Jolie was absorbing every bit of adulation and love that poured from those marvelous show people--old and young. He stopped only when the cameraman said "Ready!"

Joseph Walker recalled that there was "lots of noise, hot lights, excitement and hard work on the film. I preferred to do black-and-white pictures--with fast lenses and special developing we used very little light, about fifty or sixty foot-candles.

"No new methods of photography were used, except in the night scenes I used some blue light against the Technicolor company's advice because they preferred to get the night effect by printing. But it seemed to work out okay."

The only real problem with photography on The Jolson Story occurred when Larry Parks' early blackface appearances showed up in the rushes a little dark and indistinct, depriving the actor of some facial expression. "But don't suggest we change the make-up," Parks begged Walker. "God knows we've tried everything. This is the best we've hit upon." Then Walker noticed that when Parks stood near an incandescent work light, his visage was seen more clearly. Once again over the objections of the Technicolor consultant, Walker tried an incandescent spotlight on Parks' face in addition to the arcs. Said Walker, "That slight yellowish glow, barely noticeable, did the trick."

Betty Garrett relates, "Larry would work two or three weeks on one number, after which it would be shot." Parks learned to synchronize the songs by singing along with Jolson's recordings for the film which were blasted from loudspeakers. One of his biggest vexations was that Jolson, who frequently did several renditions of a single number, rarely sang a song the same way twice. When doing a take on "Ma Blushin' Rosie," for example, he might use the line "don't be so captivating," then in another he might replace it with "don't be so aggravating." Parks would work to get the number synchronized one way, and then along would come another take of the same song and he'd have to change the performance he'd striven to perfect. On top of that, Jolson never seemed to come in twice on the same beat.

Looking at the rushes one day of Parks "singing" "You Made Me Love You," Skolsky and Cohn detected that Jolson had hit a bad note at the end of the song. Furthermore, it made Parks look out of sync. Although it had been weeks since the recording was made, Cohn brought all the musicians and Jolson back into the studio where they spent a whole afternoon getting that one note right.

A friend of Parks, Robert Gordon, who as Bobby Gordon had played Jolson as a youngster in The Jazz Singer, was a dialogue director on The Jolson Story. Since he had closely observed Jolson at work, Gordon was hired to stand under the lens of the camera and move his arms in a way that was supposed to keep Parks on the right track with the Jolson mannerisms. Sidney Skolsky said that Parks was "too nice a guy" to put Gordon out of a job, but he really didn't pay any attention to him: by the time the director called "Action!" he had Jolson down to a T.

Parks spent a hundred and seven days before the cameras. By completion of the film he had lost almost twenty pounds and had to wear padding so the earlier scenes would match.

On the other hand, Scotty Beckett, as the young Jolson, bloomed--too much so. Al Jolson told radio interviewer Barry Gray in 1946, "Scotty caused us problems. We worried all the time. He grew like a weed while we were shooting. By the time we finished the picture, he was much taller than Larry Parks! He had to work with his shoes off."

In an interview years later, Larry Parks said, "Because

Larry Parks gets a final checking over from producer Sidney Skolsky before his first scene in The Jolson Story. Below: Jolson (Larry Parks) sings "Carolina in the Morning," a number cut from The Jolson Story.

of the money being spent, and Jolson's lagging career at the time, everyone at the studio called the picture 'Cohn's Folly' until we were about halfway through. Suddenly excitement spread over the lot: the rushes were looking good and it seemed we might have a hit."

Toward the end of January, 1946, after three months of shooting and several weeks still to go, traces of the old Harry Cohn penury began to resurface. When studio art director Stephen Goosson asked Cohn for approval of more money for the papering of a wall against which Parks and Keyes were to play a love scene, Cohn barked, "Lemme tell you something. If there's one person in this whole damn country who's looking at that wall when we show that scene, then we're in big trouble!" The wall stayed the same.

• • •

From the outset, Harry Cohn kept a tight lid on publicity. While some studios began to trickle items, even stories, on a film a year or more before release, Cohn wanted as little as possible about the project to reach print until The Jolson Story was ready to be seen. He felt the elements of discovery and surprise would play major roles in the success of the production. And, not knowing how the public would react to this unique situation, he also did not want it broadcast before the opening that his leading man would not be doing his own singing. This worked no hardships on the newspapers and the then important fan magazines which, before they got to see the film, were not exactly panting to report on a picture about an entertainer from Grandma's day that had a "B" movie actor at the top of the cast.

Principal photography on The Jolson Story was completed on March 15, 1946. A half-year of assembly followed under William Lyon, the editor of such other films as You Were Never Lovelier, No Sad Songs for Me, Death of a Salesman, The Member of the Wedding, From Here to Eternity, The Caine Mutiny, Picnic (with Charles Nelson), Song Without End, A Raisin in the Sun, and Barefoot in the Park. (Lyon died in 1974.)

For months Harry Cohn had been thinking about getting the film into New York's prestigious, 6,200-seat Radio City Music Hall which audiences then jammed not only for the

Ann Murray (Ann Todd) and Asa Yoelson (Scotty Beckett) are refused admission to Kernan's Theater by the ticket seller (Dan Stowell) in The Jolson Story, a scene cut from the film.

quality screen attractions but for the lavish stage presentations featuring the precision dancing of the Rockettes. When a rough cut of The Jolson Story had been put together he brought the manager of that Art Deco movie palace, who normally viewed prospective bookings in the Hall's mini-theater, to Hollywood to see it.

As the lights went up after the projection room screening, Phil Silvers, present with his wife, Jo-Carroll Dennison, remembered, "Radio City manager or no Radio City manager, Harry suddenly shouted to Sidney Buchman, 'When are you going to learn that you can't pull any bullshit on me? That scene where Evelyn Keyes chokes on Mama Yoelson's horse-radish is one of my favorites, and it's been cut!' When Buchman protested that it was still in the picture, Cohn, who had dozed off for a couple of minutes during the showing, bellowed, 'You son of a bitch! You tryin' to make a schmuck out of me? I just saw the picture!' I interrupted to confirm that the scene was in. 'What the hell,' mumbled Cohn. 'I must have been reaching for candy or something.'"

Eventually, many other scenes were cut. For one thing, the rough-cut film ran almost three hours, causing the otherwise admiring Radio City Music Hall representative to insist that if they were going to play the film along with their famous stage show, The Jolson Story would have to be edited down to two hours.

Cohn acquiesced. Among the first footage to be excised was the scene showing the teenage Al and his girlfriend Ann going to the ticket window of Kernan's Theater; some patter before and during Jolson's rendition of "Ma Blushin' Rosie" about going to the races and putting his money on Top Hat, "which came off!"; the song "Carolina in the Morning," used during a montage showing Jolson's rise to fame; scenes of Jolson trying to win back the grown-up Ann; and the out-of-town preparations for Julie's Broadway production number of "Liza." By the time the film was ready for its first public viewing, it was still thirty minutes longer than the Music Hall had specified.

The first preview was set for a Sunday evening in the sedate, WASPy town of Santa Barbara, California, about an hour-and-a-half north of Los Angeles. It was just far enough so that if reaction was not good the word might be kept from spreading throughout the industry until, hopefully, things could be fixed. Billed on the local theater marquee only as "Major Studio Preview," The Jolson Story was seen following the regular attraction there, the spectacular M-G-M production of Ziegfeld Follies--not an enviable act to follow. As the film of his life unreeled, Jolson, seated with his wife Erle on one side and Skolsky on the other, shook so much from nervousness that Skolsky at first thought they were in the midst of an earthquake. In spite of the competition that night, plus the fact that the print was part black-and-white and part color because a completed version hadn't come back from the

---

Jolson (Larry Parks) sings "Sonny Boy" to a youngster (Louis Traeger) in a scene cut from The Jolson Story. Below: Julie Benson (Evelyn Keyes) talks to Jolson in another scene finally omitted from the film.

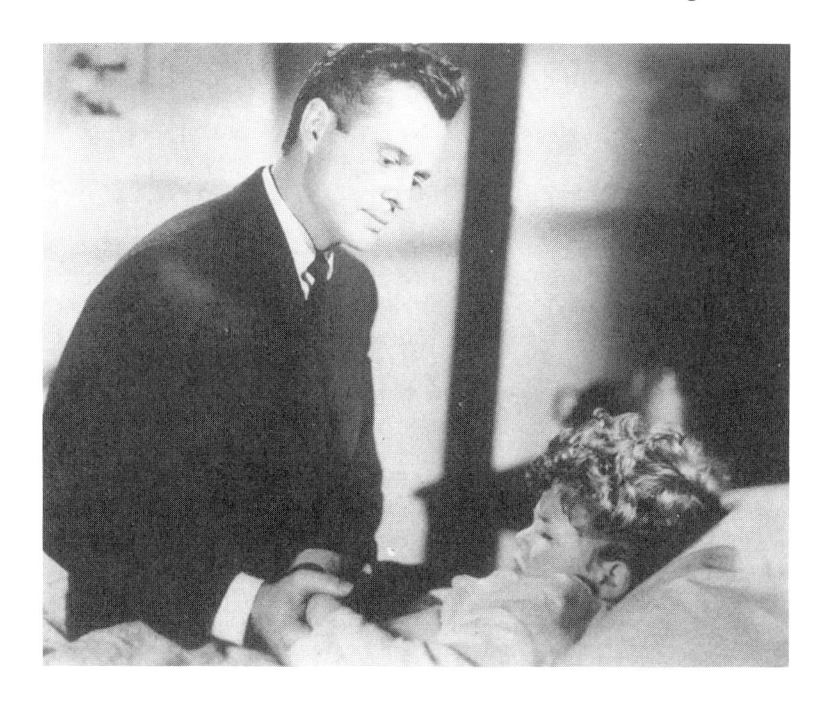

Technicolor company, the Columbia film proved a rousing success with the Santa Barbara audience.

Leaving the theater, Jolson heard an elderly woman exclaim to her husband, "What a wonderful movie! Too bad Jolson couldn't have lived to see it."

In a grimly ironic coincidence, Moses Yoelson, Jolson's father, died only months before the film was released, and so did Larry Parks' mother, Mrs. Leona Klusman Parks. When it was obvious Mrs. Parks' time was near, Harry Cohn rushed together a print and had her taken by wheelchair to a Columbia screening room where the film was shown especially for her and her son, who held her hand throughout.

Three different endings for the film had been shot and were under consideration. One picked by Sidney Buchman had "The End" flash on the screen at the moment Julie walks out of the nightclub and Jolson's life. This was used at the Santa Barbara preview. Cohn's favorite ending found Jolson, after Julie's exit, back at the Winter Garden reprising "My Mammy." Cohn had the roof taken off a sound stage so that the camera could pull way back until Jolson was a tiny figure singing his heart out down on the stage. Skolsky preferred the finale where, after Julie is shown leaving, the camera goes back to the nightclub floor where Jolson is singing "April Showers," which was sort of "their song." To make the decision, the Audience Research Institute was hired. After Institute people had viewed the three different endings, they sided with Skolsky, and, disregarding the cost that had been involved in shooting his own literally rafter-raising finale, Cohn recognized that the warm, romantic sentiment of the "April Showers" wrap-up was more in keeping with what had just gone before.

Skolsky's choice became the ending of The Jolson Story.

There were two numbers, however, that Harry Cohn insisted be cut.

One was "Sonny Boy," co-authored by Jolson himself and sung by him in the 1928 film The Singing Fool. His recording of the tune went on to become, by some estimates, the first record ever to sell a million copies, as well as one of the pieces most identified with Al Jolson. For The Jolson

Jolson (Larry Parks) sings "Chazan auf Shabbos," a Yiddish number eventually cut from The Jolson Story.

Story, they had recreated the scene from the earlier film wherein he sang the heart-tugging song to a small boy. According to Jolson, "People cried so much no one could concentrate on the rest of the movie, so it had to be cut." Cohn was more blunt: "It slowed down the picture." There were rumors that the song had actually been scissored because "Sonny Boy" was the nickname of the child Jolson and Ruby Keeler had adopted, and whom Jolson no longer saw, but since he did sing it in a different setting in Jolson Sings Again, they appear to have been merely gossip.

The other number cut was performed by Jolson in a party scene at his home. Betty Garrett recalls, "It was a charming song in Yiddish called 'Chazan auf Shabbos' ["Cantor for the Sabbath"] which Larry, a Lutheran, learned phonetically. He worked so hard on it. However, it was several minutes long and drew unfavorable comment on a sneak preview in Santa Barbara--you can draw your own conclusions."

With a couple of additional lesser cuts, including the omission of a telephone love scene between Jolson, in Hollywood, and Julie, in New York, The Jolson Story was ready for release.

On September 12, 1946, Columbia held a major press preview of the film at the studio followed by an ice cream-and-cake party at "the Schwabadero" (Schwab's drugstore) hosted by Sidney Skolsky. Outside, mobs gathered and the night was lit by "baby spots" ("to conform to Skolsky's size, y'know," said The Hollywood Reporter). Inside, Carmen Cavallaro was at the piano--ten years before he would provide the soundtrack playing for star Tyrone Power in another successful Columbia musical biography, The Eddy Duchin Story. The principal players from The Jolson Story attended the soirée, along with director Alfred E. Green, Alan Ladd, Dick Powell, June Allyson, William Powell, Louella Parsons, Hedda Hopper, John Garfield, Celeste Holm, Laraine Day, Dane Clark, Peggy Ann Garner, and Nina Foch. The festivities were broadcast live on the radio, hosted by Irwin Allen, who decades from then would become the screen's foremost producer of disaster movies (The Poseidon Adventure, The Towering Inferno, etc.).

It was decided that, regardless of the two-hour limit put on it by the Music Hall, to cut the film any further would be destructive. The final cut was to be two hours and eight minutes and, said Cohn, "If the Hall doesn't like it, it can lump it." The Hall liked it. So did the public and the press [see chapter 5]. The Jolson Story had its world première at the Music Hall on October 10, 1946, and was held over for eight weeks, concluding the still-capacity engagement on December 4, 1946, to make way for the already scheduled M-G-M production of Till the Clouds Roll By. A month after the New York opening, the film bowed in Los Angeles where it took two theaters, the Pantages and the Hillstreet, to accommodate the crowds.

"I wasn't really around during the shooting of The Jolson Story," explains Betty Garrett. "I was working on the Broadway stage most of the time. But on one vacation trip to the Coast I did get to see a rehearsal or two. When it opened in New York, some bright publicity man decided I should be the one to put Larry's name up on the marquee at Radio City Music Hall. So they put up a big ladder and one by one I took the letters spelling LARRY PARKS, which were about two feet tall, and put them up in front of the title. It was a great thrill."

"So was seeing the movie. About a month after the picture opened, interest in Larry had become so great on the part of the New York magazine and newspaper writers that Columbia flew him in to do publicity. We saw the movie together. When it was over, Larry asked me if I had liked it. I just opened my mouth and cried like a baby."

The first ads used for the film showed a silhouette in a typical Jolson gesture rather than a definite star, but after Larry Parks had been recognized for his sterling performance, his face was inserted. Harry Cohn gave him a bonus and a new Ford. Jolson sent him a telegram: "Thanks for making me a great actor."

A star was born.

A star was re-born. Jolson, thanks to the film more popular than he'd been since the twenties, recorded an album of songs from The Jolson Story for Decca Records, and a month after its release he received his first royalty payment: $400,000. It remained the label's top-selling album. He was back on Broadway, too. Record shops along that thoroughfare blared his recordings daily to passersby via loudspeakers. Often crowds would gather to listen. Young people who were not even born when Jolson was at his peak seemed to enjoy him as much as their seniors, maybe more so.

When the Academy Award nominations were announced early in 1947, The Jolson Story was mentioned six times. There was, of course, no category for Jolson, whose unbilled soundtrack contribution was unique in film history. Larry Parks won a best actor nomination and William Demarest ranked among the supporting actor candidates. Other nominations: Joseph Walker, color cinematography; John Livadary, sound recording; Morris Stoloff, scoring of a musical picture; and William Lyon, film editing.

The story of The Jolson Story had come full circle. On March 13, 1947, the Academy presentations were held at Hollywood's Shrine Auditorium, where, five years earlier, Sidney Skolsky had gotten the idea for the film while watching Jolson perform at a benefit. Parks lost the award to Fredric March for The Best Years of Our Lives, Samuel Goldwyn's timely drama of returning servicemen trying to adjust to postwar life also voted best picture of 1946 (it earned a total of seven Oscars). Following presenter Joan Fontaine's announcement that the absent March was best actor, and Best Years co-player Cathy O'Donnell's acceptance of his statuette, Betty Garrett squeezed her husband's hand and whispered, "Next time." Afterward, it was said that Parks missed getting the Oscar by one of the smallest margins of votes in Academy history.

The sole winners from The Jolson Story were John Livadary and Morris Stoloff. Demarest lost to handless war veteran Harold Russell, also of The Best Years of Our Lives. Cinematographers Charles Rosher, Leonard Smith, and Arthur Arling picked up the statuette for The Yearling, prompting a colleague of the losing Joseph Walker to lean over at the ceremonies and remark, "Joe, it took three of 'em to beat you!"

Later, Photoplay magazine corrected some of these slights at its 1947 Gold Medal Awards presentations in the Crystal Room of the Beverly Hills Hotel. As a result of a nationwide poll of moviegoers, Bing Crosby and Ingrid Bergman were selected favorite actor and actress of the year, while the most popular film was The Jolson Story.

Larry Parks and Evelyn Keyes received awards for their leads in the winning film, for which Harry Cohn accepted the venerable Gold Medal. Describing his part in the production as "just an innocent bystander," Cohn paid tribute to Larry Parks for his excellent performance; producer Sidney Skolsky for his endurance and drive throughout the project; Sidney Buchman for his invaluable assistance; and Al Jolson for living the life that made possible The Jolson Story.

Choked with emotion, Jolson said that this was the first time in all his years in show business that he had been honored with an award, and that he was especially appreciative because "it came from you ... the people." He then sang.

The event was filmed for Ralph Staub's Screen Snapshots, the long-lived, one-reel series that had been crucial to the formation of Columbia Pictures many years before.

Around the same time, Modern Screen, another leading fan publication, revealed that Larry Parks had been voted Man of the Year (1947) by the magazine's readers. "He's our all-out, all-time Popularity Poll Winner," wrote staff member

Kirtley Baskette in the January, 1948, issue, "with a record rush of ballots (200,000) that's never been matched in Modern Screen's long life!"

To Jack Warner's embarrassment, just as his studio was celebrating the twentieth anniversary of the sound revolution brought in by their film The Jazz Singer, the life of the man who had starred in it was cleaning up at the box office for Columbia Pictures.

The Jolson Story grossed $8,000,000.

References

1. Jolson was born in the shtetel, or village, of Srednik in Russian Lithuania. The most credible birth date for him is May 26, 1883, though other years a bit earlier and a bit later have been given. Jolson used to say that they didn't bother keeping such records then in his shtetel, but it's a known fact that he himself was never anxious to pin down the year of his birth.

2. When Columbia Pictures moved from its original Hollywood site in 1972, some of its old stages were converted into indoor tennis courts. Today, the property houses Sunset-Gower Studios which is used mainly for the production of television soap operas such as General Hospital and Days of Our Lives, as well as the making of television commercials.

3. Much of Columbia's "B" movie production was dispatched to Columbia Sunset, a silent-era studio taken over by Columbia two miles east of the main Gower location.

4. Jolson received no on-screen credit for his Jolson Story and Jolson Sings Again soundtracks.

5. Minstrel Man starred the old-time vaudevillian Benny Fields in what was a positively lavish production for the Poverty Row company known as PRC. Fields portrayed a Broadway star who, grief-stricken at the childbirth death of his wife, left his infant daughter with friends and dropped out of sight. Years later, he was reunited with his daughter who was now starring on Broadway herself. The story had nothing in common with The Jolson Story, but there were distinct similarities nevertheless. Fields, like Jolson, was near the end of a long career--his own life and that of his wife and partner, Blossom Seeley, would be chronicled in Paramount's Somebody Loves Me (1952), with Betty Hutton and

Ralph Meeker. In eye-rolling fashion, he performed many of the numbers in blackface. And several of the musical portions themselves--minstrel shows, a solo spot in front of a theater curtain, a nightclub performance--were done in Jolson Story-like settings. Fields' delivery was considerably lower-key than Jolson's, however, his baritone was actually closer in style to that of the crooners of the day. While not really an actor, he brought surprising sincerity and appeal to the musical sequences. It was easy to see why Minstrel Man suggested its director, Joseph H. Lewis, to those about to make The Jolson Story.

■ ENCORE ■

When men are arrived at the
goal, they should not turn
back.

Plutarch

Once again Al Jolson got the idea first for a film about his life, only this time it didn't seem so far-fetched. Observing the attendance records being set everywhere by The Jolson Story, he put the bee in Harry Cohn's fedora about a sequel.

"My life didn't end when Ruby and I divorced," he argued. "I entertained our boys overseas, got sick, recovered, met and married Erle, had my life story made into a sensational movie. I've got a lot of songs left in me, too. Whaddaya say we continue the story in another picture, Harry?"

Jolson's timing wasn't as good as he thought. It was an axiom in Hollywood that sequels were almost never as successful as the originals, which Cohn was then finding out for himself. His expensive production of Down to Earth (1947), starring Rita Hayworth and new star Larry Parks, revived the fantasy theme and certain characters from Columbia's 1941 hit Here Comes Mr. Jordan, and it was not doing very well at the box office. A dubious Cohn replied his familiar, "I'll sleep on it."

A week passed, and Jolson still had no decision from the somnolent mogul. He grew angry, feeling Cohn was not only short-sighted but an ingrate.

Then he remembered that Cohn had long been jealous of Metro chief Louis B. Mayer, not only for the riches available to M-G-M films from the parent Loew's Incorporated but because of the studio head's own rajah-like lifestyle. Indeed, he tried to emulate Mayer. Jolson went right over to M-G-M to talk about the project.

In December, 1947, M-G-M producer Edwin H. Knopf, who had made few musicals, announced that he would produce the sequel, Jolson Sings Again, at the Culver City lot and that while the film would have many songs, it would be primarily a drama. It was further reported that M-G-M star Gene Kelly might play Jolson. This alarmed fans of The Jolson Story and Larry Parks' performance, inciting an avalanche of mail to both M-G-M and Columbia to protest the casting of dancer Kelly, whose own singing voice (among musical comedy's weakest) was by now well known. Jolson's shrewd strategy of embroiling Cohn's envy of posh M-G-M plus the public outcry galvanized Cohn into action.

Completely forgetting (or choosing to forget) his own initial reluctance, Cohn phoned Jolson to ask, "Whatsamatter, you're not making enough millions with Columbia?"

Sidney Buchman, so helpful on The Jolson Story, was set to both write the screenplay and produce, while Henry Levin, who had been coming along at Columbia directing such films as The Gallant Blade (1948), starring Larry Parks, was signed to direct the Jolson sequel. Morris Stoloff and George Duning would handle the music scoring [see chapter 13]. All had hoped that Joseph Walker would again be cinematographer, but Walker recalled, "Jolson Sings Again was shot fast and cheap and was also in color, but I couldn't do it as I was on another picture, probably one with Rosalind Russell. It was in my contract that I was to be kept free of other commitments in order to do the pictures with Irene Dunne, Jean Arthur, and especially Rosalind Russell."

Fortunately, another top cameraman was available, the Technicolor specialist William Snyder, who had shot the previous year's Rita Hayworth vehicle at Columbia, The Loves of Carmen (1948), winning a color cinematography Academy Award nomination for it.

Snyder was the rare cinematographer who had started with virtually no knowledge of photography. Originally, he had sought a musical career in New York. Friends, however, convinced him that the booming Hollywood was the place to be, and as talkies arrived there, so did Snyder. He loaded cameras at M-G-M, then worked up to second cameraman followed by many years as one of the top cameramen at the Technicolor Corporation.

During the golden age of Technicolor movies, Snyder photographed (with collaborators) Aloma of the South Seas (1941), White Savage (1943), The Princess and the Pirate (1944), Wonder Man (1945), and Blue Skies (1946). At Columbia, besides the Hayworth picture and the sequel to The Jolson Story, he soloed on two other Larry Parks films, Renegades (1946) and The Swordsman (1947), as well as The Bandit of Sherwood Forest (1946), The Return of October (1948), The Man from Colorado (1948), and The Petty Girl (1950).

Snyder's post-forties work, like color cinematography in general, has been less interesting, although he was behind the camera on M-G-M's The Toast of New Orleans (1950), with Mario Lanza, and many RKO releases during Howard Hughes' regime there, including the John Wayne opuses Flying Leathernecks (1951) and The Conqueror (1956). (The latter film was a cinematography collaboration with Joseph La Shelle, Leo Tover and Harry J. Wild.)

More recently, Snyder photographed a number of Walt Disney productions, among them Bon Voyage (1962), Summer Magic (1963), The Boatniks (1970), and $1,000,000 Duck (1971).

• • •

As the starting date for the film loomed, it began to look as if Larry Parks might not be reprising his Jolson after all. He was suing Columbia to be free of his contract. "Larry Parks is an ungrateful bastard," Cohn hissed to Sidney Buchman, "but he'll need Columbia before Columbia'll need him." Jack Cole once recalled that Cohn hated all actors, that he would yell "They're all a bunch of tough shits and I could replace any one of them in a minute."

Columbia set out to do just that with Larry Parks.

One day at the Hillcrest Country Club, where Hollywood's "show biz" Jewish set congregated, Jolson mentioned the situation to George Jessel, still producing at 20th Century-Fox. He suggested that Jolson take a look at his recent film

The real Al Jolson sings "For Me and My Gal" in his September, 1948, test for Jolson Sings Again.

I Wonder Who's Kissing Her Now (1947), with Mark Stevens acting the role of Gay Nineties troubadour Joe Howard and Buddy Clark doing the actual singing on the soundtrack.

"Mark has a lot of appeal," said Jessel, "especially for the girls. Even Hedy Lamarr's after him. He might make a good substitute for Parks."

He arranged a screening of the film for Jolson and the Columbia brass. Stevens, who had been a chorus boy in Rhapsody in Blue, was emerging as a star of brief wattage, and was attractive in the Howard film biography, but the Columbia troops (and Jolson in particular) thought he lacked the requisite vitality to be convincing as Broadway's erstwhile great musical comedy star.

In the back of Jolson's mind all along was the rekindled hope that he would be able to play himself in Jolson Sings Again. Jolson was older now in the story, so he felt he could get away with it. Never one to mince words, Harry Cohn continued to resist the idea, telling him that it would come as too great a shock and disappointment to millions of Jolson

Story fans to find "some old kocker" suddenly popping up as Al Jolson--even if it was Jolson himself.

He did allow his friend to do a screen test, though, which the always cost-conscious Cohn knew could also be used as a study film for whoever would eventually portray him. In September, 1948, Jolson, in front of a stage curtain, performed in a short 8mm black-and-white test to "Is It True What They Say About Dixie?," "For Me and My Gal," "Baby Face," and "It All Depends on You." Jolson was not happy with the results. It was a pre-recorded soundtrack to which Jolson had to lip-sync, a process that had always ruffled him. He never liked to be locked into a rendition, wanted to be able to vary a song as the mood hit him (or as the lyrics would come, or not come, to mind). He believed that having physically to adjust his performance to a number recorded at another time robbed it of essential spontaneity.

After wheedling Cohn into letting him test one more time to show what he could do with an actual scene from the projected film, a month later he faced test cameras again to sing "She's a Latin from Manhattan" before some GIs in a jungle setting. The outcome was better, but Cohn remained unconvinced. (The song was not used in the final film, either.)

Then the courts decreed that Larry Parks would stay at Columbia. He signed to play Al Jolson again.

A resigned but disappointed Jolson, who had been recording songs for the film for weeks, continued the task, enthusiasm unabated. Among the other recorded numbers that did not make it to the completed soundtrack were "Lazy," "I Can't Give You Anything But Love," "Where Did Robinson Crusoe Go with Friday on Saturday Night?" and "When You Were Sweet Sixteen."

Barbara Hale came over from RKO Pictures to play Jolson's wife, Erle Galbraith, called Ellen Clark in the film [see chapter 7]. Since Mrs. Jolson was also young and darkly lovely, and had done some bits at Columbia, many wondered why she hadn't played herself in the production. Not long ago I put this question to her and she wrote back, "You are really under the delusion that I could act. I haven't a drop of talent."

Larry Parks confers with Sidney Buchman, the writer-producer of Jolson Sings Again.

The indispensable Ludwig Donath and Tamara Shayne rejoined the company as Jolson's parents, as did stalwarts William Demarest as Steve Martin and Bill Goodwin as Tom Baron. From Broadway came Myron McCormick to limn a Hollywood producer [see chapter 8].

Jolson Sings Again, with a final shooting script that was to suffer few changes this time, began filming on November 11, 1948.

Again, Parks worked on the numbers with dance director Audrene Brier. Years later, he would say, "I had one particular problem. Jolson had pre-recorded all the songs before the script was ready, and he sang every one as if he were going to drop dead at the end of it.

"Well, that was Jolson. He always sang like that, which was why people loved him. But it was difficult from an actor's point of view. As, for instance, in 'I'm Just Wild About

Harry,' which was recorded with great verve and turned out later to be used in a scene in which Jolson collapses during the song. How do you taper off at the top of your voice? I finally decided to play it as if I were singing so loudly out of desperation, struggling to get to the end of the song."

The shooting itself went smoothly and with remarkable speed for a production of its time and import. Filming was completed the day before Christmas, 1948, only a little more than a month after it had begun.

Director Henry Levin could recall only one significant quandary connected with the film, and that was quickly solved. The original ending shot had Jolson and his family and friends at dinner discussing the possibility of a sequel to The Jolson Story. At first hesitant and wanting to rest for a while, Jolson finally becomes interested when he realizes it can be the story of his great comeback and happiness with Erle. Papa Yoelson raises his glass and says, "A natural." That was the way it was supposed to have ended, but Cohn and Buchman, after viewing a rough cut, chose to end it, like The Jolson Story, on a musical note. So the benefit performance of "Rock-a-Bye Your Baby with a Dixie Melody," which immediately preceded the first closing, was now used to end the movie, and the scene in which the principals talked about a Jolson Story sequel was cut completely.

Said Levin, "The scene we cut at the end seemed anticlimactic, anyway. I've always believed that when a story is over--get out. Don't hang around to hear someone say, 'I thought it was over already.'"

Jolson Sings Again premièred in New York at Loew's State Theater on August 17, 1949, to fine reviews. Larry Parks had told everyone he thought the screenplay was superior to the first one, and some of the critics concurred. Al Jolson was characteristically unrestrained. In town for publicity, Jolson, reported The New York World Telegram, "just happened" to be passing the theater just before the first showing. At first unrecognized, he stopped to inform the "tremendous" queue, "It's worth it, folks! It's worth it! The picture's great!" He then sold the first ticket.

It was different, the paper went on, when The Jolson Story opened. Jolson had remained in a hotel room, worrying

In Jolson Sings Again, Jolson (Larry Parks) sings "Baby Face" at the Arkansas Army hospital where Ellen Clark works.

about its reception, until he read the reviews and was reassured.

"The first picture was all right," Jolson said, "but the second is much better. It's down-to-earth! It's got heart! It's wonderful! Here's a guy who's a has-been and even though he's a millionaire, he wants nothing more in the world but to sing and be loved by his audiences. It's enough to make you cry. And, brother, don't think I haven't."

Jolson shed no tears over Jolson Sings Again. As stated by Sidney Skolsky, Jolson owned twenty-five per cent of the film which grossed $5,000,000.

Disclosed Skolsky, "Cohn had promised Jolson fifty per cent of The Jolson Story because he never dreamed that it was going to gross $8,000,000. But when Cohn discovered the potential in a Jolson film biography, there was no way he was going to make the same mistake twice."

Sidney Skolsky never felt that he had been accorded appropriate remuneration for his efforts on behalf of The Jolson Story--not only as the one who brought the idea to Columbia, and was credited as producer, but as a working journalist with many media connections who was responsible for much of the production's attendant publicity and promotion. He made this known to Jolson who threw him a very small bone "as additional compensation" via several written replies that betrayed their deteriorating relationship by beginning with the salutation "Dear Sidney" and, by late 1947, ending with "Dear Mr. Skolsky." Skolsky's wife, Estelle, once said that her late husband "did not have the best head for business." A friend of the columnist's was more succinct: "Sidney was no match for a couple of old sharks like Harry Cohn and Al Jolson." Along with the conviction that he had received short money for his work, Skolsky was hurt and angry that he wasn't asked to participate in the sequel.

The Motion Picture Academy of Arts and Sciences rewarded Jolson Sings Again with three Oscar nominations: Sidney Buchman, story and screenplay; William Snyder, color cinematography; and Morris Stoloff and George Duning, scoring of a musical picture.

• • •

As soon as Jolson Sings Again was seen to be a success, talk inevitably began about a third Jolson film biography. Harry Cohn wanted Larry Parks again, but Jolson was bound to portray himself this time or forget the whole thing. He went over to RKO to propose the film to the new producing team of Jerry Wald and Norman Krasna who were setting up offices there. After discussions in which Wald-Krasna seemed agreeable, the project was envisioned as a patriotic tribute not only to Jolson but the USO, under whose auspices he so often entertained servicemen overseas. Among the titles mulled were The Stars and Stripes Forever, Let Me Sing and GI Jolson. It was still in the talking stage when, shortly after returning from performing for our troops in Korea in late 1950, Jolson died suddenly from a heart attack.

Betty Garrett remembers, "After Al passed away, Columbia spoke to Larry about the possibility of doing a third film called Jolson Goes on Singing. There were at least a couple of dozen recordings left over from the two previous ones. But then Larry was called to testify before the House Un-American Activities Committee.

"And that was that."

▪ CRITICS' CHOICE ▪

> Addison Dewitt: My native habitat is the Theatre--in it I toil not, neither do I spin. I am a critic and commentator. I am essential to the Theatre --as ants to a picnic, as the boll weevil to a cotton field.
>
> From "All About Eve"

The reviews for The Jolson Story and Jolson Sings Again were exceptional not only in their praise for the two films but because 1) movie musicals then were rarely taken seriously by critics; and 2) sequels in any genre usually fell far short, esthetically and commercially, of the originals.

Unique indeed in the thirties or forties was the musical film that received accolades similar to those garnered by The Jolson Story when it was released in 1946. The magazines were particularly effulgent.

In Modern Screen, Dorothy Kilgallen selected it "Picture of the Month." Although she felt that Jolson's real character had been whitewashed, she wrote,

> The vagaries of the screen writers can be dismissed as amusing but unimportant, since this is not their picture. The Jolson Story belongs to the music department from start to finish. These talented workers--Morris Stoloff, Saul Chaplin and Martin Fried--have created a triumphant soundtrack, fast and bright and suitable ... every yard of it deserves applause.... Al Jolson may be surprised at what he sees when he views his screen biography, but if he is any kind of a movie fan he will have a good time at it.

The Jolson Story was "Pick of the Pictures" in Liberty: "A perfect tribute to Al Jolson, this movie is as schmaltzy, spirited and unforgettable as the singer himself. One of the biggest events in show business since Asa Yoelson left home."

Look applauded it as "backstage biography at its best. Its semi-fictional account of the singer's life and loves varies little from a familiar film pattern, but the expert treatment keeps it fresh and exciting. Larry Parks duplicates the dy namic Jolson personality with uncanny skill. A memorable, nostalgic show."

Time found the film "a fine, noisy celebration of Hollywood's two decades of talking movies ... uncommonly entertaining"; while Cue called it "amusing, lively film entertainment," adding, "Evelyn Keyes is a charming and talented Mrs. Jolson."

The Jolson Story had come as such a surprise that some reviewers got their facts muddled.

Motion Picture's critic thought Larry Parks, in films for five years, was new to the screen, writing,

> For solid entertainment, this one is hard to beat. It captures what screen biographies too often fail to capture--the actual spirit of the man portrayed. Newcomer Larry Parks plays Jolson and the picture is a personal triumph for him. He has Jolson's mannerisms and gestures down so pat it's hard to believe the songs were actually dubbed in by Jolson himself.

Amazingly, Photoplay, on the other hand, was not aware that Jolson had done the actual singing. "The Jolson Story is going to leave a happy glow all over American audiences," the magazine predicted--so far so good. "The first half of the film is a masterpiece; it is only in the second half that a slowing-up becomes noticeable. Parks performs with a punch, a sincere verve that captures his audience. Furthermore, he does an uncannily good job of reproducing a living man. Even the voice seems to be Jolson's(!)."

Accurately foreseeing "terrific grosses," Daily Variety went on to rave,

Larry Parks and Evelyn Keyes in The Jolson Story, which critics called "terrific," "perfect," "delightful," "captivating" and "boffo."

One of the top musicals of the screen.... Larry Parks unquestionably will win an Academy nomination ... Evelyn Keyes enters picture when footage is nearly half unreeled, but more than makes up for her earlier absence by a lovely presence and convincing perform-

> ance, her coloring particularly highlighted by the film's tints. William Demarest gives another of his sterling roughshod delineations. Ludwig Donath and Tamara Shayne are particularly fine as Jolson's parents ... Topping all else, however, is the Jolson voice. The voice timbre of the old mammy-singer is still there to enthrall the theatre-goer and listener, and dubbed in for Larry Parks to sing, it comes out for boffo effect.

The Hollywood Reporter echoed these sentiments:

> Calling this attraction terrific is almost a deliberate understatement. Jolson is singing really better than he has ever sung before.... Larry Parks—never in the long history of Jolson impersonators has anyone else captured him so perfectly. The character called "Julie Benson" is beautifully played by Evelyn Keyes. The Jolson Story is an all-around triumph for all concerned, including Al Jolson whose personality inspired it. And a little guy named Sidney Skolsky has the right to stick out his chest and be proud.

In The New York Daily News, Kate Cameron awarded four stars to the film, lauding it as "a delightful picture" and Larry Parks for his "impressive impersonation."

"The film is essentially a testament to the excitement of show business," opined Howard Barnes in The New York Herald Tribune.

> As such, it is a captivating screen musical.... The blackface Mammy singer holds the center of the screen as he is dashingly portrayed by Larry Parks.... The songs are nostalgic and delightful. Sidney Skolsky has produced the work with affection and a deep knowledge of show business. The direction of Alfred Green is remarkably fluent for an episodic continuity and the assisting players fill in fragments of a supposed life story agreeably.... There are nicely sentimentalized portraits of the singer's parents by Ludwig Donath and Tamara Shayne.... William Demarest is a tower of strength in the wisps of drama and Scotty Beckett is fine as the boy Jolson.

Bosley Crowther of The New York Times, the dean of film critics, stood practically alone in his cool (and on at least one point inaccurate) reception to The Jolson Story and Larry Parks. Wrote Crowther,

> In this gaudy fictionalization of Al Jolson's hurly-burly life, it is not the story of the trouper which attracts the indifferently disposed, not the extreme and mawkish drooling over a popular star of stage and screen, but rather the generous sound-tracking of a sack full of familiar old songs which imparts to the film an appealing nostalgic quality.... There is little or no dramatic point--and certainly no quality of character--conveyed in this fat and fatuous tale.

Unaware that he had reviewed numerous films in which Parks had appeared, Crowther went on,

> Mr. Parks, who is new to the screen, struts and mugs in the manner of Jolson, as a bright impersonator might do. Unfortunately, his speaking voice is silken, while the singing voice of Mr. Jolson is full of sand.... Nor is Mr. Parks dynamic in the indefinable style of the man he plays. The image at no time is equal to the vitality of the sound.... Let's just say that The Jolson Story is more a phonographic than photographic job.

• • •

When Jolson Sings Again appeared, the Times was much more receptive. Crowther colleague Thomas M. Pryor commended the film as

> an occasion which warrants some lusty cheering ... at least twice as good as The Jolson Story. Sidney Buchman, who wrote and produced, has shrewdly bridged the gap between this Technicolored picture and its predecessor so that a knowledge of the 1946 production is not necessary for complete understanding and enjoyment. There is heart, humor, tragedy and a warm sprinkling of sentiment in Mr. Buchman's story. Larry Parks comes close to perfection, though his speaking voice still lacks the resonance of Jolson's singing. Barbara Hale is truly a revelation, for after

> many years in unimpressive screen roles, she finally has got hold of a part that permits her to blossom like a fresh personality.... However, in the final analysis, Jolson Sings Again is as much Al Jolson's picture as if he actually were seen in it, for without his voice on the sound track all the other remarkable efforts would have been in vain. There is only one voice like Jolson's, and it is good to be hearing it again.

Many reviewers shared Pryor's belief that Jolson Sings Again was superior to The Jolson Story.

In The Los Angeles Examiner, Louella Parsons said, "Unlike most sequels, Jolson Sings Again is even better than the first. It has more heart interest, more warmth and it flows much more naturally.... Just as the first Jolson story put Larry Parks on the map, this one will make the world Barbara Hale-conscious. She's so real, so attractive as the second Mrs. Jolson."

Cue was in accord:

> In some respects, the second in this biographical series (will there be a third?) is considerably better than the first. Its story is simpler; it seems to have more integrity, less soapy sentimentality and a good deal less of that stomach-turning adulation, awe and reverence for a plaster saint that has helped to spoil so many other motion picture biographies.... Larry Parks gives a remarkable impersonation of his alter ego.

While she thought Jolson Sings Again very good, the Daily News' Kate Cameron liked it slightly less than The Jolson Story, giving the newer film a three-and-a-half-stars rating. "The second film is not as sentimental, nor as heart-warming in its domestic scenes, as its predecessor," she explained. "It is, however, well made and more interesting

---

A letter from Mama Yoelson: Jolson (Larry Parks) and Steve Martin (William Demarest) in The Jolson Story. Below: Jolson (Larry Parks), shown making The Jolson Story, sings "You Made Me Love You" in Jolson Sings Again.

from a technical standpoint than the first, as it takes the audience into the Columbia studio in Hollywood to show just how The Jolson Story was created.... Parks, of course, does another amazing impersonation of Al."

Cameron mentioned that Sidney Skolsky's name did not appear on the screen, "although it was Skolsky who had the idea of making the original picture and it was he who brought that popular production to fruition with the help of Columbia officials and director Alfred E. Green."

Frank Quinn in The New York Sunday Mirror chose Jolson Sings Again "Movie of the Week," writing, "Once again a superb job of dubbing Jolson's singing with Parks' animation has been accomplished.... Barbara Hale is an alluring addition to the cast and provides charm, vitality and inspiration. Parks is perfect."

Barbara Hale's personal raves for her role as the "second" Mrs. Jolson were capped by an extravagant William Hawkins in The New York World Telegram. "As Ellen Jolson is played by Barbara Hale," wrote Hawkins, "she is likely to become one of the most beloved heroines in the history of moving pictures."

If Barbara Hale's Ellen didn't quite make us forget Vivien Leigh's Scarlett or Judy Garland's Dorothy or Lassie's Lassie, she did brighten 1949 considerably. She also managed to do something more practiced entertainers than she had failed to accomplish: steal scenes (and reviews) from the incomparable Al Jolson.

▪ THE PARKS STORY ▪

> Toward no crimes have men shown themselves so cold-bloodedly cruel as in punishing differences of belief.
>
> James Russell Lowell

By the time Larry Parks became an "overnight" sensation in The Jolson Story, he had paid his dues.

Following a few seasons of spotty theater work in the East, he arrived in Hollywood on September 16, 1940, with one nickel in his pocket. His first film role was as a Roman soldier in a Biblical short subject for which he received three dollars a day while a camel colleague received fifty. He signed with Columbia Pictures, and for four years prior to the Jolson film Parks was the company's busiest if least recognized utility actor, walking on unobtrusively in a smattering of "A" productions but employed mainly in more than two dozen "B" movies. Sometimes he didn't even appear in them, but was merely an unbilled off-screen voice. When he did land a prominent role, he could almost count on being upstaged by a loveable canine, or having his best scenes end up on the cutting room floor. With a rare free hour or two, he also did stunt work for some of the studio's male stars.

"Everybody he worked with got famous except Larry Parks," wrote columnist Hedda Hopper just before the Jolson film opened.

Not a few thought The Jolson Story was Larry Parks' screen debut.

Lloyd Bridges, a friend of Parks' at the studio, has recalled, "Sometimes I was in two or three pictures a week at Columbia (where I had a stock contract) just so they could make their money back on me." Janet Blair, there throughout the forties as well, feels that most of her time with Columbia was "bondage, fettered with suspensions over my refusal to accept lousy roles." Parks made no waves--for a while.

When Harry Cohn finally said, "Larry, you're Jolie," Parks was ready!

Born in Olathe, Kansas, on December 3, 1914, the actor's full name was Samuel Klusman Lawrence Parks. His parents were Frank H. Parks, an advertising man of Irish lineage, and Leona Klusman Parks, an organist of German descent. His paternal grandfather was a Kansas sheriff at the time of Jesse James and Quantrill's Raiders. When Parks was a year old, the family moved to Joliet, Illinois, where bouts with rheumatic fever and paralysis left young "Klaus" (his nickname) with a weakened heart and one leg slightly shorter than the other. Exercise, therapy and built-up shoes helped him to live normally with these problems. He attended Farragut Elementary School and Joliet High, then, inspired by the doctors who had helped him through his illnesses, took pre-med courses at the University of Illinois. Billed as Klusman Parks, he performed in numerous campus plays there, becoming increasingly attracted to acting.

"Matter of fact," he later said, "the only reason I planned to continue my medical studies was that I didn't want to be a starving actor. That was during the Depression and the German half of my nature saw very plainly that acting was a risky venture along about then. Finally the Irish in me said, 'To heck with being practical!' so I became an actor."

With a Bachelor of Science degree in chemistry, he was graduated from the University of Illinois in 1936.

Coincidentally, but not irrelevantly, the Communist Party was established in Hollywood that same year, the reasons being the prestige and glamour there, the financial support possible and the influence films had on the public. (In 1946, the year The Jolson Story was released, the Party's national chairman, William Z. Foster, told a group of card-carriers assembled at screenwriter Dalton Trumbo's home, "We can't expect to put any propaganda in the films, but we can try to keep anti-Soviet agitprop out." The next year it was charged that they had been doing very well at Red proselytizing in Hollywood films.)

After touring Illinois with a local group of actors enlisted from college, the now re-named Larry Parks answered fifty ads he found in theatrical trade papers, received three replies and accepted the highest salary offer: thirty dollars a week with Guy Palmerton's Lake Whalom Playhouse in Fitchburg, Massachusetts.

After a summer season there, Parks headed for New York City where he took a room on West 53rd Street near Tenth Avenue for $2.50 a week. He soon began a two-year association with the left-oriented, vital Group Theater, which had been formed in 1931 by Harold Clurman, Cheryl Crawford and Lee Strasberg and existed for ten years. Many of the plays produced by the Group were socially significant, the writing, acting and directing achieved with a ground-breaking realistic fervor. The esteemed director Elia Kazan has stated, "When I entered the Group in 1932, three-quarters of the Group members were left-wing." Kazan, for a while a member of the Communist Party, added, "I think the Group Theater was the greatest influence on the world theater since the great Russians of the twenties." Parks got no large parts with the Group, but absorbed much from the classes there and the camaraderie.

He played in the Group hit Golden Boy, also appearing on stage in New York in The Pure in Heart, All the Living, and My Heart's in the Highlands.

Pay was minimal, and theater jobs spaced out, so at various times he also worked as an usher at Carnegie Hall as well as a guide at Radio City and the World's Fair.

It was a time of deprivation in the United States, and this helped foster a prevailing idealization of the Soviet Union among New York intellectuals. Starting out in Manhattan in the 1930s meant being, as Alfred Kazin put it, "engulfed by Socialists ... all the most accomplished philosophers ever born to the New York streets, tireless virtuosi who threw radical argument at each other morning, noon and night." The concerned, serious Parks was a willing listener at first, then a participant.

Larry Parks and wife Betty Garrett in a publicity pose for the TV comedy The Penlands and the Poodle, aired in 1957.

During these years, Parks saw a performance by another Midwestern show business tyro, the gifted Betty Garrett, who was born in St. Joseph, Missouri, on May 23, 1919. She had won a scholarship to the Neighborhood Playhouse and was singing and dancing in nightclubs and politically slanted revues around town. Though from afar, he was immediately taken by the pretty, blue-eyed entertainer with the twangy, effervescent comic touch. Their romance would eventually blossom three thousand miles away.

• • •

When his father died in 1939, Parks returned to Illinois to help his mother. Briefly, he worked as a copywriter at an advertising agency, then was hired by the New York Central Railroad out of Chicago, "where I inspected sleeping cars before and after their runs. It's what I was doing when I was summoned to Hollywood," he revealed.

Actor John Garfield, whom Parks had met with the Group Theater and who had recently made good in Hollywood at Warner Bros., and Robert Lewis, a former Group actor-director, wired Parks, urging him to come West for a role in Garfield's next film. Parks took the bus, which was delayed an extra day in New Mexico due to floods, thus depleting his funds. Upon arrival in Los Angeles, he had not eaten for twenty-four hours. To make matters worse, he did not get the part in Garfield's film. The only thing available was some work in short subjects for an independent producer.

Ultimately, he approached Columbia talent executive Max Arnow and talked his way into a screen test. "Actually, it wasn't my test at all," Parks remembered. "I was just the foil for the man they were testing for a role in *Here Comes Mr. Jordan*. He was a character actor named Barry Fitzgerald. I'll never know why, but he didn't get the part and I wound up with a contract." That was May, 1941.

Although only of medium height, Parks was sturdily built, presentable (if possessing a somewhat Napoleonic, pugnacious look), with dark curly hair and, as Hedda Hopper once observed, "somber brown eyes." His rather swarthy appearance suggested climes more exotic than Kansas. In his quiet manner, he was also brighter and better educated than most young Hollywood players of the day, and this particularly impressed Arnow.

Managed by Samuel Briskin, Columbia's prolific, front-rank "B" department claimed Parks' services first, setting the pattern. His debut film was a melodrama called *Mystery Ship* (1941), with Parks in the supporting role of a government agent. In rapid succession that year came *Harmon of Michigan*, *Honolulu Lu*, *Three Girls About Town*, *Sing for Your Supper*, and the most interesting of the lot, an "A" romantic comedy called *You Belong to Me*. Barbara Stanwyck and Henry Fonda starred in one of Parks' more curious, ironic involvements at Columbia. Although unbilled, he had a substantial supporting role as a bespectacled department store worker who gave a radical speech protesting the employment of the wealthy Fonda. The story was by Dalton Trumbo, who later became one of the blacklisted "Hollywood Ten" screenwriters.

An interest in building started early. With a meager salary from which he contributed to his mother's support, he moved into a house with two equally budget conscious friends. One of them, an architect, owned a lot. Parks offered to raise $400 and suggested that he and his buddies build a bungalow and sell it. He borrowed the money, raised more from a finance company and went into the building business.

"The walls of the building stayed up somehow," Parks recalled. "Finally, we got the roof on. And we sold the place but quick. My share of the deal was $133."

Succeeding Parks building deals would be considerably more lucrative.

Parks' rheumatic heart kept him out of World War II, but because the draft was taking many of Hollywood's young actors he found himself in constant siege on the Columbia battlefield. In 1942, his most productive year, Parks was associated with almost twenty films. It began with *North of the Rockies*, a "quickie" Western with Bill Elliott, Tex Ritter, and Parks as the accomplice of fur thieves. In *Alias Boston Blackie*, he was an escaped convict; in *The Boogie Man Will Get You*, starring Boris Karloff, a young divorcé; in *Blondie Goes to College*, a football star; in *A Man's World*, a miner vying with William Wright for Marguerite Chapman; in *Hello, Annapolis*, a midshipman; in *Submarine Raider*, the radio operator; and in *You Were Never Lovelier*, starring Fred Astaire and Rita Hayworth, he was the tennis-playing beau of Hayworth's sister Adele Mara.

Other 1942 films included *Canal Zone*, *Harvard, Here I Come*, *Cadets on Parade*, *Flight Lieutenant*, *They All Kissed*

Larry Parks, *Jolson Story* producer Sidney Skolsky, and Evelyn Keyes between scenes of the film. Below: Larry Parks, John Alexander and Parks' terminally ill mother, Mrs. Leona Parks, during filming.

the Bride, and Atlantic Convoy. Furthermore, in that year's Blondie for Victory and Sabotage Squad, he was not seen but was a voice on the radio, in the former calling servicemen back to camp and in the latter as a Nazi.

During 1943, Parks had two roles that were harbingers of things to come in his life and career. In the potboiler Power of the Press, the more bitterly coincidental of the pair, he played a blacklisted, radical reporter. A happier precursor was the musical biography Is Everybody Happy?, the life story of veteran entertainer Ted Lewis who was portrayed by himself in middle age and by Michael Duane in young manhood. Lewis himself, however, did all the clarinet playing on the soundtrack. Parks stood out as Lewis' horse-playing, skirt-chasing partner. Another notable "B" musical of that year was Reveille with Beverly, with Parks as leading lady Ann Miller's soldier brother.

He completed 1943 as an Indian in The Deerslayer, on loan to Republic Studios, and back at Columbia also did Redhead from Manhattan, First Comes Courage, and Destroyer, with Edward G. Robinson, Glenn Ford and Marguerite Chapman. In the last-named he had a bit as an ensign on a destroyer who sighted a Japanese submarine, exclaiming, "Hey, look! Tojo!"

By 1944, Larry Parks was easing into lightweight leading man roles in "B" films. In Hey, Rookie, he was now Ann Miller's love interest, a musical comedy producer, and he performed similar duties opposite Jane Frazee in She's a Sweetheart. In The Black Parachute he was an American soldier behind enemy lines, while in Sergeant Mike he was the trainer of war dogs. The Racket Man and Stars on Parade completed his film year.

An actress preferring anonymity who was featured in a couple of Columbia "B"s with Parks recalls:

> Larry was the most conscientious actor I ever worked with, especially for one working in "B" movies. In those days, actors employed in the "quickies" took this name to heart: they did them quickly and with little thought to their character's motivation. "B"s, simply, were nothing to be taken seriously. Larry was different. He would approach something like

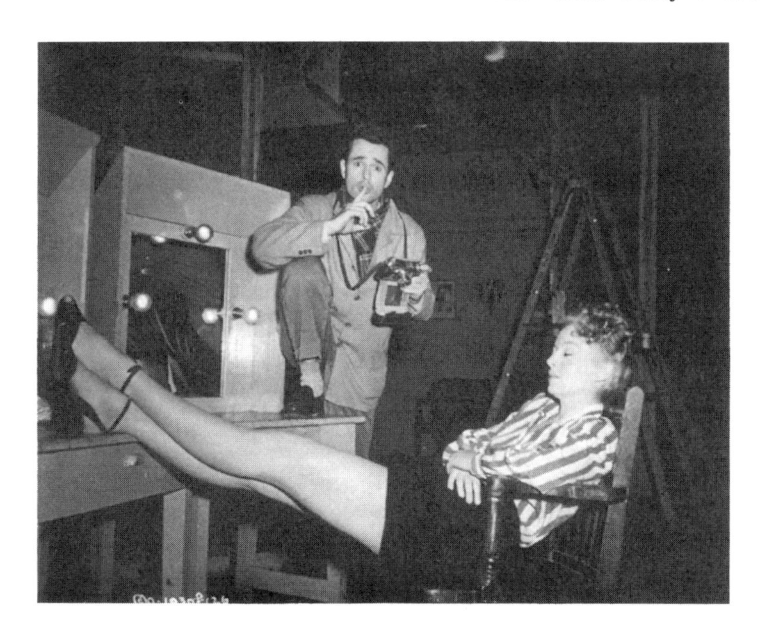

Amateur photographer Larry Parks sneaks up on dozing Evelyn Keyes during a rehearsal break on The Jolson Story.

> Sergeant Mike as if it were Shakespeare. He never dogged it. I must admit I was more than a little intrigued by this unusual intensity of his. In fact, although he was going with Betty Garrett at the time, I had quite a crush on him. I let him know it, too, by being especially ardent in our love scenes. Larry was equally ardent--until the camera stopped, when he went off somewhere to study his script. Alone, unfortunately.
>
> I don't mean to imply that he was rude or any more self-centered than any other actor. He was always congenial and considerate. But he seemed to save all his passion--in a tendency shared, I am told, with Al Jolson--for his performing.

Anxious to return to the stage, Parks had become active in Hollywood's Actors Laboratory Theater (the Actors Lab), which was sometimes referred to as the Group Theater West. It had been established in 1941 at the small Las Palmas Theater by Group playwright Clifford Odets and John Garfield, who continued to lure Group members to the film capital. Among Parks' liberal film actor friends also associated with the Lab were Lloyd Bridges, Roman Bohnen, Morris Carnovsky, and Frank Latimore.

While staging a revue there in 1944, he ran into difficulty casting a girl's role in one of the sketches. A Lab member mentioned that he'd seen Betty Garrett do the piece in New York, and that since she was in town performing at the Clover Club Parks ought to ask her to do the sketch. He did, and Garrett--fresh from Cole Porter's Something for the Boys on Broadway, where she was making a name for herself as a major talent--agreed to do the revue at the Actors Lab.

Finding they had much in common, Parks and Garrett dated for two months, fell in love and were married on September 8, 1944, at St. Thomas' Episcopal Church on Hollywood Boulevard. Then in the midst of filming Counter-Attack, Parks wore the unsightly beard stubble required by the part. Lloyd Bridges was best man. Garrett soon returned to New York to begin rehearsals for the Ole Olson-Chic Johnson revue, Laffing Room Only. For over two years, the couple was separated most of the time by their opposite-coast careers.

Parks thought his next film, the "A" production Counter-Attack (1945), would be his big break, but it didn't turn out that way. Dramatically, Counter-Attack was an unexceptional war film, although--betraying its stage origin--it was certainly more static and talky than the norm. Paul Muni starred as a simple but determined Russian soldier who, with comrade Marguerite Chapman, found himself trapped in a bombed-out cellar as captor of seven German soldiers. He obtained valuable strategic information from their officer (Harro Mellar) which, after their ultimate rescue, he was able to give to the Russians.

As Muni's friend, Parks, despite prominent billing with Muni and Chapman, had only a few brief scenes before he was killed, and those were played mostly standing behind Muni or in the shadows. His best moments, he later claimed, had been cut from release prints because the film ran too long.

In the screenplay by John Howard Lawson (who would soon be blacklisted during House Un-American Activities Committee investigations), everybody was called Comrade-this or Comrade-that; Muni made a speech about men of all races being brothers and near the end Nazi soldier Rudolf Anders, an exploited "common man" coal miner in civilian life, came over to the Russian side to help Muni and Chapman guard the other German captives.

Much more impressive was the expensive Technicolor Western Renegades (1946), in which Parks effectively portrayed Evelyn Keyes' ill-fated outlaw husband.

Then came The Jolson Story.

Parks was understandably skeptical about getting the Jolson film biography. "You see, I was always testing--for everything. I made five tests for the role of Chopin in A Song to Remember--even had the costumes fitted--but Cornel Wilde got the role. I tested for The Bandit of Sherwood Forest--Cornel got that one, too. When they told me I was testing for Jolson, I muttered a merry 'So what--who cares?' Afterwards I promptly forgot the thing because, confidentially, even at this late date, it wouldn't shock me to see my pal Cornel down on his knee, in blackface and white gloves!," Parks admitted shortly after The Jolson Story was released.

When Harry Cohn informed Parks that he had been selected to portray Al Jolson, he insisted that the actor sign a new seven-year contract.

According to Betty Garrett, "Larry rebelled. There were three more years to run on his present contract and he felt that after that he should be free to choose what he wanted to do next with his career.

"Cohn was so incensed that he declared that not only would Larry lose the Jolson role, he would be given no other good parts for the remainder of his contract. Carrying out this threat, Cohn had Larry called to report to wardrobe to be fitted for a one-day bit in a low-budget picture. Larry, realizing that Cohn was serious, capitulated. He signed as Cohn demanded and played Jolson, abetted by Jolson's own singing on the soundtrack."

Parks recognized, too, that The Jolson Story was important to his career, doing everything he could to help pro-

Larry Parks gives his impression of Al Jolson singing "My Mammy" in The Jolson Story.

mote the film when it was released. In New York the "new" star was taken on publicity rounds by a studio publicist there named Leo Pillot who reminisces, "Larry Parks was totally cooperative. I also recall escorting him to the St. Nicholas Arena for a huge rally for Bundles for Russia at which the honored guest speaker was Eleanor Roosevelt."

On April 18, 1946, Betty Garrett had opened in the Harold Rome revue, Call Me Mister, and become Broadway's darling singing "South America, Take It Away!" ("Take back your samba, ay, your rhumba, ay, your conga, ay, ay, ay ... !").

After making a brief unbilled appearance as himself in a Lucille Ball farce called Her Husband's Affairs (1947), Parks was put into another lavish Technicolor musical, Down the Earth (1947), starring as a Broadway producer opposite Columbia's biggest female star, Rita Hayworth, as the goddess Terpsichore. Photoplay magazine remarked, "Larry Parks looks sincere and able as ever, but he gets crowded right out of the picture by the big song-and-dance numbers." Although the ads proclaimed "Larry Parks Sings It His Way!," his singing was dubbed again, this time by a bland Hal Derwin.

• • •

By now, Garrett had signed with M-G-M and moved to Hollywood where her husband had bought a little white cottage in Nichols Canyon.

"It isn't unusual in our neighborhood," said Parks at the time, "to look up and find some kids standing under my favorite Chinese elm by the window dramatizing a scene from The Jolson Story for my benefit."

Parks' ailing mother, given only months to live, had moved in with her son when Garrett arrived at their hillside home to begin her first film, Big City (1948), with Margaret O'Brien. It was still the golden age of the Metro musical, and Betty Garrett left her mark in Words and Music (1948), the all-star Rodgers and Hart biography; Take Me Out to the Ball Game (1949), starring Frank Sinatra, Esther Williams and Gene Kelly; Neptune's Daughter (1949), an Esther Williams aquacade; and On the Town (1949), a critical triumph for all including cab driver Garrett and sailors-on-the-loose Frank Sinatra and Gene Kelly, who also made his film directing debut (with Stanley Donen).

To capitalize on the verve he had shown as Jolson, Harry Cohn then cast the trim, fitness-conscious Parks in two color swashbucklers. The Swordsman (1947), with Ellen

Lew Dockstader (John Alexander) hires Jolson (Larry Parks) for his minstrel show in The Jolson Story, featuring William Demarest.

Drew, was seen by Modern Screen as "a Highland Fling version of the Hatfield-McCoy feud." The magazine also reported that Parks did "some of the fanciest dueling seen in years." In The New York Times, however, Bosley Crowther wrote, "A gaudy assortment of Scottish castles, kilts, tartans, bagpipes and burrs ... is not enough to conceal that The Swordsman is just a plain, old-fashioned horse-opera."

The Gallant Blade (1948), photographed in the chintzy Cinecolor process, was liked even less. Parks appeared as "the best swordsman in France," related The New York Herald Tribune's Howard Barnes, "in a posturing costume romance, embellished with incredibly stilted dialogue. Sword fights and galloping horses provide what tiny flurries of excitement there are in The Gallant Blade." The dark beauty of co-star Marguerite Chapman was the film's biggest asset.

During the research for this book, most people contacted

who had known Larry Parks professed fondness for him. There were only two real dissenters: Joseph H. Lewis, who had directed the production numbers in The Jolson Story and directed The Swordsman; and Marguerite Chapman, the ex-Powers model who had acted in several films with Parks. Lewis would not reveal the nature of his problem with Parks, but Chapman cooperated fully.

First stressing that "Larry was a very professional, meticulous, fine actor who was easy to work with," Chapman says she has to add that "he wasn't always someone I admired personally. In the early forties, when we were playing in A Man's World, I remember that William Wright, my other leading man (also deceased now), was pretty deep into his cups. One day he was missing. The studio found him, put him in a steambath and dragged him onto the set where they literally held him up in front of everybody to get the shot they needed. They humiliated the man shamefully. They could have shot around him, or done another scene. Larry said to me, 'How dare anyone come to work like that?' I was appalled that he was so judgmental and lacking in sympathy for a fellow human being who was so obviously in trouble. I didn't like that in Larry.

"A couple of years later, we did Counter-Attack. Practically everyone in that film, excepting the director, Zoltan Korda, Paul Muni, and myself, carried a card. They would all go out together and whoop it up and have dinner parties. At the time, I was ill-informed about Communism, though, and was mainly concerned with advancing my career and getting my current part down right, so I just ignored it all then."

By 1948 Chapman couldn't ignore it. "While Larry and I were working in The Gallant Blade," she continues, "I asked if we could get together someplace to study our lines. He was married to Betty Garrett by then and I was invited over for dinner, but mainly to work. While we dined, one of the heads of the household said, 'We should run up a Commie flag from the roof.' I couldn't believe my ears, and must have shown my amazement. 'Don't you know about Communism?,' I was asked. 'Or want to learn about it?' I was shocked. Those were tense times for anyone even suspected of being Red. I had come there simply to learn my lines. I was angry to be put in such a position, and hurt because prior to this incident I felt that Larry and I were becoming friends."

In the fall of 1947, Washington's House Committee on Un-American Activities (or House Un-American Activities Committee, as it was commonly called), chaired by Congressman J. Parnell Thomas,[1] reopened its attempts to purge Hollywood of the Communist subversion it claimed was permeating the film business.[2] Hysteria reigned, careers--even, ultimately, lives--were on the line. Soon the "Hollywood Ten," or the "Unfriendly Witnesses," were called to the witness stand to answer charges that they had slipped Red propaganda into their films. When they refused to answer the Committee's now infamous question, "Are you now or have you ever been a Communist?," because they said it violated freedoms guaranteed them by the First Amendment, they were jailed for contempt of Congress. Afterward, most of them were blacklisted in the industry, along with a number of others who were suspected of being Communists. Despite writer-director Billy Wilder's quip that "Only two of them have talent, the other eight are just unfriendly," the fact is that these individuals--thought by many to have been thrown to the wolves --included some of Hollywood's top writers, especially.[3]

Meanwhile, Larry Parks and Harry Cohn had locked horns again. Anxious to do things besides the weak films Columbia had given him since he became a star, Parks sued the studio for release from his contract, charging that he had signed it under duress. The judge ruled in favor of Columbia on the grounds that Parks had enjoyed the fruits of the agreement, further stating that he should have brought suit *before* he made *The Jolson Story*. A new five-year contract was drawn up and signed, however, giving Parks permission to act wherever he wanted as long as he did one picture a year for Columbia.

While in litigation, Parks, then enjoined from working in films, starred for the Lake Whalom Playhouse in Fitchburg, Massachusetts (where he had begun in show business a decade before), in a new comedy prophetically titled *A Free Hand*, by Melvin Frank and Norman Panama.

Parks' subsequent film was the second most important one he ever made: *Jolson Sings Again* (1949), co-starring Barbara Hale. On the eve of its release, he said, "I will admit I approached a sequel to *The Jolson Story* with a certain amount of quaking. Any sequel is seldom as successful as the original.... But when I read Sidney Buchman's script

Jolson (Larry Parks) sings "April Showers" to Julie (Evelyn Keyes) in The Jolson Story.

for Jolson Sings Again, I stopped worrying about the possible merits of this picture. It's a far superior script to The Jolson Story. The songs are better, too, and with better arrangements." Parks was uncontestably right about at least one thing: the sequel did well but was not as successful as the original.

With Betty Garrett and her manager of the past decade, Louis Mandel (also their lawyer), he planned to form his own independent production company and produce his next vehicle himself, a gangster melodrama titled Stake-Out. It was never made. Instead, Parks and Garrett put together a vaudeville act (sans Jolson imitations), playing Cleveland, Ohio, St. Louis, Missouri, Scotland, and the Palladium in London. "This is the only review I'll probably every keep in my wallet," Parks told a reporter at the time, taking out a Variety clipping which read, in part, "Larry Parks and Betty Garrett...."

Songs-Comedy-Dances. Should be able to hold their own in virtually any medium."

Their sons Garrett Christopher and Andrew Lawrence were born in 1950 and 1951, respectively.

It is probably an understatement to say that Harry Cohn was not anxious to advance the career of an actor who, in Cohn's eyes, had thanked him for stardom with a lawsuit. Undoubtedly, Parks was denied good films at Columbia because of this. For example, the role of the cerebral reporter in the studio's film of the Broadway hit Born Yesterday (1950) would have suited Parks better than William Holden, whom Cohn gave the part.

Parks' next two films were inconsequential comedies: Columbia's Emergency Wedding (1950), a remake of 1941's You Belong to Me (in which Parks had had a supporting role) with the actor as a playboy who married doctor Barbara Hale; and, for M-G-M, Love Is Better Than Ever, with Parks as a New York talent agent in love with a small-town dance teacher (a teenage Elizabeth Taylor).

Josephine Hutchinson was cast as Taylor's mother. Hutchinson, who during her 1930s Warner Bros. years played opposite Paul Muni and Pat O'Brien, among others, found acting jobs scarce as World War II broke out and took to coaching young contract players at Columbia for the duration. "When I was coaching there," she recalls, "Larry Parks was under contract and getting many small parts and, as I remember, was not required by the studio to do extra-curricular work when he was acting. Soon after I left, he did The Jolson Story and was wonderful in it. His serious dedication to his work showed the meticulous study he had made, not just to imitate, but to simulate the Jolson personality.

"Larry himself did not have that inexplicable gift of charisma, and he rode in on the Jolson magic. I finally worked with him in Love Is Better Than Ever. He was a good actor, a likeable person, but he did not have boxoffice appeal when he played a straight part."

Dore Schary, soon head of M-G-M following Louis B. Mayer's ousting, had good reason to doubt Parks' audience draw at the time of Love Is Better Than Ever. After completing the film in January, 1951, Parks ran afoul of the House Un-American Activities Committee, and long-time liberal Schary, afraid of negative reaction to a Parks film at that time, held up its release for over a year. (It would prove a fiscal failure.)

On March 21, 1951, Larry Parks answered a subpoena to become the first witness to testify before the newly resumed House Un-American Activities Committee, which had been suspended while the cases of the "Hollywood Ten" wended their ways through the courts. The political climate in the nation was ominous: the very morning that Parks was called, the government had concluded its case against alleged Soviet spies Julius and Ethel Rosenberg, who were subsequently convicted of treason and executed. Parks' appearance before the HUAC was heralded by four-inch headlines in The New York Daily News.

As first witness, he received the most notoriety and, possibly, the most damage to a career already undermined by the routine quality of his starring film vehicles since The Jolson Story.

Although a reluctant witness, Parks was the first Hollywood personality to admit publicly ever being a Red.

"His stand was an unexpected one," Garrett says. "It did not conform with those who advocated taking the Fifth Amendment--that is, refusing to answer on the grounds that it might incriminate them--and I think it came as a complete surprise to the Committee, who expected him to take the stand of the so-called 'Unfriendly Witnesses.' Instead he admitted that he had been a Communist Party member." He gave the dates of his membership as 1941 to 1945, explaining that he had joined because it was the "most liberal" of the political parties but had left because of "lack of interest--of not finding things I thought I would."

He promised to tell them all they wanted to know about himself, but tearfully begged not to be forced to name others he knew to be Communists. "This is not the American way," he added.

"I have two boys," Parks went on to plead, "one thirteen months, one two weeks. Is this the kind of heritage that

Tom Baron (Bill Goodwin) and Jolson (Larry Parks) flank Steve Martin (William Demarest), whom Jolson has just asked to be his manager in The Jolson Story.

I must hand down to them? Is this the kind of heritage that you would like to hand down to your children?"

When the Committee threatened him with contempt, the meeting went behind closed doors. Two days later it was leaked to the press that Larry Parks had named names. By agreeing to talk about himself, the Committee maintained he had waived the right to refuse to talk about others.

It was said that the HUAC already knew the dozen names Parks was forced to name.

The Committee wanted to be certain that the witnesses really regretted their Communist associations, and, it claimed, only by forcing them to reveal everything could they be assured that the witnesses had repented their pasts. Despite this, many, even some conservatives, thought that some compassion might have been shown Parks, that, regardless of its legality, he need not have been made to grovel and reveal names already known to the HUAC.

Garrett relates, however, that "The Committee and its supporters were not pleased with Larry's attitude,[4] nor were the Fifth Amendment advocates. But Larry had made his choice, knowing that in the political climate of the times, it was professional economic suicide--in the film industry, at least."

After that, no alleged show business Communist called for hearings would get work (at least under his own name) unless he named names.

Wrote Victor S. Navasky in his 1980 book Naming Names,

> Larry Parks was the first man in Hollywood to inform before HUAC, but the combination of his reluctance to do so, the publicity that attended his "performance," his failure to employ an attorney like Martin Gang (a liberal entertainment lawyer who represented many Communists) to work out a behind-the-scenes advance scenario with the Committee staff and his consequent controversiality resulted in the end of a career that had been on the brink of superstardom. His memorable line, "Do not make me crawl through the mud like an informer," was remembered, and the names he named were forgotten by those in the blacklisting business.

John Wayne said, "The public will forgive Parks. I find his courage [in not taking the Fifth] commendable," but he added that Parks had waited "too long to reveal everything."

The ferociously right-wing Hedda Hopper agreed with the latter assertion. Although in 1946 she had been one of Larry Parks' biggest boosters, giving him his first important magazine and newspaper interviews, and calling him "an awfully nice guy," she turned on the actor with a vengeance when his Communist past became known, firing regular potshots at him. Spec McClure, her one-time legman, later said that while she was sometimes called vicious, "I don't think she ever wrote a damn thing that hurt anyone permanently, with the exception of Larry Parks, and that was a political thing." Right after Parks testified in Washington, saying that he didn't come forward earlier because the film industry was already "a wounded animal," Hopper gave a speech denouncing him. The self-proclaimed spokeswoman "of the mothers of 55,000 casualties in Korea," she asked, "How can anyone expect to hold his position in public who withholds valuable information until put under pressure?.... Larry Parks says he felt he'd done nothing wrong. I feel sorry for him."

She charged that four years before Parks and his wife had been asked by the FBI to give up their espousal of Communism (although Betty Garrett was never subpoenaed by the HUAC).

Small Wonder was to have been the title of Parks' next film for Columbia, but the studio claimed that its starting date conflicted with Parks' appearances before the HUAC and he was replaced by Robert Cummings. (The film was retitled The First Time.) Columbia then charged Parks with breach of contract due to an alleged inadequate accounting from his just-filmed Love Is Better Than Ever salary, a percentage of which was contractually due Columbia. As Parks saw it, "They found enough loopholes to avoid paying my salary. There was no alternative but to end the contract."

While it may be an exaggeration that Larry Parks, by the start of the fifties, was "on the brink of superstardom," as Victor Navasky opined, there would surely have been some work for him in features if the HUAC hadn't happened. But his days as a Hollywood film star were indeed over. His talented wife's career was affected, too. She had left M-G-M more than a year ago ("They never knew what to do with me there") and it would be several more before she received a motion picture offer in the film capital.

At that, the Parkses were better off than colleagues John Garfield, Canada Lee, Mady Christians, J. Edward Bromberg and Philip Loeb, all of whom died suddenly in the 1950s "shortly after the actors were ground to pieces by the HUAC," wrote Larry Swindell in his Garfield biography, Body and Soul. A couple were whispered suicides, Loeb a certified one.

"Larry was hurt by what happened after he testified, but he was never bitter," says the naturally cheerful Betty

Garrett. "Neither was I. We just wanted to get on with our lives."

• • •

Parks and Garrett trouped Canada and Europe with their act, returning to tour the United States with a play called The Anonymous Lover. They worked Las Vegas and, in the mid-1950s, guest-starred in two half-hour TV comedies, A Smattering of Bliss and The Penlands and the Poodle. When foot surgery forced Judy Holliday to relinquish the lead in Columbia's musical version of My Sister Eileen (1955), Harry Cohn, just operated on for a throat malignancy and perhaps conscience-stricken at the prospect of the imminent unknown, okayed the signing of Garrett. She rewarded him with her most delightful screen performance as the hapless would-be Greenwich Village writer Ruth Sherwood. Around then, Parks went to England to star in a low-budget feature called Tiger by the Tail (1955), as a reporter kidnaped by counterfeiters. (A couple of years later it was released in America as Cross-Up.)

After that, he played Sakini in the touring company of Broadway's The Teahouse of the August Moon, then was a star replacement in the original New York production of The Tunnel of Love. In 1957, Parks and Garrett worked together on Broadway for the first time as replacements for Judy Holliday and Sydney Chaplin in Bells Are Ringing; and in 1960, they had their own musical vehicle there, the unsuccessful Beg, Borrow or Steal.

Meanwhile, Parks was able to find an occasional job on television, notably on Suspicion, Dr. Kildare and, with particularly interesting results, The Untouchables. Entitled The Lily Dallas Story, this 1961 TV hour presented Parks as a mild-mannered, small-time bootlegger molded into a legendary gang leader by the real brains, his wife (Norma Crane). However, the memory of Al Jolson died hard: in one scene with a child, Parks, in Jolson's familiar manner, spoke with head cocked, eyes straight ahead, as if ready to break into song.

Parks returned to major filmmaking with Universal Pictures' Freud (1962), shot mainly on location in Munich, Germany. Under John Huston's direction, he had a substantial featured role as the "eminent doctor" who befriended pioneer psychoanalyst Sigmund Freud (Montgomery Clift) but disagreed

Jolson (Larry Parks) performs "Is It True What They Say About Dixie?" on Broadway in Jolson Sings Again.

completely with his controversial theory of infantile sexuality. Grey-bearded and much older-looking, Parks emoted with Muniesque dignity in this ponderous psychological primer of repressed incest, hysterical maladies, dream sequences and, yes, Freudian slips. The timing, in addition, couldn't have been worse: Freud arrived during a period in which Freudian analysis was falling from fashion. It was a box office disaster.

In 1963, Parks starred in a Broadway flop called Love and Kisses, directed by Dore Schary, himself now deposed like predecessor Louis B. Mayer as head of production at M-G-M in Hollywood. The same season, Garrett received glowing personal notices for her New York stage performance in Spoon River Anthology. While they were in town, Parks told Columbia publicist-turned-columnist Whitney Bolton:

> I foresaw--or think I foresaw--that the business

In Jolson Sings Again, Jolson (Larry Parks) sings "I'm Looking over a Four-Leaf Clover" to our servicemen in the Caribbean.

> would change and that Los Angeles would, after the war, grow even more spectacularly, spurtingly, than it was then. I took every nickel I could put away from my salary at Columbia Pictures and began buying parcels of land. In time I had associates.... When the war ended, we had the land and materials became available and we began building apartment houses--to keep. We still keep them. We are not build-and-sell people. We keep what we build and if we didn't I could not afford to be an actor. It's as simple as that.

During the next decade, Parks toured in the play Any Wednesday, and opposite his wife acted for the road in Cactus Flower and Plaza Suite.

In 1973, a play by Eric Bentley about the HUAC investigations entitled Are You Now or Have You Ever Been....?, first done at Yale University, opened off-Broadway. The New York Times critic Clive Barnes wrote, "Peter Thompson has great compassion as the baffled but doomed Larry Parks." Five years later, it was presented in New York again, with W.T. Martin cast as the blacklisted actor.

Parks' health began to give him trouble in the early seventies, when he contracted hepatitis and high blood pressure. He contented himself more and more with gardening and reading. On Sunday night, April 13, 1975, Larry Parks died of a heart attack in his Studio City, California, home. Ironically, Fredric March, to whom he had lost the 1946 Academy Award, died on the same date.

He had lived to see Betty Garrett regain the spotlight in the recurring role of Irene Lorenzo, the liberal next-door neighbor on television's All in the Family, and his son Andrew become a full-time, able actor. Later, Garrett appeared as the landlady on the TV series Laverne and Shirley, while Andrew portrayed the young W.C. Fields in the film biography, W.C. Fields and Me (1971) and guest-starred on such dramatic TV series as Hawkins, The Rookies, Hart to Hart, and Murder, She Wrote. Of Garry Parks, Betty Garrett says, "My oldest son is a musician, still in the process of forming a rock-and-roll group. He plays piano, bass guitar and composes, and I think he's very talented, but of course, I'm his mother."

When I recently interviewed Marshall A. Green, the Universal executive whose father directed The Jolson Story, he remarked, "Poor Larry Parks. He had such a sad life." I replied, "Yes, he did." Later, I got to thinking: maybe it wasn't so sad. Maybe Larry Parks knew that he had created, in his Al Jolson characterization, something that had brightened the lives of untold millions of people for a couple of generations, and would probably go on doing so. How many of us will be able to leave such a legacy? Surely this realization lightened his burden.

As Parks' long-time friend and manager Louis Mandel eulogized him: "He will not be forgotten--as long as there are motion pictures, lawbooks and a history of the United States."

Betty Garrett's unvanquished, ever-positive state today is well exemplified by the conclusion of her telephone answering machine message when to everyone she warmly intones, "I love you." She calls to mind the loyal movie star heroine of the thrice-filmed A Star is Born who, after her actor husband's neglect and death in Hollywood, attended a première where she identified herself by saying, "This is Mrs. Norman Maine." One could imagine Betty Garrett, like that film's fictional Vicki Lester, stepping up to a microphone at some gala and declaiming,

"This is Mrs. Larry Parks."

References

1. J. Parnell Thomas was jailed in 1948 for taking kickbacks from his staff.
2. From 1938-1944, Congressman Martin Dies chaired a temporary Special Committee on Un-American Activities, a less aggressive forerunner to the House Committee on Un-American Activities.
3. The "Hollywood Ten": Alvah Bessie, Herbert Biberman, Lester Cole, Edward Dmytryk, Ring Lardner, Jr., John Howard Lawson, Albert Maltz, Samuel Ornitz, Adrian Scott, and Dalton Trumbo.
4. Parks had likened the Committee's techniques to those of Nazi Germany.

■ JOLSON'S MOVIE WIVES ■

> If you want to know the secret of the perfect wife I played in all those movies, well, she was really a rascal, just like me.
>
> Myrna Loy

Once or twice in Hollywood's last lush decade, the 1940s, Mary Martin, Evelyn Keyes, and an increasingly mannered Jean Arthur were all accused by critics of playing Jean Arthur. Of the three actresses, I always thought Evelyn Keyes played her best.

Actually, Keyes' similarity to the older, already long-established Arthur was not all that pronounced. True, they were both fair and under contract to Columbia Pictures and especially adept at comedy. Each actress, too, had a vocal trick, or tic, that she employed for effect at psychological moments--with Jean Arthur, her frequent director Frank Capra rather romantically called this break in the voice like "a thousand tinkling bells."

Joseph Walker, who photographed much vintage Arthur, was also at the camera on several important Keyes films. In addition, off-camera both Jean Arthur and the politically liberal Evelyn Keyes were sometimes labeled "intellectual." [Of course, in the Hollywood of those years, when an actor ran more on instinct than introspection, the tag "intellectual" when applied to an actress could have meant that she wore cardigan sweaters to work instead of lamé.]

But Keyes' versatility was more evident than Arthur's, and found her performing personably in musicals and drama as well as comedy. She was also far more visible during that decade than the neurotic, reclusive Jean Arthur who literally

Jolson (Larry Parks) and Julie (Evelyn Keyes) on the night they meet in The Jolson Story.

had to be dragged, regurgitating, before cameras (Paramount's Mary Martin had returned, sans protest, to Broadway by the mid-1940s). Although Columbia could see little but "love goddess" Rita Hayworth during that period, Keyes was kept busy there for over ten years, a better-than-average span of time for a contract player then, and she did become a star. Many film critics and historians thought she rated superstardom, including James Agee who wrote in his Nation review of The Jolson Story, her most commercially successful film as a lead: "Evelyn Keyes has always seemed to me one of the most attractive and capable girls in Hollywood, and one of the most neglected, and it is good to see her again."

That still holds true today, when TV showings of her old movies present a forever young and delightful Evelyn Keyes to appreciative new generations.

Keyes was born in Port Arthur, Texas, on November 20, 1919, but raised in Atlanta, Georgia, the "alienated" (her term) youngest of five children (four girls and a boy). Her father died when she was two. "So, sure, I was looking for Daddy," she said in a bit of self-analysis not long ago. "That's what all those big, strong men who would play important roles in my life were all about."

During high school she studied dancing on Peachtree Street, and as "Goldie" Keyes picked up "Five dollars here, ten dollars there" dancing for the Daughters of the Confederacy, the American Legion, the Masons. After graduation she headed for Hollywood where Paramount Pictures producer-director Cecil B. DeMille put her under personal contract and into *The Buccaneer* (1938), as a drowned New Orleans belle. She next appeared for DeMille in the bit part of a telegrapher's wife in *Union Pacific* (1939). At her boss' insistence, she worked hard to lose her Southern accent, and succeeded. Keyes drew her most attention up to then, however, when producer David O. Selznick cast her as the crybaby Suellen, *Scarlett O'Hara's Younger Sister* (the inspired title of the actress' steamy 1977 autobiography), in the monumental *Gone with the Wind* (1939)--for which part, in the kind of ironic twist so craved by the writers of studio publicity, she had to retrieve her drawl.

Columbia Pictures then signed her, inaugurating her most productive epoch with the ingenue role in *Before I Hang* (1940), a Boris Karloff vehicle.

Nineteen forty-one was a big year for Evelyn Keyes. After a sensitive performance as a tragic blind girl in a Peter Lorre "B" entitled *The Face Behind the Mask*, she was given the romantic lead opposite Robert Montgomery in the comedy-fantasy, *Here Comes Mr. Jordan*, which was to reappear in 1978 as that rarest of celluloid species, the hit remake of a hit film: *Heaven Can Wait*, with Warren Beatty and Julie Christie. Keyes scored again as a flirtatious maid in the Ida Lupino thriller, *Ladies in Retirement* (1941).

Ingenue assignments ensued with the steadily climbing Glenn Ford in *Adventures of Martin Eden* and *Flight Lieutenant* (both 1942) and *The Desperadoes* (1943), Columbia's first Technicolor feature. Some of Keyes' sprightliest work, however, was in such low-budget efforts as *Dangerous Blondes*

(1943), in which she was the sleuthing wife of detective novelist Allyn Joslyn, and Strange Affair (1944), in which she was the sleuthing wife of cartoonist Allyn Joslyn.

She was moving toward the big time with the Arabian Nights "sleeper" A Thousand and One Nights (1945), stealing the spoof from Cornel Wilde and Phil Silvers. As an uncorked genie in an upsweep hairdo, she mischievously balanced her affections between the male contingent ("You have no idea how long it's been since I've seen a man!") and that new fad, the yo-yo. Decades later, Barbara Eden's title character in the long-running TV series I Dream of Jeannie was suspiciously like Keyes' libidinous apparition. Keyes' range was proved by the super-Western Renegades (1946), which found her the pregnant wife of outlaw Larry Parks. Next came The Thrill of Brazil (1946), a musically disguised version of the old Ben Hecht-Charles MacArthur play, The Front Page.

The Jolson Story followed, with Keyes as Al Jolson's/ Larry Parks' dancer wife, a role patterned after Ruby Keeler and for which Keyes had campaigned. The blonde Keyes didn't much resemble the dark Keeler, but since the character was given the name of Julie Benson it didn't really matter.

In the moody underworld opus Johnny O'Clock (1947), she again played an actress, of sorts--"Fourth from the left in a traveling girl show," as her character explained it. Costar Dick Powell would soon be her leading man again, as well as her boss.

The Mating of Millie (1948), an entertaining romantic comedy, was supposed to have re-teamed her with Larry Parks, but he was in litigation with the studio and was replaced by another familiar Keyes screen partner, Glenn Ford, her most frequent leading man. She appeared as a prim businesswoman metamorphosed, in best forties fashion, into a glamour girl.

Borrowed by Samuel Goldwyn for Enchantment (1948), she was seen as a cynical ambulance driver in wartime London who loved flyer Farley Granger. The prestigious production had a quaint, romantic charm, but in a bustling post-war world it seemed too old-fashioned and failed at the box office.

United Artists' Mrs. Mike (1949), an agreeable adapta-

Julie (Evelyn Keyes) is greeted backstage by Jolson (Larry Parks) after her Broadway opening, while the wardrobe woman (Jessie Arnold) watches in The Jolson Story.

tion of the popular novel, saw Keyes on loan-out again, this time to actor Dick Powell's production company for one of her meatiest assignments. She enacted the sought-after role of the Boston Irish girl who braved the wilderness of Mountie husband Powell. Louella Parsons predicted an Academy Award nomination for Keyes after seeing her in it--wrong again.

In the fact-based The Killer That Stalked New York (1950) back at Columbia, Keyes had perhaps her most offbeat part. She graphically portrayed a gradually deteriorating Smallpox Mary who spread disease through the city, employing, finally, a Chaneyesque horror make-up.

When studio chief Harry Cohn denied her the coveted lead in Born Yesterday, saying, "You can't play a dumb blonde because your eyes are too intelligent," she felt she had gone as far as she could at Columbia and bought her way out of her contract. She had to pay the studio twenty per cent of her earnings for years.

She has said that the best thing she ever did in films was 1951's The Prowler, made in nineteen days for Horizon Pictures, a recently formed production company owned by producer Sam Spiegel and her husband, director John Huston (whom she was then divorcing). Keyes was cast as a failed actress ("I was just a little short of talent") whose cop-lover (Van Heflin) murdered her husband. "It was a well thought-out, well constructed script," she went on. "Joe Losey directed it. Dalton Trumbo wrote it but we didn't find that out until much later because he was on the [political] blacklist." Keyes was given an interest in the United Artists release, but despite fine reviews (The New York Times: "An impressive, often exciting drama") the film flopped because it opened during the height of the Red scare and many exhibitors were frightened off by the alleged left-wing sympathies of director Losey and producer S.P. Eagle (homophone for [Sam] Spiegel). The following year Losey, blacklisted, was forced to move to Europe for work.

At Universal, Keyes co-starred with Jeff Chandler in two negligible films, Smuggler's Island and Iron Man (both 1951).

Subsequent Keyes features were helter-skelter, although she had a supporting role as the out-of-town wife in 20th Century-Fox' The Seven Year Itch (1955), starring Marilyn Monroe, and a cameo as a French tart in Around the World in 80 Days, winner of the 1956 Best Picture Academy Award and produced by her then boyfriend Mike Todd. In return for a loan from Keyes, he gave her a five per cent interest in the latter hit. It is interesting to note that while Evelyn Keyes never attained superstardom, she did appear in several of the most commercially successful films of all time.

Many (the candid Keyes included) feel her professional status would have been more significant if she had spent as much time cultivating her career as she did the opposite sex. Slender, never voluptuous, she nevertheless has been married to, or intimately involved with, a number of the most interesting, accomplished, difficult men in show business. First husband Barton Bainbridge, who was in construction, blew his brains out in 1940, about a year after they had married. In 1944 she married Charles Vidor, Columbia director of Rita Hayworth's biggest hits, Cover Girl (1944) and Gilda (1946), as well as his wife's The Lady in Question (1940), also with

Rita, and The Desperadoes (1943). They were divorced a year later.

In July, 1946, Keyes wed John Huston, director of many classic films such as The Maltese Falcon (1941), The Treasure of the Sierra Madre (1948), The Asphalt Jungle (1950) and The African Queen (1952). One day he surprised her by bringing home a thirteen-year-old Mexican orphan named Pablo whom he had adopted. (A few years later, Keyes lost touch with the boy.) Mr. and Mrs. Huston had a stormy relationship, but they were politically in tune. Both were liberal Democrats.

In late 1947, when the House Un-American Activities Committee was reactivated in Washington and began investigating alleged Communist subversion in Hollywood, some in the film capital thought the group employed "Hitlerian tactics" (as Lauren Bacall has termed it). Directors John Huston and William Wyler, screenwriter Philip Dunne and actor Alexander Knox then formed the Committee for the First Amendment to remind, as Keyes later put it, "ambitious congressmen" that the Constitution guaranteed certain freedoms. Five hundred joined the organization (not all were film people), and that year Keyes, Huston and a representative group of members flew to Washington to protest the "witch hunts" of the HUAC, as the congressional committee came to be called by the media.[1] Movie stars on the march were not taken too seriously at that point in time, though, and there was considerable jeering in the press. During the heated early 1950s HUAC investigations, the Committee for the First Amendment was labeled a Communist front organization--erroneously, says Keyes.

Following her divorce from Huston in 1950, Keyes had a long live-in affair with colorful promoter-producer Mike Todd which ended when he suddenly married Elizabeth Taylor in 1957. The same year Keyes became the eighth wife of "King of the Clarinet" Artie Shaw, from whom she has been estranged for years. George Burns was a frequent escort in the 1970s.

Keyes, after a lengthy hiatus, once again stepped in for Ruby Keeler, the toast of Broadway in the 1971 revival of No, No, Nanette. The producers remembered that she had played Keeler in The Jolson Story, and gave Keyes the Keeler role in the touring company of the musical, which she did for a couple of years.

Julie (Evelyn Keyes) dances to "Around a Quarter of Nine" in The Jolson Story.

In the 1980s, she guest-starred on TV's The Love Boat, Murder, She Wrote and, most notably, Amazing Stories, as a lively attic ghost who saw her first porno movie and sighed for us all, "I just don't understand. Clark Gable kissing Vivien Leigh--that's a movie."

With good parts for older Hollywood actresses grown

scarce, the major interest of the now grey-haired, angular Keyes seems to have become writing. For publisher Lyle Stuart, Inc., in 1971 she wrote I Am a Billboard, a novel about a not-so-innocent in Hollywood that read like thinly veiled autobiography; and then six years later, the real thing, Scarlett O'Hara's Younger Sister, primarily concerned with Keyes' real-life bedroom performances.

According to one critic of her own story, "She made more men than movies."

For starters, there was Fredric March, star of her first film, The Buccaneer, with whom she did not have an affair but who, in his dressing room, "took my hand and placed it over the bulge in front of those tight white pants." She had an affair with Anthony Quinn, who also acted in The Buccaneer and several other films with Keyes, but she found their sexual couplings "disappointing. The earth stood perfectly still. There was simply too much of Tony (yes, there, too)." Her memoirs earned her more attention than most of her films. The rare man she turned down, by her own written words, was Harry Cohn, whom she claims then sabotaged her career. Why Keyes would suddenly say no to the one man who might have helped make her a major star turned her autobiography into a mystery.

Recently, she has been writing a column, "Keyes to the Town," in The Los Angeles Times, mainly about working in Hollywood films. In one, she related that, while it was forty years since she had played the Ruby Keeler prototype in The Jolson Story, she had only just learned that Keeler was not Jolson's first wife. Evincing an astonishment that probably matched some readers' at her lack of erudition, Keyes wrote, "To my shock, Jolson had two wives before Ruby. Two, count 'em. Somehow they both got lost for our picture." She was even more stunned to find out at that very late date that Jolson was not an only child as indicated in the film, but actually had seven brothers and sisters, "all wiped out for the sake of drama."

Another time, speaking of Ruby Keeler, Keyes revealed, "We finally had a sort of nodding 'hello.' She's not one of my favorite people. Have you ever seen those awful things Ruby Keeler did in the movies? She had a squeaky voice and was forever looking at her feet!"

When Evelyn Keyes was preparing her 1977 autobiography, I offered to loan her stills for it from my collection. She wrote back with a humor that made me wonder if it weren't true after all that actors in real life are very much like their screen selves--that what you see is what you get.

"I'd be very grateful for your help with stills, as my own collection is not too complete," she said. "I had no idea that I would one day be history!"

• • •

Among her more than forty movies and scads of television and radio appearances, the film Jolson Sings Again will always be the most special to Barbara Hale.

"It came at a formidable time in my life," she explains. "My husband, Bill Williams, and I had recently had our first child, I was making headway after several years in the business and I was treated so fine by those I worked with on the picture. I have always said that making Jolson Sings Again was like a family picnic, the kind of happy event one looks back on when recalling the nice things that happened in one's youth."

Hale remembers that she got the part of the "second" Mrs. Al Jolson when Max Arnow, Columbia's talent executive, phoned her to come over from RKO, where she'd been under contract for five years. "I think you're right for this part," he told her. She then met with producer-writer Sidney Buchman and director Henry Levin and began her seven-year contract with Columbia. Hale feels that the fact that she somewhat resembled Mrs. Jolson helped cinch her for the role.

Jolson was very much in love with his young wife, Erle, says Barbara Hale, and he instructed Sidney Buchman, "This one's gotta look like Erle."

She confesses she had not seen The Jolson Story when she starred in the sequel, although she did catch up with it later.

Unlike the earlier film, there was, Hale vows, a completed script that received relatively little alteration as filming proceeded. Her recollection is that they shot very much in sequence, a rare occurrence even today in filmmaking where it is not unusual, for technical and budget reasons, to shoot last scenes first and middle ones next. "Thanks to Mr. Buchman, Mr. Levin, Mr. Jolson and Larry Parks, however, there was no one involved in the production who couldn't put an opinion into a scene. Many who worked on Jolson Sings Again had been associated with the first Jolson picture, and all were heard," she attests.

"There were three main times that I met Al Jolson," continues the actress. "The first time was on a sound stage at Columbia before the picture began. He was recording and was very busy. Max Arnow took me there. We sat in the back of the room waiting for him to finish. I was never more impressed. He didn't really have an audience, but he obviously loved what he was doing and gave his all. After he had recorded several songs we were introduced.

"When the film was completed, Mr. Jolson and I went on a promotion tour to New York. The young studio legmen on the tour, who had to travel with him to all his shows, said they couldn't keep up with him. He went through about three men a day. If he went to a theater and the audience didn't respond right away, he would not stop performing until they did. And they always did.

"After that, we did Jolson Sings Again on The Lux Radio Theater together. As we prepared for this, Mr. Jolson lapsed into his Southern accent more and more, obliging me to do the same to provide the necessary contrast. Consequently, I was much more Southern in the radio version than I was in the film!"

Asked Jolson's reaction to her screen portrayal of his wife, she smiles, "Mr. Jolson was very, very kind to me and said awfully nice things about my performance."

Hale says she learned her drawl mainly by listening to her parents, who were originally from Kentucky. "Mrs. Jolson was then most recently from Arkansas, but she was born in Kentucky, so it was close enough. After the film came out, Mother added her highest compliment. 'You were just like home-folks,' she said."

Hale adds, "I have one sweet story about Mrs. Jolson.

Barbara Hale and Larry Parks in a publicity pose for Jolson Sings Again.

When the film was completed, we had a screening which the Jolsons attended. At the end, I approached Erle and asked, 'Mrs. Jolson, did I do all right? Was it okay?' She replied, drawling heavily, 'Barbara, Ah thought you did such a good job. But why'd they make y'all talk like that?' "

Hale remembers Larry Parks with warmth and some awe. "I couldn't believe the man. He had the same enthusiasm as Jolson, working fourteen hours a day. I think he was the perfectionist of lip-dubbing; he prided himself on this, too.

"But he was not a sobersides. Once, during a crucial hospital scene, my very first in the picture, I had to come in and lean over Larry, who was ill in bed, in a concerned manner. The director yelled 'Action!,' I did my stuff and suddenly Larry sat up in bed and cried 'Boo!' This was not in the script. It really typifies the whole friendly atmosphere on the set, because this elaborate joke was staged solely to ease my nervous tension."

Ludwig Donath, who played Papa Yoelson, is also recalled fondly. "He was the dearest man. As we filmed, I was worried about myself, naturally, trying to do my job right.

I still found time to take the elderly Mr. Donath a glass of tea every now and then so he wouldn't be hurt when he moved around the cluttered, busy set. After we'd been shooting for a couple of weeks, he said, 'Barbara, you've been so kind to me. Would you like to go for a cup of coffee or tea after we finish today?' I said, 'Certainly. Shall I stop by to pick you up?' He answered, 'Wait. I'll come and get you.' Well, when the time rolled around, he came bounding up in his saddle shoes, without the make-up that made him so much older than he actually was! The whole crew, which had been aware of what was really going on, was watching as I reacted in astonishment!"

• • •

All-American girl types, as most successfully personified by Jeanne Crain and June Allyson, had their shining hour in Hollywood during that most patriotic and optimistic of decades, the forties. Dark Barbara Hale, with her wavey-haired Irish loveliness and sincere, warmly uncomplicated manner, proved the right girl at the right time. She attained modest stardom then and continues to work today, long after the disappearances of some more glittering contemporaries.

At least one friend, however, claims the actress' apple pie image is misleading. Jeff Donnell, a comedienne confidante of Hale's for more than a quarter of a century, says today, "Barbara is very funny, almost kooky. Nothing like she is on the screen."

Born in DeKalb, Illinois, on April 18, 1921, Hale spent most of her early years in the nearby city of Rockford with her father, a landscape gardener, her mother and her elder sister Juanita. After graduation from high school, she studied commercial art in Chicago, but proving unsuited to that she quickly made a successful switch to modeling in the Windy City. Ultimately, her boss sent her photo to a friend at RKO Studios in Hollywood, resulting in her trip West with a stock starlet's contract.

A natural actress, Hale was groomed slowly but surely by RKO. She was given bits in several 1943 films such as Gildersleeve's Bad Day (her first), The Seventh Victim, The Iron Major, and Government Girl. Amid a flurry of publicity, she finished up that year the envy of bobbysoxers when, as

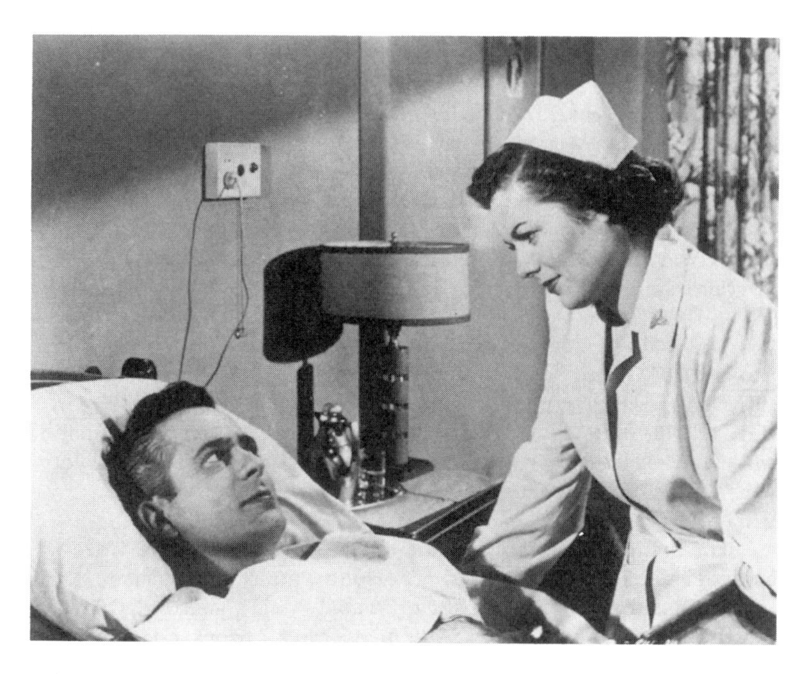

"Baby face, you've got the cutest little baby face," sings Jolson (Larry Parks) to nurse Ellen Clark (Barbara Hale) in Jolson Sings Again.

the debutante ingenue in Higher and Higher, she wound up engaged to Frank Sinatra in the first starring feature for the new generation's singing idol. He sang "The Music Stopped" to Hale who also got to warble briefly a couple of times.

Next came two leads in a popular low-budget detective series, The Falcon Out West and The Falcon in Hollywood (both 1944). Another "B", West of the Pecos (1945), opposite the stardom-bound Robert Mitchum, gave her a lively role which required her to masquerade as a boy. It also gave her a husband. While filming Pecos, she got to know fellow RKO contractee Bill Williams, who played a supporting part. Blond and sturdy, with a dimpled, boyish appeal then also in vogue, the Brooklyn-born Williams had been a champion swimmer and a member of a traveling muscle-man act; he would soon have his own bobbysox following via such films as Deadline at Dawn and Till the End of Time, both released in 1946. Hale and the divorced Williams were wed that year and are still married.

Hale was cast as a nurse in First Yank into Tokyo (1945). This time it was co-star Tom Neal who got to masquerade--as an American transformed by plastic surgery into a Japanese! The timely production, coincidental with VJ-Day, turned out to be a surprise moneymaker, paving the way for Hale's biggest break, co-starring with Robert Young in the "A" comedy Lady Luck (1946). In it, she portrayed the abstaining descendant of a long line of gamblers.

She then teamed with her real-life husband in A Likely Story (1947) and The Clay Pigeon (1946), although she had more impressive vehicles as teacher of The Boy with Green Hair (1948) and as, especially, mother of the boy who cried wolf in the "sleeper" hit The Window (1949). Her contract with Columbia Pictures and Jolson Sings Again ensued.

During the filming, Hale told a reporter there were many similarities between the Jolsons and the Williamses that helped her in her role as Erle Jolson. Hale mentioned that her husband, like Jolson, had been out of work for a long period, and it had been up to her--as it had been up to Mrs. Jolson--"to inspire him to get back in the groove again." Jolson's late-life health problems, she went on, were paralleled by her own husband's bout with arthritis, through which she nursed him--again, as had Jolson's wife. Like Erle Jolson's habit in Jolson Sings Again, Hale, too, was constantly taking off her shoes in real life. Both families lived in the San Fernando Valley.

Bill Williams joined his wife's interview to cite the biggest difference between the couples: "Jolson has $11,000,000."

Shortly, Hale was working opposite Robert Young again plus another Robert--Cummings--in, respectively, the frothy And Baby Makes Three (1950) and The First Time (1952), playing a possibly pregnant divorcée in the former and a hassled but very married new parent in the latter. Assigned the role of a physician, she was reunited with Larry Parks in Emergency Wedding (1950), going on to star in the costume swashbuckler Lorna Doone (1951). On the whole, though, she drew too few worthwhile pictures during her years at Columbia.

In Jolson Sings Again, Jolson shows Ellen (Barbara Hale) the list of Community Chest benefit stars, noting, "And many others--that's me."

Smoothly shifting from light comedy to heavy drama, she fared better on loan-out to 20th Century-Fox for The Jackpot (1950), married to James Stewart, and to Warner Brothers for A Lion Is in the Streets (1953), married to James Cagney. She played down glamour in both roles. Streets, with Hale as the Northern schoolmarm wife of Southern peddler-turned-politico Cagney, might have given her career a needed impetus, except that the film did little business. Unfortunately, a few years before, Columbia's All the King's Men, starring Broderick Crawford and also obviously inspired by Louisiana demagogue Huey Long, had covered similar terrain, winning the best picture and actor Academy Awards. "Barbara Hale did her best work as Verity Wade," wrote Homer Dickens in his 1972 book The Films of James Cagney.

Hale has appeared in just about every film genre. There were Warner Bros.' Unchained (1955), a factual prison tale, and Columbia's The Houston Story (1956), a crime syndicate quickie. Her many Westerns include Paramount's The Far Horizons (1955), with Charlton Heston, and a pair with Joel McCrea: Universal's Lone Hand (1953) and Allied Artists' The Oklahoman (1957). In 1970, she turned up as Dean Martin's wife in Universal's record boxoffice hit, Airport. Five years later, she and husband Bill Williams were prominent in Transcentury Pictures' science fiction release, The Giant Spider Invasion.

Despite all this, Barbara Hale may be best known as Della Street, the sidelines-confined (often annoyingly so) Girl Friday of TV lawyer-sleuth Perry Mason (Raymond Burr). For her part in the show, which premièred in 1957 and ran nine years, Hale won the 1959 Emmy Award as best supporting actress in a dramatic TV series.

Hale has done considerable television work, and, still attractive and endowed with a disarming Midwestern credibility, she became familiar in recent years as the video spokesperson for Amana kitchen appliances. In 1978 Hale played a foster parent in the Walt Disney TV movie The Young Runaways, while in a Warner Bros. theater feature the same year called Big Wednesday, she appeared as the mother of her own son, blond actor William Katt (father Bill Williams' real name). Katt co-starred with his mother, resuming as Della Street, in the 1985 television movie entitled Perry Mason Returns, with Raymond Burr once again portraying the unbeatable legal eagle. Happily, this time Hale was very much the center of attention as Burr and Katt had to prove her innocent of a murder charge. Critic Tom Shales wrote: "Hale is more than hale as Della. Prior to the filming, Hale broke her hip in an accident and so did the whole movie sitting down. Whenever you see Della moving around, that's a double. What a trouper! And she's as sweet as ever, too." Perry Mason Returns was the highest-rated TV movie of 1985. More Mason features were planned.

Bill Williams, remembered for his title role in the 1950s television series Adventures of Kit Carson, has become very active in real estate development. He and Barbara Hale Williams, who has always put family before career, live in Sherman Oaks, California, and have three grown children (in the order of their appearances): Jody, a speech therapist; William, star of the early-eighties television series The Greatest American Hero (in which Hale guested to play his reel mother again); and Nita, a nursery school teacher.

Despite the accolades that came Barbara Hale's way when Jolson Sings Again was released, at least one important critic, the actress remembers, remained unimpressed: her then two-and-a-half-year-old daughter Jody, who slept soundly through a preview showing of her mother's favorite film.

Reference

1. The Washington protesters included Larry Adler, Robert Ardrey, Humphrey Bogart, Jules Buck, Richard Conte, Philip Dunne, John Garfield, Ira Gershwin, June Havoc, Sterling Hayden, Paul Henreid, David Hopkins, Marsha Hunt, John Huston, Danny Kaye, Gene Kelly, Evelyn Keyes, Joseph Sistrom, and Jane Wyatt.

▪ THE JOLSON "CHARACTERS" ▪

> You're handsome now, but if you give me any more trouble I'm going to make a character man of you.
>
> Director William A. Wellman speaking to star Ronald Colman while making "The Light That Failed."

From the diverse worlds of vaudeville, Vienna, Russia, radio, and Broadway came the five seasoned, now deceased character players featured in both Jolson film biographies. There was no culture shock, however, nor any clash of styles. The motley troupe boarded a sometimes tempest-tossed ship and helped to keep it afloat with their expertly blending, unflappable professionalism.

"The part was custom-made for me," stated irreplaceable William Demarest who portrayed Al Jolson's sidekick Steve Martin and who was, as Alfred E. Twomey and Arthur F. McClure wrote in their book The Versatiles, "one of the master exponents of the fish-eyed stare, crusty voice and baleful countenance."

Demarest went on:

> The Jolson Story even had me playing a cello, an instrument I have been using in show business since 1905, when I played on the porches of Asbury Park (New Jersey) hotels. I liked the part, too, because it took me away from my usual type of comedy role. I liked the fact that Steve Martin grew more sympathetic as he grew older. The whole picture took me back to my days in vaudeville. I was barnstorming

> at the same time Jolson was, playing the same towns, and on the set we often swapped stories.

Born in St. Paul, Minnesota, on February 27, 1892, little "Willie" Demarest was the son of a second-hand furniture dealer. He began his theatrical career as a pre-school cellist with his older brothers, pianist Reuben and violinist George. Then the family returned to its roots in New Jersey, where the lads helped to support themselves and their recently separated mother by performing not only on porches but on streetcorners and at church socials. They soon learned it was wiser to mix comedy with their music. Among their songs were "It Takes the Irish to Beat the Dutch," "I Am the Bosom Friend of Albert, Prince of Wales" and a number about the prison at Ossining, New York, "Dear Sing Sing" (one line went "In there you never get the measles because they can't break out").

When Reuben was seriously injured in a New York traffic accident, the trio became a duo re-christened "The Demarestio Brothers, European Entertainers." Later, William Demarest toured for several years with his first wife, Estelle Colette, whom he married in 1923, and also had a short boxing career as "Battling McGovern." His Broadway appearances included the Earl Carroll revues _Sketch Book_ (1929) and _Vanities_ (1931). A frequent headliner at the Palace Theater in New York, Demarest was master of ceremonies when that show business mecca closed its two-a-day vaudeville policy in 1932.

Demarest already had broken into motion pictures. "I made the first talking picture, _A Night in Coffee Dan's_, early in 1927 at Warners," revealed the actor. "I also made the second talking picture, _Amateur Night_, and also the third, _The Mail Man_. They were all short subjects. _The Jazz Singer_, in which I appeared with Jolson and which is always called the first talkie, was really about the twelfth. It was actually the first _musical_ talkie. For the erudition of anybody who's interested, Warners' _Lights of New York_, in which I did not appear, was the first full-length, all-talking picture."

A kind of Damon Runyon version of Scrooge, his pseudo-serious scowl and growl made him a comic natural from the start in films, where he worked with amazing regularity over the decades, save for a year's hegira as a talent agent in the mid-thirties when he took credit for discovering actresses

Jolson (Larry Parks) goes on for a drunken blackface singer in The Jolson Story, with William Demarest.

Jane Wyman and Ellen Drew. His thirties films include Diamond Jim, Hands Across the Table, Charlie Chan at the Opera, Wake Up and Live, Easy Living, Rosalie, Rebecca of Sunnybrook Farm, and Mr. Smith Goes to Washington. He was under contract to Paramount for sixteen years.

Demarest's most productive and rewarding period began at that studio in 1940, when the erratic, slapstick-obsessed but brilliant writing-directing satirist Preston Sturges gave him a supporting role in The Great McGinty as the crooked politician who helped ambitious hobo Brian Donlevy become governor. Minus name stars, with scenarist Sturges himself still unproved as a double threat, the film turned out to be a surprise hit and for a few years thereafter auteur Sturges wrote his own ticket at Paramount.

Demarest became the cornerstone of his envied stock

company, usually as characters named Bildocker, Heffelfinger, and Murgatroyd. He appeared for Sturges in Christmas in July (1940), as the frazzled foreman of a coffee slogan contest committee; The Lady Eve (1941), as ale heir Henry Fonda's "bodyguard and governess"; Sullivan's Travels (1941), as the studio publicist assigned to slumming director Joel McCrea; The Palm Beach Story (1942), as a drunken, rifle-blasting Ale and Quail Club member on the train to Palm Beach; Hail the Conquering Hero (1944), as the Marine who got phony war hero Eddie Bracken deeper into his unwilling masquerade; and, most effectively, The Miracle of Morgan's Creek (1944), as the understandably dour, small-town Constable Kockenlocker whose elder daughter (Betty Hutton) found herself pregnant by an unknown soldier after an all-night spree with departing servicemen.

In the memorable latter film, he took one of the screen's best-timed and executed pratfalls (a specialty of Demarest's well into middle age). When the constable attempted to kick his insolent adolescent daughter (Diana Lynn--"Papa, can't you learn to be a little more refined?"), she blithely escaped through a screen door, leaving Demarest to miss her backside with an astonishing aerial flourish and land flat on his porch. "The picture reaches its perfection in William Demarest," wrote James Agee in Time, "whose performance is one of the few solid-gold pieces of screen acting in recent years."

Despite the glory each had brought to the other's career, Demarest and Preston Sturges had a falling-out in the mid-forties and never worked together again.

The Jolson Story came along in 1946, bringing with it a best supporting actor Academy Award nomination for William Demarest. He remembered a fan letter he received for his favorite part. It came from Canada and read: "You are now a member of my farmyard. After seeing you in The Jolson Story, I named a pig after you. But don't feel badly; you are in good company. I have two other pigs, named Bing and Bob. But you, I think, are the cutest pig of all."

In the fifties, sixties and seventies he brightened such pictures as Riding High, When Willie Comes Marching Home, What Price Glory?, Dangerous When Wet, Escape from Fort Bravo, Lucy Gallant, Pepe, Son of Flubber, It's a Mad, Mad, Mad, Mad World, That Darn Cat, Won Ton Ton, The Dog Who

Tamara Shayne and Ludwig Donath play Jolson's parents in The Jolson Story.

Saved Hollywood, and the TV movie The Millionaire. He made, by his count, one hundred and thirty-eight films but is perhaps most easily recognized by younger audiences for six-and-a-half years in the television series My Three Sons as the carrot-topped "teen-sitter" Uncle Charley ("the little squoits").

According to Frank Capra, who directed him several times, "Bill is what I would call an anchor man. A director likes to find a strong actor around whom he can build a scene." Discussing the many great stars with whom he worked, Demarest said, "They liked me. I never played tricks on them. Many supporting actors are either too nervous or too tricky. I played straight and they liked me."

At age ninety-one, William Demarest died of a heart attack on December 28, 1983. He and his wife of forty-five years, Lucille, had lived in Palm Springs, California, since 1968, and though plagued with emphysema and eye and hearing trouble he managed to play golf right up to the end, often for charity. His business card read: "When I have the urge to work, I lie down until the urge passes."

He had a bottomless file of quips on aging. In 1979, TV host Merv Griffin asked him if there were any joys in being old, and Demarest replied, "If there are, I don't know what the hell they are!" In 1981, he told Johnny Carson, "I've been takin' so many treatments for so many ailments that when I die I'm going to die healthy!"

William Demarest also grumbled in that distinctive, poker-faced manner that endeared him to generations of moviegoers, "If I had known I was going to live this long, I'd have taken better care of myself."

• • •

"Besides the top romantic pair," wrote Variety in that paper's review of The Jolson Story, "Ludwig Donath as Cantor Yoelson and Tamara Shayne as Mrs. Yoelson are the cast's outstanders."

Although a Jewish refugee from Nazi Germany whose major recognition was as the gentle and devout Papa Yoelson in The Jolson Story and Jolson Sings Again, the distinguished Ludwig Donath had a whole sub-career portraying Adolf Hitler. He not only played Hitler in the film The Strange Death of Adolf Hitler, he also provided the voice of the great dictator in Margin for Error and The Moon is Down (all 1943) as well as on many Armed Forces Radio broadcasts. He appeared, too, in several films concerning Hitler.

Born in 1900 in Vienna where he was graduated from the Royal Academy, Donath made his professional acting debut as Lysander in A Midsummer Night's Dream, performing the role about five hundred times in various European cities. In addition, as a young actor at the State Theater in Berlin he sang in several operettas. He fled the Nazi holocaust in 1940 and quartered in Hollywood where he signed with Columbia Pictures, establishing himself as one of the film capital's most respected character actors. Among his movies are Hangmen Also Die, The Seventh Cross, The Hitler Gang, The Story of Dr. Wassell, The Master Race, Blondie Knows Best, Gilda, Renegades, The Return of Monte Cristo, To the Ends of the Earth, The Fighting O'Flynn, The Great Sinner, The Killer That Stalked New York, Journey into Light, Sirocco, Sins of Jezebel, and The Torn Curtain.

Just before the tender exigencies of The Jolson Story (for which he unaccountably received no Oscar nomination), the versatile Donath had one of his showiest, least sympathetic assignments in Counter-Attack (1945). Wearing a crew-cut toupée, he essayed a Nazi prisoner, a professor affecting a nonsensical spiel to camouflage himself as, it was ultimately revealed, the scourge known as "the butcher." [In the meantime, Donath's character gibberish sounds today almost certain to have inspired the wacky nightclub, TV and film comic called Professor Irwin Corey.]

Nineteen fifty-one found him back in a successful film biography of a musical personality, this time M-G-M's The Great Caruso, starring Mario Lanza. Although Donath played "the great tenor Brazzi" who, upon losing his voice, became the great Caruso's manager, he was not required to sing in this part.

New York audiences saw Donath on stage in The Dybbuk, Abie's Irish Rose, The Sea Gull, Only in America, The Deadly Game, and She Loves Me, and his many television appearances include the role of the German judge in the Playhouse 90 production of Judgment at Nuremberg. In later years, he directed the New York City Opera's The Marriage of Figaro and developed new talent for the NBC Opera and the Metropolitan Opera. He also coached actors and singers.

Ludwig Donath died of leukemia on September 29, 1967. His wife survived.

The memory of the Jolson film biographies had lingered on. One of Ludwig Donath's better late performances was on a segment of TV's Bonanza series. Once again crowned by a yarmulke (the skull cap worn by Jewish males), he portrayed an orthodox European Jew who tried to understand our Old West and sang (probably dubbed) the "Sholem Aleichem."

Interviewed shortly before her fatal heart attack on October 23, 1983 (ironically, the same month and day on which Jolson had died thirty-three years before), Tamara Shayne remembered her time as Mama Yoelson as "the most wonderful professional experience of my life."

The stately actress, born in Perm, Russia, then recalled (evidently somewhat conditioned by studio-manufactured forties publicity):

> Mr. Jolson was a very nice and warm person. During The Jolson Story, he was on the set where we worked every single day. He just couldn't stay away! Besides, he worked very hard with Larry Parks, and they did achieve such amazing results.
>
> The director of Jolson Story, as well as Mr. Jolson and the casting office, tried many actresses for the part of Mr. Jolson's mother. One well-known character lady actually came to the reading wearing an old-fashioned long dress of the period in the story, on the arm of a bearded old gentleman wearing a yarmulke! Although I believe this woman was born in England and was a Christian, she spoke only with her idea of a Russian Jewish accent the whole time.
>
> "If we used that woman," Bruce Humberstone, the first director on the film, whispered to me, "we'd have to change Jolie's birthplace to a shtetel in Shropshire!"
>
> I was among the last actresses seen and read the part for them. They engaged me the next day, or maybe the day after that. I don't exactly remember --it is all so long ago. Someone told me that after my reading Mr. Jolson said, "I want her. She looks like my mother." When I heard what he said, I didn't know whether to be flattered or not: Mr. Jolson was many years older than I! But I was delighted to get the best part I ever had on the screen.[1]
>
> As a company we were all very close and liked each other very much. It was a real joy to work with all

> of them, including absolutely everybody, down to the very last stagehand. And yes, we all felt it would be a success.

Shayne, who died at eighty, came from a theatrical family. Her brother was Konstantin Shayne, a fine character player in many Hollywood films of the period such as Orson Welles' The Stranger, released the same year as The Jolson Story and in which her sibling portrayed the Bible-clutching ex-Nazi. Tamara Shayne came to America in 1929 with her future husband, the soon Academy Award-nominated actor Akim Tamiroff, whom she married in 1932. They had both made films in Europe, and on Broadway Shayne appeared in The Cherry Orchard, Judgment Day, and These Few Ashes. Among her United States films: Mission to Moscow, Song of Russia, Pirates of Monterey, It Happened in Brooklyn, Northwest Outpost, The Snake Pit, Walk a Crooked Mile, Thieves' Highway, The Red Danube, Black Magic, I Can Get It for You Wholesale, and Anastasia.

In 1961's satiric Romanoff and Juliet, she played opposite her real-life husband, Tamiroff, as a Russian ambassador's wife who coveted a "subversive" fancy black hat. Coincidentally, twenty-two years before she had played Garbo's Russian roommate in Ninotchka--who yearned to borrow her comrade's Paris-bought silk slip.

When Tamiroff died in 1972, she retired to Palm Springs. Although gone slightly deaf, she enjoyed traveling in the decade before her death.

As was the case with Ludwig Donath, none of Tamara Shayne's other movies brought her anywhere near the affection and appreciation of the two Jolson biographies.

• • •

San Francisco-born Bill Goodwin, who came from a long line of lawyers, quit college at seventeen to go on the stage. His first real break came a couple of years later, in 1930, when he joined an Oakland, California, stock company run by character actor Leo Carrillo. Jobs were scarce in all areas then, and he was soon obliged to try radio, where, he liked to say, for a while he swept up the studios. By 1934, he was working with George Burns and Gracie Allen in an airwaves association

Bill Goodwin as Tom Baron in The Jolson Story.

that would last almost twenty years. While he also acted on radio, Goodwin was best known during these years as a mellifluous-voiced announcer with an agreeably extraverted personality all his own.

Others with whom he worked on radio were Bob Hope, Frank Sinatra, Paul Whiteman, Eddie Cantor, and Edgar Bergen.

Goodwin's film career really got underway in the forties, when the big, good-humored actor with "that wide-open smile" (Betty Hutton's description of him in Incendiary Blonde) appeared, often for Paramount, in Wake Island, Blondie in Society, So Proudly We Hail, No Time for Love, Riding High, Bathing Beauty, Spellbound, Hit Parade of 1947, It's a Great Feeling, and The Life of Riley. In the fifties, he was prominent in Tea for Two, The First Time, Lucky Me, The Opposite Sex, Bundle of Joy, The Big Beat, and Going Steady. He always said that his pet role was Tom Baron, Jolson's pal, in The Jolson Story and Jolson Sings Again.

His next most prized part was that of Tim Callahan in Paramount's Incendiary Blonde (1945), another film biography of an early twentieth-century entertainer, nightclub queen Texas Guinan (Betty Hutton). Goodwin's supporting role was the journalist who married Guinan, guiding her career from rodeo stunt rider to Broadway entertainer to legendary speakeasy hostess famed for her hearty "Hello, suckers!" Goodwin's newsman left her when he felt he was becoming "Mr. Guinan," and amid the musical comedy format the actor was able to limn a dimensional character who could be both breezy and sensitive. For the same studio later that year, Goodwin worked with Hutton again when this time he portrayed the real-life night club host, Sherman Billingsley of New York's swank Stork Club, in The Stork Club.

In 1946, besides appearing in The Jolson Story, Goodwin was featured in Paramount's To Each His Own, for which star Olivia de Havilland won the Oscar. He played a brash "drummer" (salesman) in love with small-town girl de Havilland, whose character described him thus: "He travels in wines, spirits and gents' toiletries."

On May 9, 1958, Bill Goodwin was found dead in his car, apparently of a heart attack. He was forty-seven. He left a widow, ex-actress Philippa Hilber, and four children--plus a creditable list of pleasant screen performances.

• • •

While he made a number of movies, the late Myron McCormick, who played the serious role of the Hollywood producer in Jolson Sings Again, was primarily known as a stage actor whose forte was comedy. The Jolson film completed shooting on De-

Jolson (Larry Parks) is approached by producer Ralph Bryant (Myron McCormick) to make a film about his life in Jolson Sings Again.

cember 24, 1948, and on April 4, 1949, McCormick opened on Broadway in perhaps his best remembered part, Luther Billis, the "dame"-anxious Seabee promoter, in Rodgers and Hammerstein's South Pacific. McCormick stayed with the Pulitzer Prize musical for its almost five-year run. In a tearful speech following all the bows at the last performance, he told the audience that the curtain would never be lowered on South Pacific, departing while the curtain remained up.

McCormick was born in Albany, Indiana, in 1906 and attended Princeton University, where he became Phi Beta Kappa and where James Stewart and Joshua Logan, later director of South Pacific, were classmates. During summer vacation in 1928, the University Players was founded on Cape Cod by McCormick and other collegians whose roll eventually boasted Stewart, Logan, Henry Fonda, Margaret Sullavan, Kent Smith, Mildred Natwick, and Barbara O'Neil. A number of them and McCormick made their Broadway debuts in the 1932 production of the Cape Cod-tried Carrie Nation. For a time during those Depression years, McCormick, Stewart, Fonda, and Logan shared a small apartment in Manhattan.

There, McCormick, jug-eared, puffy-eyed and generally looking as if he had just come off a lost weekend, was soon an in-demand character actor appearing regularly in such plays as Goodbye Again, Yellow Jack, Winterset, Small Miracle, Paths of Glory, Thunder Rock, Storm Operation, Soldier's Wife, State of the Union, Joy to the World, The Damask Cheek, No Time for Sergeants, The Time of Your Life, and 27 Wagons Full of Cotton.

His film credits, more widely spaced out, include Winterset, One Third of a Nation, China Girl, Jigsaw, Three for the Show, Not as a Stranger, The Man Who Understood Women, and The Hustler. McCormick's finest, and funniest, screen performance was the recreation of his Broadway role in Warner Brothers' No Time for Sergeants (1958). He played the quiet-craving, jowl-joggling Air Force sergeant whose life was upturned by a well-meaning but trouble-prone "plowboy" inductee (Andy Griffith).

On July 30, 1962, cancer finally lowered the curtain on the life of Myron McCormick, but not, thanks to warm memory and film, on his work.

Reference

1. Another advantage Tamara Shayne had over others in contention for the role of Mrs. Yoelson: Jolson already knew her casually from the previous decade when her husband, Akim Tamiroff, supported him in the Broadway musical The Wonder Bar.

■ ASA LOVES ANN ■

"Why, why did you put me in pictures when I was three years old?," a teenage Darryl Hickman asked his mother.

"But, dear," she replied, "it's what you always wanted to do."

During the thirties and forties, Scotty Beckett (who played young Asa Yoelson in The Jolson Story) and Ann Todd (as his girlfriend, Ann Murray) were two of the busiest, most appealing child actors in Hollywood whose careers not only often crossed but also paralleled each other. It is hoped, however, that Ann Todd, whose adult life is a question mark, has escaped Beckett's tragic ending.

Born in Oakland, California, on October 4, 1929, Scott Hastings Beckett was about three when he moved with his family to Los Angeles. The cherubic, almost pretty lad was inducted into the movies when a casting director observed him singing a popular song of the day to cheer his hospitalized father. Scotty's first film was Gallant Lady (1933), with Ann Harding, followed by regular appearances--cap askew, in baggy sweater and pants--as foil for rotund "Spanky" McFarland in the Our Gang (Little Rascals) shorts.

In features, he gained recognition playing sons of an astonishing assortment of star parents, as in Dante's Inferno, with Spencer Tracy and Claire Trevor; Anthony Adverse, Fredric March and Olivia de Havilland; Conquest, Greta Garbo and Charles Boyer; The Bad Man of Brimstone, Wallace Beery; Listen, Darling, Mary Astor; Marie Antoinette, Norma Shearer and Robert Morley; My Favorite Wife, Irene Dunne and Cary Grant; Our Neighbors--The Carters, Fay Bainter and Frank Craven; The Youngest Profession, Edward Arnold; and My Reputation, Barbara Stanwyck.

Ann Murray (Ann Todd) looks on proudly as Asa Yoelson (Scotty Beckett) sings "On the Banks of the Wabash" in The Jolson Story.

Another specialty of Scotty's was portraying various film stars as children. In Whom the Gods Destroy, he was Robert Young as a youngster; in My Son, My Son, Louis Hayward; Kings Row, Robert Cummings; Heaven Can Wait, Don Ameche; and in both Aloma of the South Seas and Ali Baba and the Forty Thieves, he represented the youthful Jon Hall.

With his aristocratic looks, it was perhaps inevitable that Scotty would be cast as royalty; Universal saw to this twice in 1944. In Ali Baba and the Forty Thieves he was the outcast ruler of Baghdad raised by the fabled Forty Thieves; and in The Climax, a Boris Karloff vehicle, he was the young king spectator beguiled by soprano Susanna Foster.

Scotty proved his versatility by playing "Junior" in The Life of Riley, the forties radio situation comedy hit starring William Bendix as his blue collar dad.

Despite all this, he reached his zenith essaying Larry Parks/Al Jolson as the adolescent Asa in The Jolson Story. His baby fat and angelic countenance having given way almost overnight, it seemed, to lanky, ingenuous young manhood, he got the best public and critical reception of his career. Dorothy Kilgallen, in her Modern Screen "Picture of the Month" review, appeared to favor him above all the other players in the film. "Scotty Beckett gives a touching, enchanting and to all indications, accurate performance as the boy Jolson," added the celebrated journalist.

He was now ready to court Peggy Ann Garner in Junior Miss, Elizabeth Taylor in Cynthia, and Jane Powell in A Date with Judy and Nancy Goes to Rio.

Other important Scotty Beckett films around this late-forties/early-fifties time were the war story Battleground, a comedy with Ronald Reagan called Louisa, and The Happy Years, a tale of teenage schoolboys. The latter title was prophetic, because Beckett's own happy years pretty much ended with his teens.

After roles in the short-lived Gasoline Alley "B" series, pictures became scarcer and scarcer for Beckett. He married, divorced, married, had a son named Scott, Jr., divorced, married. He was arrested on numerous occasions for passing bad checks, carrying a concealed weapon, suspicion of possessing "dangerous drugs," suspicion of burglary and drunk driving. In 1958 he was taken unconscious to a Hollywood hospital following an apparent overdose of drugs. In January, 1964, he received a suspended jail sentence for allegedly hitting his stepdaughter over the head with a crutch. Inactive in films for more than a decade, he entered a Hollywood rest home on May 8, 1968, after a serious beating, and died--it could hardly be called suddenly--two days later. Pills were found in his room, but the exact cause of his death was reported as unknown.

Much has been written about the unpleasant outcome that can befall a child put out to work in show business, and nowhere is there more horrifying validation for this theory than in the Scotty Beckett story.

The attention lavished on the children who manage to become stars may tend to spoil them severely, whereas youngsters such as Scotty Beckett, who work regularly but never quite make it to that high plateau, are open to more frequent rejection. Survivor Darryl Hickman, a talented, active contemporary who never really achieved name-above-the-title status either, recalls, "Nobody outside the profession has any idea what it was like. We lived in an adult world and were treated like adults. Not like children, to be loved and kept safe. Is it any wonder that all of us grew up with problems? Some producer, or a studio executive, would walk up and say, 'You were lousy in that last film.... Why don't you do something about that hair of yours?.... You're stupid. You can't act worth a damn.... You're fired.' ... And this sort of thing happened to me when I was ten years old. Can you imagine what that does to a kid's ego, his sense of security?"

The child actor--whether featured player or star--often faces _total_ rejection by the time he attains his majority. Some are equipped to deal with this, and some are not. Scotty Beckett, sadly, was not.

• • •

Ann Todd, a few years younger than her _Jolson Story_ childhood sweetheart, Scotty Beckett, was born in 1932. She became Ann _E_. Todd in the late forties, to avoid confusion with British actress Ann Todd who had recently become an international star in _The Seventh Veil_.

The daughter of Mr. and Mrs. Albert Mayfield of Longmont, Colorado, Ann Todd Mayfield modeled children's fashions in her home town. She was brought to Hollywood when her father had to relocate for his health. While acting in a church play, the bright-eyed, ebullient little girl was discovered by an agent who took her to director George Cukor, then casting Paramount's _Zaza_ (1939), starring Claudette Colbert. Cukor hired Ann to portray Herbert Marshall's daughter in the film.

A contract ensued with 20th Century-Fox, the studio whose curly-topped little Shirley Temple recently had been the number one boxoffice attraction for several years. When her expensive _The Blue Bird_ (1940) failed to draw customers, Shirley left the studio, and Fox proclaimed that they were going to groom Ann, four years younger, as successor to the fast-growing, erstwhile moppet superstar. In 1941, Hollywood

Fast-growing child actor Scotty Beckett as the teenage Asa Yoelson in The Jolson Story.

columnist Harrison Carroll announced, "Now the studio is going to build Ann a bungalow on the lot similar to the one Shirley Temple once occupied." But the studio did not come up with vehicles for Ann, invariably using her instead in supporting parts. Fox chief Darryl F. Zanuck was not yet able to forget the flop of Shirley's The Blue Bird--Ann Todd and Scotty Beckett, coincidentally, had played small roles in the production. The next authentic child star was M-G-M's Margaret O'Brien, who clicked with Journey for Margaret (1942).

Blonde ringlets did not sit well upon Ann's cheerful hardiness; she was quickly allowed to be her own dark-haired self. The public liked her naturalness, and she was able to work not only at 20th Century-Fox but just about all the other Hollywood studios as well.

Remember Ann, age seven, as the daughter of successful concert violinist Leslie Howard in Intermezzo (1939), winking at him as he labored over the title piece? Or, now thirteen, lathered up and being shaved by war hero John Garfield in Pride of the Marines (1945)? Oh, she could be a trial, too, as when, at eleven, she ignited a World War II incendiary bomb in her apartment in Dixie Dugan (1943). She worked steadily, appearing with Scotty Beckett in, besides The Blue Bird and The Jolson Story, the films Kings Row, My Reputation, and Dangerous Years.

Like Scotty, she frequently played stars "as a child." She was early Ann Sheridan in Kings Row; Linda Darnell in Blood and Sand; Dorothy Lamour in Beyond the Blue Horizon; Rosalind Russell in Roughly Speaking; and, of course, Jo-Carroll Dennison in The Jolson Story. If the mind boggled when Garbo and then Wallace Beery brought the cute Scotty Beckett into the world, it was even more of a shock for audiences when the open-faced, wholesome little Ann Todd, via the magic of the movies, suddenly became the oomphy Sheridan, the beauteous Darnell, the exotic Lamour, and the chic Russell, not to mention Miss America-of-1942 Dennison!

Among her other films: Dr. Ehrlich's Magic Bullet, Destry Rides Again, All This and Heaven, Too, Bad Men of Missouri, How Green Was My Valley, Remember the Day, The Men in Her Life, Brigham Young--Frontiersman, Cover-Up, Perfect Strangers, and The Lion Hunters.

Some film historians have stated in cast listings that Ann Todd portrayed Barbara O'Neil's daughter in Tower of London (1939), but it was actually Ann's contemporary, Joan Carroll, who appeared unbilled as the little princess in that film. Both quite small at the time, they were similar types and scarcely well known, so the mistake is understandable. Ann was the daughter, however, of Jeanne Crain in Margie (1946) and, in 1948, of Jeanette MacDonald in Three Daring Daughters, one of Ann's last films. Elinor Donahue (then Mary Elinor Donahue) played Ann's sister in the latter production, with Jane Powell completing the sibling triumvirate.

Today, Donahue, best known as Robert Young's daughter in the fifties TV series Father Knows Best, does not know what happened to former colleague Ann Todd.

"I can only dimly remember hearing of Ann's plan to follow a career as a concert pianist," says Elinor Donahue--Ann Todd began studying piano, like acting, at a very early age and occasionally got to play in some of her movies, notably Three Daring Daughters and Intermezzo.

Dickie Moore, a peer of Scotty Beckett's who also appeared in the Our Gang shorts, put the situation into perspective once when he said, "What do you do when you are eleven years old and your peak earning years are behind you? You hit the road. I tackled vaudeville."

■ THERE SHE IS, MISS STONED AMERICA ■

A husband is a man who often
finds that words flail him.

Anonymous

When I approached Phil Silvers, who had been a Columbia player then and friend of Harry Cohn, for any information he might have of the story behind The Jolson Story, he gave me a few anecdotes and some personal opinions, all useful. When asked how to contact his ex-wife, Jo-Carroll Dennison, who actually played in the film, Silvers declined to help, writing back, "Jo-Carroll Dennison, a former Miss America, was my first wife who cared very little for show business, and I really don't think she could supply you with any interesting material."

I located her anyway. Fortunately.

She was living in the same city as her ex-husband: Los Angeles.

Jo-Carroll Dennison, whose Miss Texas title led to Miss America of 1942, married comedian Phil Silvers in 1945, divorced him in 1950. In his autobiography, Silvers described the first meeting between Dennison, a Christian, and his mother, a Jew. The scene, with his new wife bravely ingesting such Jewish delicacies as stuffed derma and horseradish, was an exact replica of the scene in The Jolson Story in which Al brings bride Julie home to dinner.

Taking the comparison further, to believe Silvers he and Dennison broke up for reasons similar to those that finally separated Jolson and his wife in the first film biography: Silvers' compulsion to work while his wife was left waiting alone at home.

Jo-Carroll Dennison appeared in several other films. For 20th Century-Fox, she did Ladies of Washington, Winged Victory, State Fair, Something for the Boys, and Billy Rose's Diamond Horseshoe, the latter pair with Silvers. For Columbia, Beyond the Purple Hills and Pickup. Eagle-Lion released Prehistoric Women. Family always meant more to her than acting, and, after divorcing Silvers, she married TV executive Russell Stoneham, bore him two sons and has contented herself being on the fringes of show business in Bel Air, California.

Asked how she got the second female lead in The Jolson Story, Dennison replies, "I was a friend of Harry Cohn's. Actually, Phil Silvers, to whom I was married at the time, was his friend. It was 1944-45, and we would dine at Cohn's house often. So would Al Jolson. Columbia was going to make the movie about Jolson's life, and Al was after Cohn all the time to let him play himself in it. Jolson would always sing at Cohn's place, which was marvelous, because he was a great entertainer--as well as, reputedly, an egomaniac. He seemed ancient until be began to sing, then he was magic. I have been in and around show business all my life, and can say without qualification that Jolson was the most magnetic performer I have ever seen. It was my understanding that Cohn agreed to let Jolson do the singing on the soundtrack of The Jolson Story as a result of the response he would always get at these impromptu evenings. Cohn seemed to adore Jolson."

One day Cohn called Dennison and said, "You're in it."

"That was all," she shrugs. "I imagine I was chosen because I was around a lot during the formation of the picture. I was under contract to 20th Century-Fox at the time, so Cohn called Darryl Zanuck, the head of Fox, to get me loaned out. I was astonished to find myself important enough to be 'borrowed' for a picture, and a major one at that. I hadn't really done anything very big in movies. And there were plenty of girls already under contract to Columbia who could have done the role.

"I was on The Jolson Story for a long time, considering that my part was not that big. Although there were many weeks of prior musical preparations which didn't involve me, my scenes in the picture took about six weeks to shoot, I think, and I worked steadily. Some of my part wound up on the cutting room floor--guess the finished product ran too

Mama Yoelson (Tamara Shayne), Ann Murray (Jo-Carroll Dennison) and Papa Yoelson (Ludwig Donath) waiting to hear how Jolson's Broadway show is going in The Jolson Story.

long. There was a sequence in which Al returned from the road to find his childhood sweetheart, me, bent on marrying someone more stable, and tries to win be back but fails. His efforts to do so were cut from the final print.

"I'm sure my character of Ann Murray was fictional, a device created to make Al more sympathetic. From what I have heard, I don't think Jolson ever loved anybody except himself (although he was always pleasant to me). And if he did, I doubt she would have jilted him as my character did.

"Jolson was not on the set while we were shooting the story portions; at least I didn't see him. But I understand he worked with Larry Parks a lot on the musical parts. Or so we were told, anyway."

Ann Murray (Jo-Carroll Dennison), at far right, brings her fiancé (Jimmy Lloyd), second from right, to meet Jolson (Larry Parks), at center, in The Jolson Story. Others: William Demarest, Ludwig Donath and Tamara Shayne.

She continues, "Except for the delightful and sweet people I came to know on it, my memory of the picture is rather vague"--her recall actually is exceeded only by her modesty. "Larry Parks was one of the nicest people one could know, terribly eager for his big break. He was a good friend of mine for many years. The director, Al Green, was a lovely, grey-haired man who had been a good director but was old and terrified of Cohn now. Cohn made his life miserable with constant memos. Cohn took a personal interest in all his pictures, but I think more on this one because of his relationship with Jolson. It was a very 'personal' picture. But the director was lovely to me and everyone else and enormously helpful to Larry, especially, since the main focus was on the part of Jolson.

"The Jolson Story was constantly being re-written--by writers, by Cohn, by Jolson. I don't remember that my part was changed much, but everyone else never knew what the next day's shooting would bring. Cohn not only sent memos to the director but to the writers and anyone else he could think of who needed instruction on how to do their job. There was little rehearsal for the story parts, just terrible pressure to hurry."

She has pleasant memories of Ludwig Donath, "a very cultured man and fine actor who was so kind to young actors. Which was not true of the assistant director, whose name escapes me [Wilbur McGaugh]. An assistant director would *have* to be tough to work with Harry Cohn, of course, but I had only known the extremely nice ones at 20th, so he scared me to death. The one at Columbia was one of the rudest, crudest men I've ever known.

"One morning I phoned the A.D., as the assistant director was called, to tell him that I could not come in that day because I had unbearable menstrual cramps. That sometimes happened to me, whereupon I would stay in bed with lots of codeine. Well, he got me out of bed in a hurry with an endearment such as, 'Get your ass over here in twenty minutes or I'll send the police for you! You're in the first shot, goddammit, now GET OVER HERE!' So, on the day they took all the close-ups of me at the dinner table with Al and his parents, I had so much codeine in me that it was all a dreamy haze."

Laughs Dennison, "The other day someone told me my performance in *The Jolson Story* was my best. Maybe this was the reason. I was stoned!"

Jo-Carroll Dennison also remembers, "I got to know Jolson's wife, the former Erle Galbraith. We became friendly, so one day I invited her to lunch and she said she'd love to. Later, she declined, explaining that Al said she couldn't because that was the way he lost Ruby--girlfriends of Ruby's talking against him."

In trying to discourage me, then, from interviewing his ex-wife, Phil Silvers may simply have wanted to remain the star in the family. On the other hand, if he truly thought she had never really been interested in show business and would have no worthwhile recollections from having worked on *The Jolson Story*, it is not surprising that they were divorced: he never really knew the lady.

■ GREEN AND LEVIN: THE QUIET MEN ■

If you wish to know what a man is, place him in authority.

Yugoslav proverb

Although separated by about a generation in age, directors Alfred E. Green and Henry Levin nevertheless had more in common than their respective films, The Jolson Story and Jolson Sings Again.

Green, a pioneer motion picture director, plied his trade for forty-eight years. Born in Perris, California, in 1889, he started with that state's first movie studio, the Selig Polyscope Company, and what many consider the first real action approach to serials, The Adventures of Kathlyn (1913). He did Mary Pickford's Little Lord Fauntleroy (sharing credit with her brother, Jack Pickford), as well as George Arliss' Disraeli, The Green Goddess, and Old English, plus 1935's Dangerous, for which Bette Davis won her first Academy Award. In addition, he directed Ella Cinders, Silver Dollar, Colleen (with Ruby Keeler), Thoroughbreds Don't Cry (with Judy Garland), The Duke of West Point, The Gracie Allen Murder Case, East of the River, Flowing Gold, South of Pago Pago, Badlands of Dakota (the latter three with Frances Farmer), The Mayor of 44th Street, Mr. Winkle Goes to War, Strange Affair, A Thousand and One Nights (the latter two with Evelyn Keyes), Tars and Spars, Copacabana, The Fabulous Dorseys, Four Faces West, The Jackie Robinson Story, The Eddie Cantor Story, and Top Banana, among dozens of films.

Green, then, was an unpretentious journeyman director in all genres who worked as consistently as anyone in the business, every now and then coming up with a surprise hit.

D-D-1020-P.36

Actress Marguerite Chapman, who calls the Green-directed Appointment in Berlin (1943) her favorite among her thirty-odd films, recalls the director as "a great guy. Very easy-going. You were never aware that he was carrying the whip, that he was the leader. While you were waiting for a set-up and thinking of your next scene, he liked to tell corny, silly little jokes, jokes that lightened the tension but were trivial enough not to distract you from your concentration on the scene to be played."

Marshall A. Green, Vice President and Executive Production Manager of Universal Pictures, feels that his father has never been justly recognized for his direction of The Jolson Story.

"Nobody wanted to be associated with the film in the beginning, but when it became a smash everybody claimed they had directed the whole thing. I've always been quick to correct them. A number of years ago I was sitting in the café at the Goldwyn Studio when my father came in and joined me. I heard someone nearby say, 'That's Al Green. He directed The Jolson Story.' Another guy at his table replied, 'No, he didn't. Sidney Skolsky put that whole thing together, wrote and directed every scene. He told me so.' I straightened them out and then mentioned the incident to Sidney, who, saying he'd been misunderstood, apologized," related Marshall Green.

"In 1962, Larry Parks made his comeback for us (Universal) in Freud. It was directed by John Huston in Munich, but they had to come back here to the studio to do some dubbing and other work. I was assistant production manager at the time. Larry went to the trouble of looking me up. He came into my office, sat down and said, 'The Jolson Story would never have been made if it weren't for your father. I wouldn't have been able to get through it without him.'

"Somewhere along the line, I worked with Ludwig Donath,

Director Alfred E. Green, Larry Parks and Al Jolson between scenes of The Jolson Story. Below: Jolson (Larry Parks) is told by manager Steve Martin (William Demarest) to slow his work pace and have a life outside the theater in The Jolson Story.

who played Jolson's father, and he said the same thing, adding, 'Don't ever let anyone tell you your father didn't direct The Jolson Story.'"

Marshall Green believes his father won the Jolson Story assignment because he had just directed A Thousand and One Nights at Columbia. Although no one expected it to amount to much, Nights became a box office winner.

"It wasn't easy for Dad," he goes on. "I was in the service overseas during most of the shooting of The Jolson Story, but I visited the set once when I came home on leave. I remember Dad undergoing particular abuse from Harry Cohn that day. Cohn was something else--one tough baby. When we went home that evening, I asked him, 'Why do you take this?' Dad answered, 'I'm going to ride this out. I think the picture's going to be a smash. I can take it.'"

Marshall Green states that director Green had left Columbia by the time the sequel, Jolson Sings Again, got going, and was "probably busy somewhere else. He'd changed agents, as I recall, and gone with MCA, where they were into packaging independent pictures. They'd put a director with a package and sell it. My father went to Universal in 1949 to do Sierra, with Audie Murphy, and I went with him as second assistant. I've been at Universal ever since."

Alfred E. Green's reputed outward calm must have covered a steely interior. During Bette Davis' first decade in films, the thirties, he directed her more than any other director would ever manage--seven times. This, in a period when the tough-minded Davis was, as an acquaintance put it, "someone only a mother could love"--if not a daughter: many years later Davis' only natural child, B.D. Hyman, wrote a hate-filled best-seller about her parent entitled My Mother's Keeper.

After Davis, in the late-thirties/early-forties Green graduated to the erratic, now deceased Frances Farmer, guiding her, too, through more films than anyone else. About the young Farmer, who went on to spend years in mental institutions, William Wyler, co-director with Howard Hawks of her best film, Come and Get It (1936), said, "The nicest thing I can say about Frances Farmer is that she is unbearable." For these two protracted associations alone, many thought director Green deserved, if not an Oscar, at least a Purple Heart.

"Dad never said much. He was very modest, reserved. (That's why there probably weren't as many photographs released of him at work on The Jolson Story as there were of some others. He would head in the opposite direction when he saw the photographer coming.) But I think The Jolson Story was his favorite of all his many pictures. He liked Disraeli, with George Arliss, for its artistic aspect, but I honestly think he still favored the Jolson picture," says Marshall Green.

After the Jolson job, Green directed several other film biographies, including 1953's The Eddie Cantor Story, back again with producer Sidney Skolsky and Warner Bros., the studio at which he had spent much of the twenties and thirties. "If that was my life, I never lived," said Eddie Cantor, who dubbed the vocals à la The Jolson Story for his on-screen counterpart, Keefe Brasselle. None of Green's succeeding films had the impact of the Jolson chronicle--but then, what director could really expect two Jolson Storys in one lifetime?

Alfred E. Green, age seventy-one, died in Hollywood on September 4, 1960, after a long illness.

• • •

Henry Levin, director of the less challenging Jolson Sings Again, was, like his predecessor on The Jolson Story, a prolific director of program pictures. Their personal working styles were similar as well: each did his job with quiet competence. It would not be stretching matters too far, in fact, despite their crowded field, to call the younger man Green's successor in general.

Furthermore, recalled Levin much later, "When I first went under contract to Columbia in the early forties--as a dialogue director fresh from New York--my first assignment to an 'A' film was as a dialogue director on a production Al Green was directing. I worked with him two or three more times, and he was one of my strongest boosters, urging the studio to give me a directing opportunity." After sixteen months, he became a full-fledged director.

Henry Levin, director of *Jolson Sings Again*.

Born in Trenton, New Jersey, in 1909, Henry Levin was raised in his parents' theatrical boarding house. Almost inevitably, he went on the stage—at the age of two. Later, after being graduated from the University of Pennsylvania with a B.S. degree in economics, he stage-managed for the Theatre Guild, ran a summer theater in Massachusetts and acted whenever he could.

At Columbia Pictures, he directed such disparate fare as Sergeant Mike and The Gallant Blade, both with his subsequent Jolson Sings Again star, Larry Parks, as well as The Bandit of Sherwood Forest (sharing credit with George Sherman), The Guilt of Janet Ames, The Mating of Millie, The Man from Colorado, And Baby Makes Three (with Barbara Hale), and The Petty Girl.

He then signed with 20th Century-Fox, where he directed several of the lot's major female stars: Jeanne Crain in Belles on Their Toes, Betty Grable in The Farmer Takes a Wife and Susan Hayward in The President's Lady. In addition, there were three Clifton Webb vehicles: Mister Scoutmaster, The Remarkable Mr. Pennypacker, and Holiday for Lovers.

Levin proved especially adept at handling pop recording stars of the fifties and early sixties, directing Pat Boone in his three best features, Bernardine, April Love, and Journey to the Center of the Earth; plus, at M-G-M, Connie Francis in her film pinnacle, Where the Boys Are. For Metro, he also did Come Fly with Me and (sharing credit with George Pal) The Wonderful World of the Brothers Grimm; returning to Columbia, Genghis Khan and Murderers' Row.

Jolson Sings Again remained one of his top favorites among the fifty-odd features he directed. "One reason I think of it fondly has to do with my childhood," Levin explained only weeks before his death by heart attack in 1980 while directing a TV movie titled Scout's Honor. "I was a song-and-dance kid and an actor, playing in family burlesque, vaudeville and many benefit amateur productions. And one of my acts consisted of donning blackface and singing Jolson songs, like 'My Mammy,' 'Rock-a-Bye Your Baby with a Dixie Melody' and 'April Showers.' Therefore, to meet Jolie and work with him and direct a film about him was a moving experience for me."

Levin continued, "The story of how I got the job is a simple one. I was under contract to Columbia at the time, and one day my agent called and said, 'How would you like to direct the Jolson sequel?' Naturally, I was excited; it was my best break to date. When my euphoria kept me from answering right away, my agent informed me, 'It's your next assignment.'

In Jolson Sings Again, Ellen Clark Jolson (Barbara Hale) tells Papa Yoelson (Ludwig Donath), Jolson (Larry Parks), Henry the butler (Eric Wilton), and Steve Martin (William Demarest), "Oh, there's a benefit show for the Community Chest next week."

"Jolson recorded all the songs especially for the film. Old recordings were not used. And he was in great voice for these sessions. I recall so well that when we were recording, the orchestra used to applaud him after each take. And he would amuse them with stories and anecdotes and jokes. He was always 'on.' Without an audience, he wasn't quite alive. An audience, any audience, was more than food and drink and possibly sex to him. I believe the only thing he loved--truly loved--more than himself was an audience.

"I remember the day Harry Truman won the Presidency. I don't know what scene we were filming, but I do recall that Jolson had bet me 250 to 1 that Thomas Dewey would win. Later I heard that he wired a congratulatory telegram to Truman saying that one of his favorite songs was 'I'm Just Wild About Harry.'"

The newly elected President of the United States, in turn, informed Jolson that when the entertainer had toured the hinterlands in 1911 in his first Broadway show, La Belle Paree, it was also the first Broadway import the then young Missourian Truman ever saw.

Henry Levin remembered Larry Parks as "a gentleman and a talented actor who listened carefully to anyone who was there to help him. He was a tireless worker, especially when it came to rehearsing the Jolson songs. During the days of preparation, he would work for hours in front of a great mirror, rehearsing the movements and the synchronization for the songs which were blasting forth from the two enormous speakers at a level so high that the recordings could be heard outside the sound-proof stage. Larry insisted on this high level for both rehearsing and shooting, because in that way he could sing at full voice without hearing himself--only the voice of Jolson.

"And the hours of rehearsing paid off. Never has the synchronization of lips and sound been truer than in those two films. And Larry was not essentially a man of impeccable rhythm. He was not at heart a song-and-dance man--therefore, his accomplishment in those films was all the more remarkable."

As for any significant problems encountered directing Jolson Sings Again, Henry Levin said, "There are no 'easy' films. There are always crises--daily--and somehow they are always met and conquered. But at this late date, I can't recall any particularly dire problems. Unfortunately, I didn't keep a diary to record what my memory has failed to retain."

If Henry Levin and Alfred E. Green *had* been so prescient as to keep diaries of their Hollywood years, their words could have provided an insightful, panoramic history of the motion picture industry.

■ WRITERS TO THE LEFT AND RIGHT ■

> In Hollywood, a writer puts on a sport jacket and takes off his brain.
>
> Ben Hecht

In the mid-thirties, soon after the censoring power of the Motion Picture Production Code had been strengthened, mogul Samuel Goldwyn anted up $50,000 to purchase Lillian Hellman's The Children's Hour, which he planned to film shortly. When a more erudite, shocked member of his publicity department asked former glove salesman Goldwyn if he knew that he had just bought a play about a couple of lesbians, Goldwyn shrugged, "So what? I'll have my writers make them a couple of Americans."

That's how it was in Hollywood. The first chapter of the Gospel of St. John realized that "In the beginning was the word," but the writer's social standing in the City of the Angels was at best third-class.[1] In his autobiography, Heyday, Dore Schary put it this way:

> [In Hollywood], failure always has a father--the writer. To the dictum "When the going gets tough, the tough get going" should be added "and the tough always go for the writer"--the schlimazel of motion pictures. He is the first to be sprayed with the odor of failure.

The writer was--is?--a hired hand often called on "to lick," as it was inevitably phrased, any story problems. If one writer couldn't do it, there were plenty more available from a pool that at various times at various studios included such distinguished (if grappling) literary names as Raymond Chandler, William Faulkner, F. Scott Fitzgerald and John

Steinbeck. To the producer and director, no matter how illustrious the scribe, they were simply, condescendingly, "my writers."

Well enough was rarely left alone. There is an applicable story that has gone around Hollywood for years. A producer and screenwriter are marooned on a desert island, and the producer asks the screenwriter to write a message for help. When the producer reads the message, he shakes his head and says, "Sorry, but I'm going to have to call in another writer."

In 1929, for instance, Mary Pickford and Douglas Fairbanks filmed The Taming of the Shrew, containing Hollywood's most notorious credit line: "By William Shakespeare/Additional Dialogue by Sam Taylor."

So it was with The Jolson Story.

• • •

Marjorie Walker, owner of an advertising-public relations agency in Hollywood, recalls an incident relevant to this book. Not only does her story present a more sensitive Al Jolson than real-life legend has provided, it indicates--through Jolson's apparently spontaneous recognition of many of the events depicted--that The Jolson Story may be more factual than it has been given credit for, even by its own writers. At the very least, Marjorie Walker's recollection lends support to the screenwriter Stephen Longstreet who likes to say that the film was "true to his spirit." She says:

> When I was a young girl I attended the preview of The Jolson Story at the Pantages Theater on Hollywood Boulevard, and found myself seated next to Al Jolson. We were in the second row of the balcony.
>
> The picture, of course, was advertised only as a "Major Studio Feature Preview." My father had called me from the studio and told me that the Jolson picture was being previewed that night, and where, so a friend and I decided to go. The Pantages was very crowded--a few "insiders" who knew what the picture would be, but mostly the general public.
>
> Half-way through the picture I noticed the man sitting next to me, still wearing his camel's hair coat.

Stephen Longstreet, who gets the major screenplay credit on The Jolson Story.

The light from the screen reflected on his face. He was crying. Then he was laughing--a lot--and then the tears started down his face again. I realized it was Al Jolson, and he was alone.

The movie was a big hit with the audience. They clapped after several scenes (a common practice at previews for films that were liked), such as the singing scenes and the production number where Evelyn Keyes danced down the stairs. The audience whistled and clapped more when the film was over. The lights went on.

Mr. Jolson sat there for a minute with his head down, wiping his face. Then he got up and started up the balcony steps to the aisle. Suddenly someone recognized him and came over to shake his hand, exclaiming, "Jolie! Jolie! What are you doing here? The picture was wonderful!" Then everyone turned around--"There's Al Jolson!" His head had been down, but now he looked up and started shaking everyone's hands.

By the time we saw him in the lobby a few minutes later, he was strutting like the king of the mountain. Everybody crowded around him--a few people from the studio and the public. I don't think anyone else knew he had been crying through most of the picture.

Preparing the biographical essentials for whomever would write the screenplay, Sidney Skolsky spent much time with Jolson but said that the entertainer changed the facts of his life story every time they met. [As a Hollywood reporter, Skolsky himself was no slouch at mangling facts. In a 1947 Photoplay article he by-lined on Larry Parks, he erred claiming that Parks was the only person tested for the lead in The Jolson Story. And in a 1955 piece on Jolson, he incorrectly wrote that his subject was born in St. Petersburg, Russia.] The columnist-turned-producer alleged that he wound up interspersing with Jolson's most repeated recollections fragments from Skolsky's own childhood. There was also one other not inconsiderable dilemma: how to make loveable a man well-known to be extremely self-centered.

There were at least a dozen writers eventually hired to work on The Jolson Story, but only three were finally accorded screen credit.

The first person approached to write the screenplay was Andrew Solt, a young Hungarian émigré who had sold a play to Columbia and was brought to the studio as a contract writer at $250 a week. Not long after his arrival Solt had the following dialogue with studio chief Harry Cohn:

COHN: What do you know about Al Jolson?

SOLT: I remember going with my mother in Budapest to see The Jazz Singer.

COHN: What else?

SOLT: I saw Jolson some years ago when I was living in New York. He was in a play, a musical, and the little I remember is that it wasn't very good.

COHN: What else?

SOLT: I hear he's washed up.

COHN: Is there anything else you know about Al Jolson?

SOLT: No.

COHN: Good. I want you to work on the script of The Jolson Story.

Cohn felt that a Hungarian would be less likely to romanticize the American legend known as Al Jolson. Solt, who says that "Al Jolson hardly ever visited the set. I used to go to see him at the Beverly Hills Hotel," opines that the biggest problem confronting the screenwriter(s) on Jolson's story was an ending. Jolson's career was thought to be pretty much over, which was too downbeat a note on which to end his movie life. However, it was World War II and Jolson was then touring United States military bases in Europe. Certain studio personnel discussed the fine dramatic finale they would have if Jolson's plane would crash while entertaining the troops.

Solt adds that he liked Harry Cohn. "He could behave like a monster," Solt explains, "but he would do so to your face, so that you always knew where you stood."

As it turned out, an insufficient amount of Solt material was used for him to be listed as screenplay writer. His final acknowledgment was only a shared adaptation credit. He consoled himself by writing--with others and alone--the screenplays for Without Reservations, with Claudette Colbert and John Wayne; Ingrid Bergman's Joan of Arc and June Allyson's Little Women; one of Humphrey Bogart's best but least-known vehicles, In a Lonely Place; and For the First Time, the final film of another famous singer, the late Mario Lanza.

Papa Yoelson (Ludwig Donath) asks young Asa (Scotty Beckett) why he was late at the synagogue, while Mama (Tamara Shayne) looks on in The Jolson Story.

Cohn next reversed his thinking, perhaps at the suggestion of Jolson who had Cohn's ear and may have reasoned that the writer of a screenplay focusing on aspects of Americana really ought to have a nodding acquaintance with same. Cohn hired Lawrence Hazard, writer of middle period Joan Crawford screenplays but now known for his horse-oriented Americana scripts (Thoroughbreds Don't Cry, She Went to the Races, etc.). Jolson's widely publicized predilection for "the sport of kings" might have suggested Hazard to Cohn, who often went to the races with the entertainer. Hazard also is believed to have worked on the infamous, multi-handed re-write of the screenplay for Three Comrades (1938), the first draft of which was done by noted novelist but alcoholic, failed screenwriter F. Scott Fitzgerald. [A number of literary lights who tried their hands at writing for the movies were defeated by the terseness required by the medium, as well as the crassness of their mogul employers.] Hazard got no credit for Comrades, nor for any of his work that may have wound up in The Jolson Story, though he was mentioned as the sole writer at one point in early publicity for the film.

Stephen Longstreet--with whom Hazard drove to the studio in a wartime car pool--was hired to write the first Jolson film biography. It is Longstreet who gets major on-screen credit as having written the screenplay for the picture.

A jazz and art critic, painter and prolific author of novels like The Gay Sisters (later a Barbara Stanwyck movie), New York City-born Longstreet sometimes wrote the screen versions of his books, such as Stallion Road, which starred Ronald Reagan. In 1957, he did another film biography of a theatrical personality. "I worked on The Helen Morgan Story, but it was a dud," he admits. "The actress playing Helen, Ann Blyth, was too refined and not able to catch the full seamy character, and the director, Michael Curtiz, was Hungarian and had no idea of Americana. It was, by the way, one of Paul Newman's first pictures. He was only fair."

Other films on which Longstreet received varied writing credits: The Greatest Show on Earth, with Betty Hutton; The Strange Affair of Uncle Harry, with George Sanders; Silver River, with Errol Flynn; Duel in the Sun, with Jennifer Jones; and The First Traveling Saleslady, with Ginger Rogers. He also wrote the book (from his own novel) for the hit Broadway musical featuring Phil Silvers, High Button Shoes.

Proof that Stephen Longstreet came to the Jolson project early is found in a November, 1944, issue of Motion Picture, two years before the release of The Jolson Story. The magazine contained the first of many whimsical articles therein by Longstreet on the Hollywood scene, and the following provocative excerpt is from this initial piece:

> I suppose the climax of my life with the Hollywood stars came just this week. I had been working on Jolson at the Columbia Studios. (It's no secret that Jolson is The Life of Al Jolson.) And Al and I had been talking all afternoon on casting the picture.
> "It's very simple," said Al.
> "Yes?," I said.

"All we need is an actor for the part."

"Yes, all we need is a new Al Jolson from the ages of twelve to twenty. And they happen about once every thousand years."

I was driving down past Milt Gross' house and Milt was on his front lawn painting sets for the new Bing Crosby-Betty Hutton picture, Here Come the WAVEs. I waved to Milt. I was just wondering if he could play Jolson when a low touring car, built like a tank, came out of a side street and almost drove me onto Milt's lawn.

"Why don't you look where you're going?," said the Army major behind the wheel of the car.

I said, "How long you been back?"

Clark Gable backed up the car and ground his gears. "Short time. Sorry if I almost ran you down."

"It's all right ... my fault.... I was casting a picture."

Clark went off in a cloud of dust. Milt Gross put down his painting and came over to me.

"Milt, what do you think of Clark playing Al Jolson in a picture?"

"Come inside," said Milt. "You been standing in the sun too long."

Maybe Milt was right ... but think of the novelty of Clark Gable in blackface!

Today, Stephen Longstreet, although a resident of affluent Beverly Hills, sounds bitter. In a chapter called "Schmucks with Underwoods" from James R. Silke's history of Warner Bros. Studios titled Here's Looking at You, Kid, Longstreet recalled of Hollywood's halcyon years: "The studio chiefs didn't trust us. They needed us. They needed us to sew the dialogue into the action, because basically that was what movies were--action. We had no real power. No writer ever stopped a scene to tell the director it was being done wrong. The studio always put three or four writers on the same project. You didn't know that. You'd be off doing your version and they'd be off doing theirs. Credit-stealing was going on all over the place. It was easy to steal a credit from a writer--particularly if you were a smart producer." Longstreet said producers managed this simply by adding a few lines and then convincing the front office they had written most of the script. This went on before there was a strong writers' union, he asserted.

Longstreet tells me, "Hollywood is built on lies. It's their business. About The Jolson Story I've heard a hundred versions. I wrote the script alone. There were other scripts, but I didn't read them. The people who got some story credit I never read, but someone felt it was policy to add a few names. The picture was really made by Sidney Skolsky who had the idea, got Jolie and Harry Cohn together. After the success of the picture everyone tried to grab credit. Sidney Buchman claimed a lot, but he really did the sequel, Jolson Sings Again. I didn't write that because I felt it a stupid idea, a poor story and not worth doing. But Buchman seemed to go around claiming The Jolson Story when he was called by the House Un-American Activities Committee in Washington to explain his radical past.

"Harry Cohn hated the picture until it was a big success, then he, too, took bows. Skolsky really deserves all credit, but he's been overlooked.

"I got to know Jolie very well. He was a ham, a great performer, not much of a human being. All ego and bluff, but damn great on stage.

"The film is made up. I created a legend: 'Let me sing and I'm happy. Off-stage, I'm a failure, can't cope.' It's fiction, really: I doubt his father was a cantor,[2] we left out a couple of wives, as well as brothers and sisters who hated him. The spirit was there, if not the facts. I was on the set a lot, making some cuts, but in the main, as usual, no one really cared for a writer's opinions. That's why so many films are so bad. I was well paid. I got a lot of honors, including the Gallup Poll Photoplay Gold Medal award, and probably would have gotten an Academy Award nomination, but at that time musicals were considered frivolous and were frowned on as contenders. Jolson was happy and promised me a great gift. All he sent was a photo of himself signed, 'To Steve who took my life....' We hung it over a toilet."

Longstreet advises, "If you look at the sets you'll notice the picture was made for very little money. Jolie owned half of it so he did well. It's revived from time to time, and also plays TV often, but I don't get any extra cash. The Screen Writers Guild numbly gave away free to television all those films made before 1960. Screwing writers is a great art.

"I had a happy time writing the picture, however. Skolsky was bright and the ideas worked. I got along with Jolie very well, but never liked him as a human being, though I greatly admired him as an entertainer. It proved my idea: if there is someone of note that you like, don't meet him."

Sidney Buchman, the studio's executive producer, wrote patches here and there of The Jolson Story, as well as writing the whole screenplay of Jolson Sings Again. In King Cohn, the biography of Harry Cohn, author Bob Thomas alleges that it was Buchman who came up with "the key to the story" for the first film when he heard of an incident during the marriage of Ruby Keeler and Jolson. On the first night in their new ranch home in bucolic Encino, California, where Keeler hoped he would retire from show business, a restless Jolson said he had to get out for a while. He didn't return until early morning, having spent the time entertaining local firemen in their station.

"This story is a love affair. The lover is applause. Jolson's wife could handle another woman, but she was no match against the applause," Buchman told the writers.

Betty Garrett says, "Both pictures were very strongly supervised by Sidney Buchman, so in effect he really was the director behind the scenes--and even the writer, as many scenes were written the night before they were shot in a back room of Schwab's drugstore with Sidney Buchman, Larry, and Evelyn Keyes."

During interviews in the 1960s, Larry Parks sometimes forgot (or neglected to mention) who actually received on-screen credit for writing The Jolson Story and gave the honor solely to the uncredited Sidney Buchman.

Buchman refused on-screen recognition for writing the film because, Sidney Skolsky reported, "he said he didn't want credit for a movie he had written only a couple of scenes for."

It is Harry Chandlee who shared with Andrew Solt the lesser adaptation credit. Chandlee, like the previously discussed Lawrence Hazard, was an Americana specialist and worked on the screenplays for Our Town, with William Holden;

In The Jolson Story, Jolson (Larry Parks) interrupts his Broadway show by saying, "I think I got another dozen songs in me, and I'm rarin' to go!"

Sergeant York, with Gary Cooper; and The Adventures of Mark Twain, with Fredric March. He died in 1956.

• • •

After World War II, concern mounted in the United States over the spread of Soviet influence through Eastern Europe. The House Un-American Activities Committee, spotlighting a fervid young freshman congressman named Richard Nixon, was reactivated in Washington, focusing its investigations of suspected Red subversion on Hollywood because, allegedly, of the film colony's influence on the public. Some thought the HUAC was publicity-hungry and that the idea, as writer Anthony Lewis has said, that "those conservative film factories were turning out Communist propaganda was laughable." Others saw the crisis as more economic than political: the establishment film industry, long dedicated to entertainment alone, against the young upstarts with a social conscience who were coming on strong.

But these opinions were far from the vocal majority in the Inquisition-like climate of the day.

According to Sidney Skolsky in his autobiography, Don't Get Me Wrong--I Love Hollywood, the unlikely John Howard Lawson wrote at least three-fourths of the final Jolson Story script. Brought to the project by Sidney Buchman, Lawson later was called by Hedda Hopper the leader of Hollywood Communism in the thirties and forties. Unfortunately, Lawson's radicalism had begun to get him into hot water by the time of the first Jolson film. Although Harry Cohn was a Republican (who cared little for politics--it was strictly for status), Columbia had risen to prominence as one of the most liberal of Hollywood studios, thanks to the films of director Frank Capra and screenwriter Sidney Buchman; but the conspicuous, proselytizing Lawson was clearly another matter.

As early as 1942 there was apprehension about Lawson at Columbia, where he'd come to write the Humphrey Bogart tank warfare vehicle Sahara. Inspired by a 1937 Soviet film called The Thirteen, Lawson, wrote Bernard F. Dick in his book The Star-Spangled Screen, "envisaged Sahara as an allegory of brotherhood, a common theme in films of the Hollywood Ten." Dick added that while Lawson's screenplays may have been "touched" with propaganda, "a touch is not a brushstroke, and Lawson's touches were put in with a fine hand."

One day during pre-production of Sahara, Columbia Vice President B.B. (Ben) Kahane and studio legal counsel Mendel Silberberg marched into Harry Cohn's office.

"Harry, you've got to fire John Howard Lawson immediately," Kahane pleaded. "Just get him off the lot—fast. He's spouting Communism everywhere and alienating everybody. This Communist thing could blow up in our faces. We've got to be in the clear."

Cohn thought a few seconds, then replied, "No, I'm not going to fire him. I've got Cole Porter on the lot, and *he's* a fairy!"

The retired Jolson (Larry Parks) relaxes with manager Steve Martin (William Demarest) and wife Julie (Evelyn Keyes) at their country home in The Jolson Story.

Nevertheless, by 1945 Communism was becoming an increasingly risky doctrine in Hollywood. That year the United States Chamber of Commerce reported on "Communism Infiltration in the U.S.," warning particularly of Red inroads in the Screen Writers Guild. When Cohn heard this, he finally acceded to his executives' entreaties and, charged Skolsky, fired Lawson before the Jolson Story screenplay was finished. "He's only a goddam writer. This town's full of writers, and so is this lot. I'm tripping over the goddam know-it-alls!," rationalized Cohn, who publicly had extolled writers as more important to the creation of good movies than stars or directors. Later, he refused to give Lawson screen credit on the film.

"Whatever Harry may have felt personally about Lawson didn't matter when the welfare of Columbia appeared to be at stake," said Skolsky, adding that Sidney Buchman completed the script.

The year before he was barred from Columbia, Lawson had written the pro-Russian film Counter-Attack at the studio; the year after the Jolson film he was the first of the Hollywood Ten who refused to cooperate with the House Un-American Activities Committee. The emotional spokesman of the Ten, Lawson, wrote Peter Biskind in Cineaste, was "dragged" from the hearing by Federal officers for insisting that investigations mastermind/Chairman J. Parnell Thomas "accord Lawson the same courtesy Thomas had extended to the long parade of cooperative witnesses who had been encouraged to give lengthy testimonials to their own patriotism and the treason of others.... He set an example for those who followed him before the HUAC. He served nearly a year in prison for contempt of Congress." The remaining nine Unfriendly Witnesses were jailed for similar periods as well.

Lawson's other films include Our Blushing Brides, Dynamite, Blockade, Algiers, Four Sons, and 1947's Smash-Up, The Story of a Woman, the latter written for liberal producer Walter Wanger and Universal-International Pictures and starring Susan Hayward as an alcoholic singer in what some feel was her finest performance.

But the one that evidently got him into trouble with the HUAC was the 1943 Warner Bros. production, Action in the North Atlantic, starring Humphrey Bogart. Jack Warner testified that Lawson had written leftist propaganda into the scenario. Viewed today, the noisy film is almost entirely anti-Nazi sea battles, although author Bernard Dick has said that in structure North Atlantic follows the Russian classic Potemkin. Only once near the end is Lawson's political philosophy actually audible above the din, and it could hardly have constituted a threat to national security. As a bedraggled American Merchant Marine tanker bringing needed materials to Russia finally chugs into port there, the crew is greeted with joyous on-shore cries of "Tovarich!" One American seaman asks, "What does that mean--Tovarich?" His ecstatic companion exclaims, "That means comrade! That's good!" That is as subversive as things actually got in Action in the North Atlantic, made, after all, when the Soviets were our allies.

The author of the talked-about, avant-garde play Processional (1925), John Howard Lawson was co-founder of the short-lived (1927-28), radical New Playwrights Theater in New York, where he subsequently wrote for the Group Theater.

He was one of the first stage writers summoned to Hollywood when talkies (and the need for polished dialogue) came in. He was also the author of many books on playwriting, film-making, and criticism. In 1933, he organized and became the first President of the Screen Writers Guild, only weeks later serving as consultant on the founding of the Screen Actors Guild.

After being released from prison in 1951, Lawson was forced to write for the screen on the "black market" (anonymously). He died in 1977 at the age of eighty-two.

When he was excommunicated from Columbia Pictures, he dined with Sidney Skolsky, who claimed he worked very closely with Lawson on the Jolson film. Swore leftist Lawson, "Sidney, I've just got one thing to tell you. You trusted me, and I didn't violate that trust in anything I did. You'll find that when you run *The Jolson Story* that there's only one thing red in the entire picture. The red velvet curtain at the Winter Garden."

John Howard Lawson was *right*--for once in his life.

References

1. In the late forties-early fifties, when the House Un-American Activities Committee was chasing Communists in Hollywood, it should have startled no one that the ten persons jailed were mostly screenwriters.

2. The record shows that Moses Yoelson, Jolson's father, *was* a *chazan*, or cantor, in his native Russia as well as in America.

▪ LOOKING FOR A BLUEBIRD AND ▪ LIST'NING FOR HIS SONG

> Everybody here in Hollywood knows his business, plus music.
>
> Alfred Newman

Louis Armstrong. Fred Astaire. Janet Blair. Judy Canova. Carmen Cavallaro. Frederic Chopin. Bing Crosby. Alfred Drake. Duke Ellington. Jane Frazee. Rita Hayworth. José Iturbi. Gene Kelly. Kay Kyser. Frankie Laine. Ted Lewis. Ann Miller. Grace Moore. Frank Sinatra. Rudy Vallee.

None of Columbia Pictures' features spotlighting this extraordinary range of musical artists presented as great a challenge to the studio's music department as The Jolson Story, with its cornucopia of songs and unequalled dubbing requirements, related Morris Stoloff, department head and music director on both that film and Jolson Sings Again. "Or one that meant more to me personally," he added.

"A lot of people at the studio were concerned about The Jolson Story, wanted it to be good," said Stoloff just months before his death in his eighties in 1980. "We held meetings and decided to go for as much perfection as possible. It's a little hard to remember the details now, frankly--I was at Columbia twenty-four years and worked on several other pictures at the same time as I worked on The Jolson Story. It is one of my favorites, of course; I won an Oscar for it. The success of The Jolson Story was important to my career in that it had the effect of sustenance, of staying on. Now I don't mean to imply my position at Columbia was shaky, but it was definitely solidified by the first Jolson picture. And, I need hardly add, we were all working with the most remarkable talent: Al Jolson."

Columbia Pictures Music Director Morris Stoloff conducts the orchestra for Al Jolson as they record the musical soundtrack for The Jolson Story.

Stoloff denied persisting rumors that the Jolson voice had deteriorated to the point where bits and pieces of his old recordings had to be interspersed with the new recordings. "His recordings for The Jolson Story and Jolson Sings Again were completely new," assured the music director, "although occasionally we did have to do several takes for one reason or other before we got what we wanted. But this was the procedure with Crosby and Sinatra, too. Remember, Jolson had never used a mike on stage in his life. He didn't have to. His was not a delicate instrument easily damaged by time. Even in his sixties, he was still a forceful belter who was more than up to the recording for the Jolson biographies."

Continued Stoloff, "One of the biggest challenges on the first film was helping Al to find a way to bring his singing style up to date, which was the way we had decided to go, without sacrificing its unique vitality. He didn't like it, but I forced him to sit down one afternoon and listen to some of the top crooners of the day. He certainly didn't copy them, but it brought home to him the need for a slight adjustment to the times. His voice, which had once been a tenor, luckily had deepened with the years into a baritone, which was closer to the popular singing style of the forties. Obviously, we were able to pull it off.

"Furthermore, I found Al quite different, personally, from the way he was painted."

Stoloff refuted stories that Jolson was stingy. In 1947, shortly after The Jolson Story had become a smash, Jolson signed for several appearances on Bing Crosby's Philco Radio Time show. He said he wanted to bring along Morris Stoloff as his musical director, but the producers said no, Crosby always used John Scott Trotter. Jolson protested that he needed Stoloff for his arrangements, so they let him bring him to the show as "advisor." Stoloff went to every session and never did a thing, he said, "But you ought to have seen those checks he gave me. I've never known a man more generous. I did absolutely nothing."

Jolson felt Stoloff had done plenty. He was the man responsible for the more modern, commercial sound that had helped bring Jolson a whole new career.

Stoloff also won Academy Awards in the category of Best Score (Scoring of a Dramatic or Comedy Picture) for Cover Girl (1944) and Song without End (1960). Born in Philadelphia, he concertized on the violin throughout the United States at age sixteen and played with the Los Angeles Philharmonic, going on to found the Stoloff String Quartet. He entered films in 1928 as conductor of the Paramount studio orchestra, becoming head of music at Columbia in 1936.

Among those assisting Morris Stoloff on The Jolson Story was Saul Chaplin, who toiled in various capacities on this film and Jolson Sings Again. The composer of such songs as "Please Be Kind," "Bei Mir Bist Du Schön" and "Until the Real Thing Comes Along," Brooklyn-born Chaplin, after leaving Columbia, won Academy Awards for his scoring of the M-G-M films An American in Paris (1951) and Seven Brides for Seven Brothers (1954) and the United Artists release West

Side Story (1961). He was associate producer on the latter and The Sound of Music (1965), and was full-fledged producer of Star! (1968).

During his forties period at Columbia, Chaplin has observed, the music department had four or five people on staff who did "everything." One of these was George Duning, then recently arrived from the Cincinnati Conservatory of Music who today claims to have scored more than two hundred films. "On The Jolson Story," he says, "I did several arrangements of his songs, had numerous meetings with him and Morris Stoloff while working out the arrangements." In 1949, Duning, with Stoloff, received an Oscar nomination for scoring Jolson Sings Again.

Describing work in Columbia's music department at the time of the Jolson films, Saul Chaplin has said that one week it would be "a couple of songs for a quickie musical, the next arrangements and choral work for one of Harry Cohn's big musicals, like The Jolson Story or Cover Girl. That is where I really learned the movie business." Later, at M-G-M, he couldn't believe he was only working on one project, sometimes for months at a time. "One picture--such luxury!," he exclaimed.

Song possibilities for The Jolson Story were tested for familiarity by The Audience Research Institute, an organization founded in 1935 by Dr. George Gallup that pioneered in testing small cross sections of the country on specific matters and mathematically projecting the results for a large percentage of the population.

Obtaining rights, at non-prohibitive prices, from publishers for the many songs finally required for The Jolson Story (and Jolson Sings Again) proved a tricky transaction. According to Sidney Skolsky, when the word was out that a movie about Jolson's life was in preparation, publishers raised their prices on every Jolson song. One use of "Sonny Boy" reportedly cost $50,000, and it ultimately was cut from the first film. Harry Cohn's ingenuity and background in the music business kept things from getting totally out of control here.

A number of classic Jolson tunes had to be omitted from The Jolson Story because there just wasn't room for them, or because they didn't fit the scenario.

George Duning, who did some of the musical arrangements for The Jolson Story and worked with Morris Stoloff on the scoring of Jolson Sings Again.

Or because the producers felt they had dated and would not be acceptable to forties audiences. One of the latter was "Who Paid the Rent for Mrs. Rip Van Winkle (When Rip Van Winkle Was Away)?," popularized in 1913 by Jolson in the Broadway musical The Honeymoon Express and recorded for,

Saul Chaplin assisted Columbia Pictures music chief Morris Stoloff on The Jolson Story and Jolson Sings Again.

but not used in, the first picture about his life. For the film's soundtrack, as a recently released LP of Jolson Story outtakes revealed, he sang the brief piece straight at first, then in an expert but by 1946 passé low-Dutch comedy accent he rendered a lip-smackingly bawdy interpretation that also might have been a tad suggestive for what was planned as a "family movie" ("The landlord always left her with a smile on his face"). It was decided to let "The Spaniard Who Blighted My Life" represent all of Jolson's comedy numbers in the film. Many other songs that were used had to be given new arrangements that would combine the best of the old with contemporary post-war tastes.

Saul Chaplin says he never worked harder than on The Jolson Story, beginning months before filming actually started. He acquired old Jolson recordings from a woman collector in Pasadena and spent part of each day listening to them in his office, familiarizing himself with the Jolson style and repertoire.

At the first recording session, Jolson did "April Showers" and everybody cheered. Chaplin knew something was wrong: Jolson had left out the talking part, or recitative, in the second chorus. Noticing Chaplin's restraint, Jolson asked if he had liked it. He replied that it was okay but not like the record he remembered. At this, Jolson took out a big roll of bills and said, "I made this in show business; show me yours!" They argued, and Jolson went home angry. Eventually, he came back, Chaplin persisted and Jolson capitulated; he did the song Chaplin's way. After that, Chaplin claims, he was teaching Jolson how to do his own songs!

Evidently, Chaplin could be a stickler. Russ Tamblyn, who was featured in Seven Brides for Seven Brothers and West Side Story, recently admitted that, although he (Tamblyn) sang, he was rarely allowed to do so in his musicals. "In West Side Story, I did use my own voice in the 'Officer Krupke' number, but not in the 'Jet Song.' I could have, but the man in charge of the music--Saul Chaplin, he had done Seven Brides, too--didn't like using any actors to do singing," said Tamblyn.

"Chaplin liked using professional singers. He always brought them in--for everybody.... He's known for that. He even wanted to dub Al Jolson's voice--do you believe that? --when he did a Jolson movie 'way back in the forties. He's out of it, that way."

While the songs were being recorded for The Jolson Story, Jolson, giving tirelessly in a soundproof glass booth, was heard only by Morris Stoloff, wearing headphones. Evelyn Keyes said, "I remember just standing and staring, watching Jolson perform. It was uncanny. He was in the booth singing, but we could see him moving about and the people there were just overwhelmed."

Not long after the filming got underway, Jolson repaired to his Miami Beach home. But, recalled Larry Parks, "Jolson returned to Hollywood in time to see me play some of the scenes. As I finished one of his songs, he said, 'No, no, that's not it, son. Don't you remember how I used to do that?' I told him I'd never seen him perform, which didn't thrill him. Then he said, 'Well, you're doing too much.' To show me how to put the number across, he sang it. He almost wrecked the room. He practically hung from the chandelier. When he finished the song, perspiration was dripping from his forehead. 'There,' he said. 'You see? I didn't move a muscle.'"

The "Anniversary Song," which became the song hit of The Jolson Story, was initiated by Sidney Buchman. He felt that Larry Parks as Jolson needed "a little throwaway number," a bit of romantic nostalgia to be used simply as background to the dialogue at the anniversary party for Jolson's parents.

One day while Sidney Skolsky and Jolson were listening to playbacks, Skolsky noticed that Jolson, during the breaks, was hugging himself and humming a peculiarly catchy minor key melody.

"What's that you're humming?," asked the producer.

"I'm not humming," replied Jolson.

"Yes, you were," said Skolsky.

"If I was, I didn't realize it. Stop me the next time I do it."

After a while Jolson was absent-mindedly humming the melody again, and Skolsky mentioned it to him. The song turned out to be one Jolson's mother had sung to him as a child. Further investigation revealed it to be a waltz called "Danube Waves" that had been popular in Eastern Europe during Jolson's childhood. Written in the decade of his birth, the 1880s, by a Rumanian named J. Ivanovici who had died in 1902, it was now in the public domain.

Jolson may also have remembered an earlier, more bizarre instrumental performance of the tune when Marlene Dietrich, awaiting execution by firing squad in Dishonored (1931), gave a fierce rendition on the piano in her cell.

Over lunch with Saul Chaplin, Jolson said he had a song with just the right "old world" sentiment Buchman wanted for the anniversary scene. He hummed "Danube Waves" and Chaplin agreed that the melody was perfect. Chaplin set off to write new lyrics, and after about forty-five minutes of work performed them for Buchman, who liked the number and gave permission for Jolson to record the re-titled "Anniversary Song" for The Jolson Story. It worked so well that the scene in which it was to be used was re-written to feature the tune. Chaplin then wanted to improve the simplistic words, written more or less off the top of his head, but Buchman said, "No, you're going to re-write it into a failure. It sounds fine now."

Jolson had come up with the idea for the first line of the song. So, Chaplin claims, Jolson cut himself in for half of the royalties on the sheet music. Apparently, this kind of deal was nothing new with the entertainer. It has been alleged that, in Jolson's prime, when certain composers came to him to introduce their songs, he sometimes did so with the proviso that he be named co-author and thereby be permitted to share in the royalties. To have a song sung by Al Jolson, the songwriters often agreed to his terms. This practice existed with other important performers, too, such as Eddie Cantor, and it still goes on today.

"I didn't mind Jolson cutting himself in on the royalties of 'Anniversary Song,' because as it turned out he got us a marvelous royalty deal from the publishers," continues Chaplin. "I thought he was crazy at the time--there hadn't been a waltz hit for maybe twenty years! Jolie made it into a hit."

The number has become the most lucrative of standards: one can scarcely go to a wedding or anniversary party without the orchestra going into the melody that is often accompanied by the words "Oh! How we danced on the night were wed/We vowed our true love though a word wasn't said."

Then there is the subsequent parody, almost equally familiar to generations. It goes:

> Oh! How we danced on the night we were wed.
> We danced and we danced 'cause there wasn't any bed.

Evelyn Keyes dances and sings to "She's a Latin from Manhattan" in The Jolson Story.

The song's enduring recognition factor is further attested to by its reference in the 1979 film spoof of the Dracula legend titled Love at First Bite. When the vampire and his bug-eating henchman invaded a blood bank, the latter hummed, "Oh! How they danced on the night that they bled ... "

Said Sidney Skolsky, "Jolson made more money from 'Anniversary Song,' I think, than Larry Parks made playing him."

• • •

Jack Cole, who became Marilyn Monroe's choreographing amanuensis, had a distinct avant-garde/balletic style. As this approach matured, he appeared to favor hand movement over feet, which may be the reason non-dancer Monroe favored him. In his biography of Cole, Unsung Genius, Glenn Loney wrote that some colleagues who were close to Cole and Monroe swear that it was explosive, demanding Jack Cole, not some studio or Method Svengali, who really helped Marilyn develop her screen personality, teaching her how to move and deliver her lines and songs.

Cole seems to have been chosen to create the necessarily old-fashioned dances for The Jolson Story for three main reasons: 1) the dancing would not be extensive; 2) since he was working at the studio then and teaching dance on the lot, he was handy; and 3) Cole worked well with women and Harry Cohn had taken a personal interest in Evelyn Keyes, who had not danced professionally in years.

One of Cole's pupils would soon be Gwen Verdon, who became his assistant and with whom, during their seven years together, he had several fistfights. Carol Haney and Bambi Linn also trained with Cole at various times.

So did Ethel Martin, who had danced for Jack Cole on Broadway in 1943's Something for the Boys, which he choreographed. In Hollywood she was among the first of Cole's group of dance trainees at Columbia.

Ethel recalls, "We were under contract to Columbia, my husband George Martin and I and the others. In 1944, Jack had made Harry Cohn realize that if he sponsored a group of dancers at the studio, he wouldn't have to import them from New York or wherever when he needed them. Our contracts were unique. We were on salary, paid to be trained, and we didn't have to do any other work at the studio. We also had acting classes.

"I had recently married George when we did The Jolson Story. (We met a short time before dancing in a Roy Rogers film called The Yellow Rose of Texas.) We danced in several numbers throughout the Jolson film. In one I remember, Rod Alexander (who was also a trainee) and I did a brief dance solo in a nightclub scene and George appeared in a blackface duet with Larry Parks. It was kind of hectic. We were doing three pictures at the same time then: Jolson Story, Tars and Spars, and a 'B' whose title I can't recall.

"We had no problems with Harry Cohn, though. Behind closed doors there may have been an order to 'Use this lady.' But once we got into rehearsals, all we knew was the work.

Jack Cole, who staged the dances for The Jolson Story, is photographed on the set of M-G-M's The Merry Widow, a 1952 film starring Lana Turner and Fernando Lamas which Cole also choreographed.

Harry adored Jack. When some people mention Jack, they say, 'Oh, Jack Cole--East Indian. Jack Cole--extreme jazz.' But Jack was far more rounded as a dancer and teacher. When he didn't think he could give us something specific, he brought someone else in to teach us.

"I worked for Jack Cole for twenty-three years, and co-choreographed with him as well. Jack was a taskmaster and could be mercurial, but I loved him." Ethel's first job in Hollywood was doubling some of Merle Oberon's dancing in The Lodger (1944). Ethel and George Martin also danced in Tonight and Every Night and Down to Earth.

Born in New Brunswick, New Jersey, Cole was a star dancer with partners Alice Dudley and then Florence Lessing in smart supper clubs of the thirties and forties. His jazzy, exotic choreography was also a strong influence on the era's musical stage where he devised the dances for--besides the aformentioned Something for the Boys--Kismet, Jamaica, A Funny Thing Happened on the Way to the Forum, and Man of La Mancha.

In films, Cole was associated with some of the screen's most glamorous female stars, including Rita Hayworth in her peak efforts, Cover Girl, Tonight and Every Night, Down to Earth and, most memorably, Gilda, with, wrote Hayworth biographer John Kobal, "the number that has become a cornerstone in the mythology of the forties," the enduringly sexy "Put the Blame on Mame." Cole worked, too, with Marlene Dietrich in Kismet; Lana Turner in The Merry Widow; Betty Grable in Moon over Miami, Meet Me After the Show, The Farmer Takes a Wife, and Three for the Show; Kay Kendall in Les Girls; the insistent Marilyn Monroe in Gentlemen Prefer Blondes, River of No Return, There's No Business Like Show Business, Some Like It Hot, and Let's Make Love.

His theatrical achievements notwithstanding, not everyone was as enchanted with Cole as Marilyn Monroe, Harry Cohn, and Ethel Martin. In his study of the films of director George Cukor, Cukor & Co., Gary Carey, discussing Les Girls (1957), starring Gene Kelly, wrote, "Choreographer Jack Cole's combination of neo-native, sub-Martha Graham dance patterns is the nadir of the American musical's flirtation with 'culture.'"

Jack Cole also danced in several films himself, notably Moon over Miami, Eadie Was a Lady, Tonight and Every Night, The Merry Widow, and Designing Woman. He died on February 17, 1974, at the age of sixty-three.

• • •

The song numbers in Jolson Sings Again were staged by a Columbia dance director named Audrene Brier, who also did some uncredited coaching of Larry Parks and Evelyn Keyes on The Jolson Story.

A diminutive blonde, Brier was a Los Angeles native who was discovered by Gus Edwards, becoming a child actress at age three. Many small roles in films followed, but, after years of studying ballet with Ernest Belcher and tap with Nick Castle, she turned to chorus work in films. In 1941 she joined the Columbia dance department and stayed there throughout the decade.

Brier had been helping Jack Cole map out some dances for Rita Hayworth when he asked her to assist him with The Jolson Story. She and Parks worked especially well together, and after the second time, Jolson film publicity was saying that "Around Columbia when Larry Parks sings, Audrene Brier's throat contracts--they're that close, professionally."

After Jolson Sings Again, Brier explained their modus operandi: "Larry's songs are sung to resemble the way Jolson sang them; but make no mistake, apart from the voice itself they're Parks songs, not Jolson songs. The action surrounding them is created to give an 'impression' of the great blackface entertainer without trying to do what would be impossible for anyone--reproduce it exactly."

She said she devised the actions for the numbers from the Jolson songs themselves, not from the pictures in which Jolson appeared. During preparations for both Jolson films, Parks worked with her at least nine hours a day, six days a week.

Audrene Brier went on to create the underwater choreography for M-G-M's spectacular Esther Williams vehicle, Million Dollar Mermaid (1952), the biography of Australian swim star Annette Kellerman.

• • •

Fred Karger had just begun his twenty-eight-year career as a musical supervisor at Columbia Pictures when he worked on The Jolson Story. The son of violinist Maxwell Karger, co-founder of the early Metro Pictures Corporation which evolved into the monolithic Metro-Goldwyn-Mayer, Karger *fils* also married actress Jane Wyman *twice* following her 1949 divorce from Ronald Reagan.

"I worked mostly with Larry Parks on The Jolson Story," revealed the conductor-composer-arranger-accompanist before his death in 1979 of leukemia. "I helped him to synchronize to Jolson's recordings. As I recall, I also wrote a little piece

Fred Karger, right, pictured with Ethel Merman and his then wife, Jane Wyman, in the mid-1950s.

of Latin music that was used in a backstage scene; later we gave it lyrics. I think my biggest help was criticizing Larry. I didn't work with Jolson at all, but it was part of my job to be on the recording stage when he was recording his songs. I had to be there so that I could help Larry to interpret the numbers afterward. Larry learned every one of the songs working with me. This was before stereo and hi-fi, and he used these two gigantic Lansing speakers which were deafening. Larry sang all the songs in his own voice but Jolson's voice coming from the speakers would drown him out completely.

"I have great memories of Larry. 'Fred!' he would exclaim, bursting into my office at Columbia. 'You've got to drop everything and come down to see me do this number and tell me what you think.' I'd go and say, 'You were great,' which he usually was. 'I'm *not*,' he'd insist and go at it again. He was very tough on himself."

Reflecting a few seconds, Karger continued, "Larry was so definite in that part that I think it hurt his career later on. He was always associated with Al Jolson. That happened, too, with Robert Alda, who played George Gershwin in Rhapsody in Blue around the same time. Of course, Larry's political problems didn't help, either. No, they did not help at all. He did not get a fair shake from life, and you can quote me on that."

At Columbia, Karger worked on everything from the big Rita Hayworth and Kim Novak movies to the Gidget movies; while at M-G-M later on he did several Elvis Presley vehicles, finding time as well to write many songs, including the title tune for From Here to Eternity.

"I worked on Jolson Sings Again, but not as much as on The Jolson Story. By then I was busy on other projects, too," added Karger, who led his own big band as well. "I was also deeply involved in a romance with Marilyn Monroe around the time of Jolson Sings Again. She was just starting out and had come to Columbia for a featured role in a 'B' picture called Ladies of the Chorus. As with Larry, I was assigned to work with Marilyn on her songs. Harry Cohn thought she had nothing and afterward let her go. She went over to 20th Century-Fox. The rest is history."

• • •

Milton Delugg may be remembered as the bandleader on television's first late-night program smash, Broadway Open House, with Jerry Lester. Recently, he drew a similar post with The Gong Show. More to the point, he played Al Jolson's/ Larry Parks' overseas accordionist in Jolson Sings Again.

Claims Delugg, "I also did most of Al's arrangements for the film. Al and I worked together constantly in his office in Beverly Hills. I remember he just wanted to sing all the time. We must have recorded at least thirty songs that didn't get in the movie. Singing seemed to make him stronger. He told me he was sixty-seven years old and I really thought he'd live to be a hundred. I also did his radio show.

"After we did the picture we went to New York to promote it. I picked up seven fellows for a band and we did seven Loew's theaters a day (August 10, 11, and 12, 1949). I was also doing the Abe Burrows radio show at the time and was exhausted. Like I say, though, the more Al sang, the stronger he seemed to get.

"I got Jolson Sings Again this way. I was working in a little jazz club on Vine Street in Hollywood. We did remote radio broadcasts from there, which, what with the noise and smoke and everything, had to sound awful. Al heard me on the air and called me to be in the picture. He had to have been drinking!"

Delugg calls Larry Parks "a very, very nice man. Al used to get mad because everybody thought Larry was Al and nobody knew who Al was. He used to mutter, 'I could'a taken Mark Stevens....' Of course, if he'd taken Mark Stevens to play him it would have been the same thing as with Larry."

Delugg also wrote the music for an aborted Broadway musical about the life of Al Jolson called Joley that was tried out on Long Island in 1979, starring Larry Kert.

Much earlier, he'd been with Matty Malneck's orchestra for a while, and worked with the late composer Frank (Guys and Dolls) Loesser. "Frank had a wonderful ear," says Delugg. "He was the best lyric writer around but he couldn't always put down the music which he also wrote. I helped him to do this. In return, he wrote the lyrics to the first hit song I composed, 'Hoop Dee Doo,' and then wrote the words for my next one, 'Orange-Colored Sky.'"

Delugg has appeared in numerous films since the late 1930s, so many he can't remember them all ("Whenever a hot accordion player was needed, they called me"). In one, 1950's Let's Dance, he was cast as himself and again entertained servicemen in a World War II setting. Introducing him on screen, star Fred Astaire remarked, "Milton Delugg.... Of whom the great Stokowski once said, 'What's that name again?'"

• • •

None of the Columbia music department's achievements on the Jolson films would have been possible without the expertise of the sound department, run by John Livadary from 1928 until 1959. During that time Livadary picked up three Academy

Awards: one for The Jolson Story and the other two for One Night of Love (1934), which successfully presented the previously uncinematic opera star Grace Moore, and From Here to Eternity (1953), which resuscitated Frank Sinatra.

Now New York-based, Dede Allen, celebrated for her editing of such contemporary films as The Hustler; Bonnie and Clyde; The Godfather, Part II; and Reds, was a youngster who had just begun working in the sound effects department at Columbia when The Jolson Story was made. "John Livadary was, in fact, the man who upped me from messenger to the sound department when I was unable to get into the film editing department. He was a remarkable man with a great feeling for young people."

She continues, "I knew Larry Parks both at Columbia and at the Actors Lab, where I worked backstage evenings and weekends. Parks worked extra hard, as I remember, not only as an actor but particularly on perfecting 100 percent lip-sync for the Jolson part."

• • •

> To Truck--Without you I never could have done the picture--I'm sorry to say!! Love & kisses, Larry

This message was written by Larry Parks on a blackface photograph of himself from The Jolson Story to Truck Krone, a sound man at Columbia from 1941 until 1950. Krone, after that a cameraman for a while, has been a lighting director at ABC Television in Hollywood for years.

"Larry Parks and I started out together at Columbia," Krone reveals. "I was a sound man and he was a 'B' movie actor. We didn't have much money, so we roomed together for a while. When The Jolson Story came up, there was a bunch of guys after it. Dick Conte, for one. But Larry got it. (Janet Blair probably came closest to getting the girl's part finally played by Evelyn Keyes.) I was assigned to be playback operator and coach for Larry on the film. The important thing for me was to watch how he looked while he worked on the musical numbers, to make sure he was getting the synchronizing and gesturing properly. A woman named Audrene Brier worked with him on the dancing (we were both

Larry Parks, observed by playback operator Truck Krone, rehearses for one of the musical numbers in Jolson Sings Again.

on Jolson Sings Again a few years later, too). By the time of The Jolson Story, Larry was making about $500 a week, while I pulled down $87.50. Actually, not bad money, when you compare it to what the rest of the country was making in 1945-46.

"Warner Brothers wouldn't loan Columbia any of the old Jolson films, but I had a friend there who sneaked out prints of Jolson's The Jazz Singer and The Singing Fool and maybe one other title. We got these great chunks of film over to the house where Larry studied them on the Movieola [the machine used for editing and scrutinizing film]. Larry may not have been the world's greatest actor, but he was a little like the Japanese: he could copy anything.

"Originally, The Jolson Story was to be shot in black-and-white. It filmed that way for about a week. Then one day Larry came home, mystified and very dejected, and said, 'The picture's off!' They resumed shortly, though, this time in Technicolor, with a new director and a bigger budget--and all on the power of the black-and-white rushes they had seen of Larry's great job.

"When we began the picture the first time, Al Jolson was not exactly in demand in show business anymore, but he would come on the set and be dictatorish. This was very upsetting to Larry. After the shut-down, when the picture resumed in color the edict went out: keep Jolson away. Jolson intimidated people. He was domineering. That's why he had that great effect on audiences."

Asked to name the biggest problem he faced on the Jolson stories, Krone answers, "Larry's perfectionism. I don't believe he was ever happy with his own work. Christ, his job on 'Mammy' was sensational--there were sixteen takes, and I think they printed the first.

"But it was never good enough for Larry. He'd come over to me and say, 'How was it?' Now on the set the director is supposed to be the boss. I was just a kid; the director was the one to ask. That was the veteran Al Green. Al would see this going on and say to me, 'Let me wink at you, Truck, if Larry's going to put all his faith in you'--meaning, facetiously, that he, Green, would signal me if Larry's scene was okay."

[The distinguished actor Paul Muni, who at the time of *The Jolson Story* had just left Columbia after three pictures, was notorious for the subtle signals that passed between him and Bella Muni, his wife and director-*sans*-portfolio. After each take, he would glance for the verdict not to the director but to Bella. As Muni biographer Jerome Lawrence wrote, Bella then had "a Yiddish way of shrugging with her face." Even if the director had liked the scene, when Muni recognized Bella's disapproval, he would request another take.]

Truck Krone continues, "We had to pump Jolson's recordings back over the Lansing speakers at almost pain-barrier, because Larry didn't want to hear his own voice while learning the numbers. He had the worst singing voice in the world. No real musical ability at all. That's how fine an *actor* he was.

"'You ain't heard nothin' yet!' was the toughest line Larry ever said. He just didn't believe it. He was too unsure of himself. He did have trouble swinging his arms as Jolson. If you see the picture again, you'll think: if he could only put his arms in his back pocket.

"But Larry was dedicated. If the blacklist hadn't happened, I think he might have developed along the lines of a Paul Muni. Larry didn't chase girls, even though he was a good-looking guy and could have done well. When we were on Jolson Sings Again, Ava Gardner lived up the street from Larry in Nichols Canyon. One afternoon while Larry and I were alone at his place, Ava dropped by in an old Army shirt, with no bra--very unusual in those days. I was going crazy, but Larry didn't even bother to look up from the Movieola; he couldn't have cared less.

"He was a physical fitness nut. He felt that his body was important to his work and jogged and did push-ups regularly.

"As for the Communist thing, I'm sure there were guys who wanted to overthrow our government, but Larry sure as hell wasn't one of them. He was no more of a Communist than I was. Sidney Buchman, the studio's executive producer, was the one who first invited Larry to a cell meeting, I believe. In fact, Larry invited me to go along, but I was busy or something. It was just that Larry worried about people starving in the world. He was a very serious, sincere guy."

Krone notes that "Harry Cohn, the head of the studio, intimidated Larry. Me, too. He was tough. During The Jolson Story, I was up on a boom one day, smoking--a no-no. Cohn came by and said, 'I can retire. Can you?' Sidney Buchman was so powerful at the studio and yet so gentle. I often think he ran Columbia Pictures. He was the one who came down whenever there was a problem.

"Al Green was a well-loved, down-to-earth guy. Henry Levin, who directed Jolson Sings Again, was very quiet."

Asked if he could venture an opinion why Parks always said he preferred Jolson Sings Again to The Jolson Story (a choice that few moviegoers would second), Krone answers,

"Because the spotlight was on Larry more in Jolson Sings Again. After all, he was an actor."

And the name Truck? "It's a nickname. I played football at USC. I wasn't the fastest thing in the world, so...."

▪ THE INVISIBLE STARS ▪

Illusion is the first of all pleasures.

Voltaire

As the 1980s approached, Hollywood columnist George Christy asked Evelyn Keyes if "tinsel town" had changed. She replied, "The big studios aren't there, where there were dozens of starlets under contract.... Their schools shaped our speech and how we looked. If you want to make it today, you can't be another pretty face or body. You have to sing, dance, emote in front of a camera. In my day, we didn't worry about not doing something right. Big Daddy would dub us, or fake it. The studios crippled us that way, as well as our personal lives, because Big Daddy was the super-stud who took care of everything. I remained a child until middle age. I didn't know how to buy an airline ticket."

Before shedding tears over the plight of movie queens of yore, it is more relevant to note that few motion pictures have "faked it" as much as The Jolson Story. Or as brilliantly.

And few studios were as practiced in the fine art of dubbing and doubling in musical films as Columbia Pictures. There was the company's biggest star of the period, Rita Hayworth, who became a musical comedy star despite the fact that her singing was almost always dubbed, usually by Anita Ellis, Martha Mears, Nan Wynn, or Jo Ann Greer. In 1943, the studio produced a "B" musical based on the life of clarinettist-entertainer Ted Lewis entitled Is Everybody Happy? Larry Parks had a featured role, but the lead was enacted by Michael Duane with Lewis himself dubbing the clarinet playing. In 1945, Columbia's most successful film was the Technicolor super-production of A Song to Remember, the

Miriam Franklin doubles Evelyn Keyes' dancing in the "Liza" production number in The Jolson Story.

romanticized biography of composer-pianist Frederic Chopin in which Cornel Wilde became a star. Although concert artist José Iturbi actually did Wilde's piano playing on the soundtrack, the stocky Iturbi's hands were deemed too chunky to represent those of the lean leading man, so a third party was employed to provide the digits shown in close-up on the keyboards, one-time child prodigy Erwin Nyiregyhazi.

Coincidentally, the whole thing actually started with Al Jolson's The Jazz Singer, made by Warner Bros. in 1927 and the film that ushered in talking pictures. The singing of Bobby Gordon, who played Jolson's character as a child, and Warner Oland, who played his father, was dubbed, but very differently from what became the accepted mode of recording the musical tracks first and then later having the actors pantomime the numbers when the cameras got rolling. The artists who sang for Gordon and Oland had to be on the set during shooting because their vocals were recorded simultaneously with the scene action. That this was all still very new to all concerned was especially evident in Master Gordon's numbers. His mouthing of the lyrics was so glaringly out of "sync" with the actual vocalizing that, to obscure this fact, the camera cut away from him as often as possible.

Virginia Rees, who dubbed the vocals for Evelyn Keyes in The Jolson Story, and Cantor Saul Silverman, who sang for Ludwig Donath in both The Jolson Story and Jolson Sings Again, became reliable "ghosts" around the Hollywood studios. This kind of work proved a one-time-only arrangement, however, for choreographer-dancer Miriam Nelson, who did the stepping for Evelyn Keyes in one difficult number, and for Rudy Wissler, the singing actor who dubbed the songs for young Scotty Beckett in The Jolson Story.

Miriam Nelson was married to dancer Gene Nelson when she got the Jolson Story job, and, as Miriam Franklin, had performed in several movies. Among them were Ginger Rogers' Lady in the Dark; Preston Sturges' Hail the Conquering Hero; Masquerade in Mexico, with Dorothy Lamour; and the star-filled Duffy's Tavern, all four produced at Paramount. Today, she thinks Duffy's Tavern (1945) contains "the best thing I did in pictures," a "tap-ballet" production number featuring Johnny Coy as a returning war hero and Miriam Franklin (Nelson) as his hometown sweetheart.

On The Jolson Story, she explains, "Originally I was hired only to choreograph the 'Liza' number for Evelyn, because the film's choreographer, Jack Cole, did not tap. I was under contract to Paramount when the job came up and had to be loaned to Columbia, where I had danced in Cover Girl a short time before.

"The story point was told me of Evelyn dancing down only a few stairs on this high staircase, almost falling and then being given the courage to go on when she hears Jolson singing out from the audience. I was given the record of Jolson singing and put on a sound stage with the stairs, which were then in two sections. I was assured that I would never have to have them one on top of the other, going all the way up. By 'movie magic' they would make it appear as if the stairs reached the ceiling.

"I rehearsed all alone for four weeks. Then everyone--about fifteen people--came to see the number, including Al Jolson. You can imagine how nervous I was. After I showed the number, they all started talking to each other but not to me. They all talked to each other again. Finally, they seemed to agree on something. Harry Cohn asked me if I would double Evelyn. It was the first time anyone had said anything to me. Of course I said yes. They were happy that Evelyn, who had done little or no dancing in films, didn't have to risk her important neck in this (I would learn) possibly dangerous number. She wound up doing only a few shots in it: striking a dance pose at the top, the one of fear and the bow at the end where she blows a kiss to Jolson in the audience.

"The day before we shot it we were to rehearse with cameras on the shooting stage. When I arrived, to my chagrin there were the stairs, piled one on top of the other--about forty feet high! I had to go up and down these stairs so the director, Al Green, could figure out how to shoot it.

"The next day, the big day, I got out of bed and almost fell down; my legs had such cramps I could hardly walk. I called the assistant director and he said he would have a doctor at the studio, 'But get here.' I did and he did, and the doctor worked the cramps out with heat and massage. You would think that after four weeks my legs would have been used to it, but I guess I overdid it. I have always loved to dance, so I had a wonderful time in spite of the cramps."

She continues, "For me, the most important thing about the whole affair occurred the day everybody came to see the routine for the first time. Afterward, when everyone got up to leave, Jolson came back to me and said, 'Everyone loved the number. I'm sorry no one told you.' So of course I have fond memories of Al Jolson."

Nelson did not work with Evelyn Keyes, but taught Larry Parks one dance step Jolson did that she learned from watching an old Jolson film.

Asked if she had any idea that The Jolson Story would be such a hit, she admits, "I think I was too young at the time to really know. Almost all musicals were pretty big in

Rudy Wissler, left, shown with Joan Carroll, Skippy Homeier, and Patsy Ann Thompson in the United Artists film Tomorrow the World! (1944), dubbed the singing for Scotty Beckett in The Jolson Story.

those days. But Jolson's name was very important and we knew Larry was doing a great job. It remained for the audiences to accept him."

Miriam Nelson's marriage to Gene Nelson lasted from 1942 until 1952. They only did one film together, The Daughter Rosie O'Grady (1950). "It was the first of many for Gene at Warner Bros.," she adds. "He was featured, but I only did a bit, a little cross-over. By then I was a choreographer and have been ever since."

She staged Doris Day's dance routines in early-fifties musicals, and in 1955 choreographed the sexily memorable William Holden-Kim Novak picnic dance in Picnic. More recently, she has choreographed many nightclub acts and TV shows, as well as "a dozen or so" pictures produced by Mike Frankovich, such as Bob and Carol and Ted and Alice and Cactus Flower. Her TV movies include Ziegfeld: The Man and His

Women (in which she also played a small role--a choreographer) and Irwin Allen's Alice in Wonderland. She was one of the founders (in 1953) of SHARE, Inc. (Share Happily and Reap Endlessly), the Hollywood charity organization for retarded children, and stages its annual benefit show. Remarried, she is now Miriam Nelson Meyers of Beverly Hills.

Rudy Wissler's film career goes back to a choir boy bit in Angels with Dirty Faces (1938), a harbinger of Jolson scenes (and vocals) to come.

He had been acting for some time when, he recalls, "My agent learned that Columbia was looking for someone to dub Scotty Beckett's vocals as the young Jolson in The Jolson Story. I had always sung, so an audition was set up with Saul Chaplin and Morris Stoloff of the music department, and I was selected. I was about eighteen, but sounded younger, which was what the part required. I worked on the film for a five- or six-week period.

"For a while it looked like I might get to play the part, too. When Jolson learned that I would be doing the actual singing but not the acting, he couldn't understand why I wasn't going to do both. He was told my resemblance to Larry Parks was not strong enough, but he insisted that the studio try to correct this via make-up. Columbia's make-up chief had me in his chair for almost three hours, as I recall, trying to build up my nose. That was the major problem: my nose was more of a 'pug' type while Parks' nose was fine and straight, almost classical. When the 'operation' was over, I'm afraid I looked more like a Halloween mask. It was a major disappointment for me, naturally, because I was otherwise completely qualified to do the part myself."

A member of the music department told me that in looks, Rudy was just too much of a street kid type. The studio wanted someone more clean-cut and immediately appealing to audiences, someone in the "cute" Hollywood mold to appear as the young hero, and that was Scotty.

Wissler says he worked "very closely with Jolson during the scoring, or pre-recording, process. For the sake of authenticity, he insisted on being on hand when I was working. But everything came to a halt every day in the afternoon to allow him to go to his dressing room to hear the horse race results on the radio.

"One day, while I was recording 'When You Were Sweet Sixteen' and Jolson was sitting with the producer and other executives at a table a short distance away, he suddenly started singing the song with me. Of course it ruined the take, and he was chided for his mistake. He knew he shouldn't have done it, but he explained that he just got carried away, and *had* to sing it."

Wissler affirms that Jolson himself did the whistling in the musical numbers--"I don't think anyone could have duplicated it."

About the tragic Scotty Beckett, he observes, "I knew Scotty very well. We were both quite active at the time in films, and had worked together on previous occasions such as in the film *Good Luck, Mr. Yates*, also at Columbia. I was not aware that he had any problems in those days, and I don't believe he did. As for there being competition between youngsters in films, I would have to say there was--for all of the natural reasons: the money, the recognition, etc. I suspect that the sense of competition was strongest among the most successful of them."

Wissler has two younger brothers who also appeared in films, although not as conspicuously. He worked in pictures until 1950, then went into the Army. "When I was discharged in 1952, I worked in a couple of pictures until I decided to go back to school. I don't do any professional acting anymore--though I *could* be tempted. For a quarter of a century now, my career has been in broadcast sales, radio and television stations," he recently revealed. He made many films, including *Men of Boys Town*, *Cover Girl* (as one of a young gang after Rita Hayworth's autograph--"Maybe we can catch her out in the alley!"), *Boys Ranch* (in which he got to sing for himself), the Gas House Kids series, *Gallant Journey*, *My Girl Tisa*, and *San Diego I Love You* (in which city, married and father of three, he now lives).

Among his movies, Rudy Wissler prefers (*Tomorrow the World!* (1944)--in which he played the important supporting role of the Polish-American schoolboy who finally thrashes Nazi youth Skippy Homeier--and one in which he did not actually appear: *The Jolson Story*.

• • •

Virginia Rees did the singing for Evelyn Keyes in The Jolson Story.

Virginia Rees, who dubbed Evelyn Keyes' vocals in the film, recalls, "Eons ago I was an extra in the Our Gang comedies and much later sang with Horace Heidt's big band. After that I was with the Merry Macs, the first quartet, I think, to be comprised of a girl with three boys. The first record I made with the Macs was in 1946, 'Sentimental Journey.' It was a No. 1 hit until Doris Day and Les Brown came out with their version. Later, we had *the* No. 1 record with 'Laughing on the Outside.'"

She got the Jolson Story job because a few years earlier she had dubbed Marlene Dietrich in The Lady is Willing at Columbia.

"Morris Stoloff, a real fan of mine, remembered me," she says. "I had helped them out when they ran into a problem with the Dietrich film at the preview. After one of her songs, Fred MacMurray, who starred opposite her, had to say something like, 'I didn't know you could sing.' This got a big laugh from the preview audience, because she had been just a hair off-key. I was in the choir in the background of the number in question, and Morris Stoloff, who liked my work, asked me to dub Marlene. So there I was, singing the back-up for myself."

She claims that "Marlene was easy to imitate: she had a throaty voice not too different from my own.

"Dubbing for Evelyn Keyes in The Jolson Story was much harder, because she had a very soft, little voice. I remember I had to dub the imitation her character did of Jolson at a party, when she gets down on one knee and belts out 'California, Here I Come.' I took Jolson's record home and studied it. Jolson was there when I recorded it and was pleased with the job I did because it sounded like him. Evelyn didn't say anything, but I really didn't sound much like her. But then, come to think of it, that was the point: she was supposed to be singing like someone else."

Rees also dubbed Keyes' vocal in the production number "She's a Latin from Manhattan," in which Keyes did all her own dancing.

The singer worked two days on the picture, with the process coming off in the by-then prescribed fashion. Explains Rees, "I recorded the vocals before shooting began, then Evelyn mouthed to my recordings later when the scenes were filmed."

She concludes, "Wish I could tell you more, but in those days you did your job and went on to the next one. No publicity; it was all rather hush-hush that a star had to have someone sing for them. Remember back in the thirties when Jack Haley became a star after Buddy Clark sang for him in Wake Up and Live? When the studio, 20th Century-Fox, put him in a musical on his own, he bombed. It was a tricky business but I loved being part of it."

Now married, retired and living in Los Angeles, Virginia Rees, during the forties and fifties, also dubbed the vocals for Lucille Ball in Easy to Wed, Adele Jergens in Ladies of the Chorus, Marie Windsor in Hellfire, Vera Ralston in Timberjack and, in 1946, for Angela Lansbury in The Harvey Girls--just two decades before Lansbury became Broadway's song-and-dance queen!

Fred Karger, of the Columbia Pictures music department during The Jolson Story and Jolson Sings Again, remembered Cantor Saul Silverman, who sang for Ludwig Donath as Cantor Moses Yoelson, "very well. Cantor Silverman was very active doing that sort of thing in films. He was a very serious, religious man, but not dogmatic. And he had a beautiful deep baritone voice."

The Columbia publicity department thought Cantor Silverman's unusual "double life" a good publicity gimmick, so he received dollops of attention in the press--considerably more than other film dubbers of the day. (Donath, after all, was not a star, merely one of Hollywood's legion of character actors, so the "revelation" that he had not done his own singing could hardly hurt his image.)

Born in Russia, Cantor Saul Silverman's early years were steeped in Hebraic studies which did not abate when the Silverman family moved to America, settling in Detroit. Studying voice, he began singing at religious services, soon branching out to include radio, symphony orchestras and opera. He was also known for a time as Detroit's Singing Cab Driver.

Cantor Silverman and his wife Mollie moved to Los Angeles in 1923, where he continued to combine religion with singing for the general public, giving concerts not only for many Jewish groups but in such places as the Hollywood Bowl. He was a music teacher plus advisor to various Jewish organizations as well.

When Al Jolson died in 1950, thousands filed past his open coffin at Hollywood's Temple Israel, to which Cantor Silverman would belong for thirty-seven years. In 1967 at the California School of the Hebrew Union College, Cantor

Cantor Saul Silverman dubbed the vocals for Ludwig Donath in The Jolson Story and Jolson Sings Again.

Silverman presented the Temple's music award established in his name to that year's winner: his son Richard, selected by the College's Sacred Music Department as the "top student." Richard Silverman is Cantor at a temple in Lafayette, California.

Cantor Saul's widow recalls that "Cantor Silverman was chosen to dub the singing for Ludwig Donath in the Jolson pictures because his voice matched the speaking voice of Mr. Donath. Al Jolson was buried at Hillside Memorial Park and Cantor Silverman sang at his service. He admired Al very much for his ability and also for the many nice things he did at various times."

Cantor Silverman not only sang for Eduard Franz (as the aging cantor) in Danny Thomas' 1953 remake of Al Jolson's The Jazz Singer, he also appeared in the film, as did the three Silverman children. In later years, he worked on such TV series as Marcus Welby, MD and The Waltons.

Cantor Saul Silverman died in 1976. One eulogist called him "a hero of Los Angeles Jewry," which suggests that The Silverman Story could be the title of a worthwhile movie.

Unthinkable as it may sound, even Al Jolson once had his vocals dubbed by someone else. Early in 1928, The Jazz Singer was released as a silent picture to theaters not yet equipped for the new Vitaphone (sound-on-disc) process. A singer named Ben Gold was employed to sing the Jolson songs "live" for one silent booking of the film, but audiences soon objected to this and the idea was abandoned.

■ LARRY AND JOLIE WERE NOT SWEETHEARTS ■

Friendship is almost always the union of a part of one mind with a part of another; people are friends in spots.

George Santayana

Almost every day Jolson was on the set of The Jolson Story advising Parks. To help him get into the spirit of things, he took him to the racetrack and to a synagogue.

Jolson, by Michael Freedland

For The Jolson Story, Larry Parks spent three months as Jolson's constant companion, aping the older man's tricks, watching his movements.... He even went to the synagogue with Jolson, to acquire a knowledge of the ritual.

Louis Berg, journalist

To prepare for his role, Parks lived for three months with Jolson, studied his mannerisms.

Cue Magazine

> Jolson spent five months grooming Parks.
>
> *Liberty* Magazine

> Parks and Jolson were inseparable while he (Parks) was preparing for the part and playing it. They went to ball games, shows, races and fights together.
>
> Sidney Skolsky,
> *Photoplay* Magazine

> Larry and I became Hollywood's first pair of Siamese twins.
>
> Al Jolson, Columbia Pictures
> Publicity Release

None of the above assertions suggesting that Al Jolson and Larry Parks became bosom buddies was true, according to Betty Garrett, Parks' widow. Merely lily-gilding figments of the Columbia publicity department's imagination that attempted to make even more authentic Parks' peerless performance. Incredibly, some members of the cast were taken in as well, believing to this day that Jolson guided Parks through the shooting of *The Jolson Story*. And the myth was still being perpetuated in 1978 when, on a segment of the TV series *That's Hollywood!*, narrator Tom Bosley, over a clip of a Parks number from *The Jolson Story*, stated, "Jolson personally coached Larry Parks."

Recalls Garrett, "Jolson had one session with Larry for *The Jolson Story* in which all he did was to 'perform' the song and then he flew off to Florida for most of the rest of the picture. Much later, Larry did one radio broadcast with him on Jolson's show, *The Kraft Music Hall*, after which we had dinner with Mr. and Mrs. Jolson. I became friendly with his wife, Erle, who was a lovely person."

There were a number of photographic poses circulated of Jolson and Parks together taken in connection with *The*

Jolson Story and Jolson Sings Again--Parks sitting on Jolson's knee, Jolson and Parks playing golf--but they were all evidently just that: poses, for purposes of publicity.

Parks confirmed all this in a TV interview a few years before he died. He said he had only seen Al Jolson a few times before shooting began on The Jolson Story. Furthermore, once filming had started Jolson did not come on the set to help him at all, he swore. Parks saw him a couple of times afterward for promotion and publicity, but said that stories that Jolson had worked with him on his characterization were all studio-engineered fantasy.

In an interview with The Los Angeles Herald-Examiner, Evelyn Keyes recently indicated to writer Richard Cuskelly that Jolson dropped by the set frequently, but added, "He wasn't crazy about Larry. Jolson wouldn't have liked any actor playing him. But he treated me well." On her first day of filming when she had to burlesque Parks imitating Jolson singing "California, Here I Come," Jolson ruined the first take by applauding and shouting from the sidelines, "Great! Great!" Then, Keyes went on to say, "He bawled out the extras for not applauding. They'd already seen me do it eight times in rehearsals."

In 1978, Keyes guested on the Joe Franklin TV show in New York to plug her autobiography. When host Franklin, an honorary member of The Original Al Jolson Society, asked her if Jolson was a "nice guy," she snapped, "Of course he wasn't a nice guy. Anybody who gets into the position he was in can't be a nice guy. The competition's too tough.... I was there while Larry was making his test for The Jolson Story. Jolson groaned and moved around. He wanted to play the part himself."

Jolson, intimidating when he was around the Jolson Story set (and just how often around is debatable), made the more introverted Larry Parks uncomfortable. And vice versa. One thing is certain: they were never close. Henry Levin, director of the sequel, Jolson Sings Again, explained, "Jolson came on our set fairly often. Perhaps one or two hours each week. His main problem was one of jealousy. He had always been jealous of other performers who received great acclaim--even his friends, Cantor and Jessel. But to see Larry Parks performing as Jolson himself was almost more than he could bear. I believe he had admiration for the job Larry was doing, but he was constantly wishing that he were up there doing it, and not that young fellow in his place, singing his songs, answering to his name."

George Burns, who has repeatedly called Al Jolson the greatest entertainer in his experience, once cracked, "Jolson didn't like other actors. He wanted to be the only person in show business. And he only went around with untalented people, because he wanted to be the star. I was one of his closest friends."

"Old acquaintance" and Jolson eulogist George Jessel seconded Burns' opinion of him as a talent, but added that "Jolson was so insecure that if he heard another person was being applauded, he would drown out the noise in his dressing room by turning on the water faucets."

Although Jolson was obviously thrilled when The Jolson Story turned out well, he probably had mixed emotions when he read comments such as Jack D. Grant's in his Hollywood Reporter review: "Parks' performance is so delightful that Jolson should make him one of the leading beneficiaries in his will." Needless to say, Jolson--who was soon joking (?), "The kid is so good that when I die they're going to bury him"--did no such thing.

[Nor did he, upon his death four years later, bequeath "even a tiny ring or a cufflink, a pin or a portrait" to the three devoted friends who were with him at the end, reported George Jessel. Inexplicably, continued Jessel, Jolson left a fortune instead to "colleges and organizations with which he had no association or admiration." In his will, Jolson explained that, while alive, he felt he had given more than enough to the three intimates in question, Louis Epstein, Harry Akst, and Martin Fried. John Schneckenberger, Jolson's accountant, was the only member of his entourage to be remembered in the will. A multi-millionaire, Jolson provided for his wife and children privately.

[His elder brother Harry surfaced in the Hollywood Hills soon after Jolson's death to voice some displeasure at being left the relatively small sum of $10,000 in Jolson's will. He also told a reporter, "People are surprised to learn about me, because I wasn't in the Jolson pictures. I always tell them

Al Jolson in the 1928 Warner Bros. film, *The Singing Fool*.

that while Al and my mother and father were playing their scenes in our dining room, I was out in the kitchen washing dishes." Harry commented that the two deceased Jolson sisters, Rose and Etta, were not portrayed in the films, either. Left out, too, were Al Jolson's half-sister, Gertrude, and three half-brothers, George, Myer and Emil, born of the second and also unmentioned marriage of Jolson's widower father, Moses Yoelson.]

Show business chronicler Maurice Zolotow remembers the time after The Jolson Story opened when he and Jolson tried to walk backstage at the Warner Theater in Atlantic City. The doorman stopped Jolson, who was headlining the stage show there.

"Who are you?," he asked.

"I'm Al Jolson," the star answered.

"Don't kid me," replied the doorman, who had obviously seen Larry Parks in the movie about his life. "You don't look like Al Jolson."

Another time, also circa The Jolson Story, the young daughter of a friend of Jolson's gaffed, "Gee, Mr. Jolson, you're much better looking on the screen!"

It was Larry Parks, half Jolson's age, who had become the movie star and the darling of the movie magazines, where story after story on him appeared.

There's no doubt that all this got to the veteran entertainer. And he was not very successful at hiding his pique. In a time when the Hollywood studios were still powerful enough to control virtually everything their people said in public, and long before the trend to celebrities telling all, Jolson could be quite outspoken. In public conversation he would usually praise Larry Parks, but before long his true feelings would seep through. In a famous middle-of-the-night radio interview with Barry Gray soon after The Jolson Story opened in New York, Jolson commended Parks' "great" job, then went on to mention an incident concerning the new star on the recently completed Down to Earth, a Rita Hayworth musical. He said Parks was unhappy when Buddy Clark was proposed to dub his vocals in the newer film. "I don't like these 'hot' singers. I don't sing like that," protested Parks, according to Jolson.

"He 'don't sing like that'," Jolson chortled mockingly to host Gray. "He don't sing at all."

In 1949, on the eve of the Jolson Sings Again première at the Pantages Theater in Hollywood, Jolson guested on Steve Allen's off-the-cuff radio program there. He took charge completely, overwhelming, for once, the flatulent Allen to demonstrate a gift for one-liner jokes and fast repartée generally ignored in the film biographies. Possessed of a vital, indeed compulsive-seeming presence barely able to contain itself, he referred to the infant television as "smellevision," blaming it for the recent demise of his radio show, The Kraft Music Hall. Between quips and songs Jolson got in a few light jabs at both Larry Parks and Harry Cohn.

At one point he identified Cohn for listeners as the President of Columbia Pictures, quickly adding, "If I do another Jolson film biography, I'll call it Jolson Strikes Back."

Later, more seriously, Jolson announced, "If I do another one, I want to play myself." When the studio audience finished applauding, he explained, "I got a couple of kids; don't want them to grow up and say, 'Larry--I want to tell you something.'"

When Allen asked him to sing, he replied, "I'd pay you to let me sing." After his rendition of "Sonny Boy," he got in another slight Parks zinger: "If you want to hear that song really sung, you come to the Pantages tomorrow night and hear Larry Parks sing it."

Ironically, as Sidney Skolsky put it, "to sustain his new life with contemporary music fans Jolson had to modify his exuberant singing style and do what amounted to an imitation of Larry Parks."

• • •

To an extent, it was tougher for Larry Parks, who, after all, was not a rich, globally renowned artist with a legendary career already behind him. It worried him. Soon after The Jolson Story was released, Parks said, "I loved playing Al. But that Jolson fellow is world-famous and millions of people know his every gesture and vocal inflexion. I had to be on my toes every moment to be Al before the cameras. And then I began to notice that I was adopting the Jolson mannerisms. It was fine before the cameras. But when I got home at night, I'd catch myself using such Jolsonisms as 'You ain't heard

Jolson (Larry Parks) sings "April Showers" for Julie Benson in The Jolson Story.

nothin' yet!,' and that frightened me. After all, no actor minds submerging his own personality, but he'd certainly hate losing it once and for all."

Parks' situation was a matter of considerable speculation in Hollywood. In a 1947 Photoplay article, Louella Parsons reported the following dialogue from "one of Hollywood's most important producers--at a rival studio":

> The case of this boy is a heart-breaker because he hit and hit big with another star's personality. Not only was Larry singing with Al Jolson's voice, but he had been loaned the Jolson personality, been coached [sic] in the Jolson mannerisms, and then to top it all off, he had Al's life story thrown in. He gave a magnificent interpretation of another man's success story.

However, Parsons rebutted in her piece, "The first interview we had was just before the release of The Jolson Story, and this kid had been jumping and jiving. It wasn't Al Jolson's personality he turned on me full force in that first flush of anticipating fame after years of striving. It was Larry's own brand of enthusiasm coming out of him."

Parks told Louella Parsons he was unhappy with his two films since The Jolson Story, namely Down to Earth, top-billing Rita Hayworth, and The Swordsman. "I think it was a mistake to put me into Rita Hayworth's picture and allow me to sing with my own voice[1].... Many people who do not follow inside stories about picture-making never knew that it was Al's voice on the soundtrack when I sang. And it came as a shock and a surprise to hear me singing in a totally different way.... Then I went into The Swordsman, a swash-buckling costume movie. That isn't my cup of tea, either." He said he'd like to specialize in comedy (though in truth his earnest manner made that a curious choice) and proceeded to initiate a long legal hassle with studio boss Harry Cohn mainly, he insisted, to be able to do outside things.

On the afternoon of New Year's Eve, 1948, a week after completing Jolson Sings Again, Parks officially ended months of squabbling with Columbia by signing a new five-year pact with the studio. "Under the new contract I will make one picture a year for Columbia," explained Parks, "which can cover a period of seventeen weeks. The other thirty-five, I'm a free agent. I can make my own commitments with other studios, stand on my own judgment, and together with Betty and our manager, Lou Mandel, have my own producing company ... which has long been my tall dream.... I still make the same money, but that's all right with me. My fight was never for money, but for freedom, which has always been a gold-weighted word to me."

Nevertheless, columnist Erskine Johnson reported in Motion Picture earlier that year, "What's driving Parks crazy is that he could earn around $250,000 a year, in addition to having his choice of pictures, were he a freelance actor."

After the court decision he spoke again to Louella Parsons to publicize formation of his Lou Mandel Productions. Early on, she observed that while he was very careful what he said, she could see that he would just as soon forget the

Jolson (Larry Parks) talks Julie (Evelyn Keyes) into co-starring in a film with him, while Dick Glenn (William Forrest) and Steve Martin (William Demarest) look on in *The Jolson Story*.

Jolson sagas which brought added fortune and a comeback to Al.

Well into the interview, Parks asked, defensively, "I didn't say I didn't like portraying Al Jolson, but would *you* like losing your own personality and becoming another person? I figure the Jolson stories did more for Jolson than they did for Parks.

"Al is over sixty-five years old, and until *The Jolson Story* he had made up his mind that he was practically through. Now he is going stronger than ever. He is an amazing person. When he was recording the soundtracks for the films, he would sing for three hours at a time without stopping, which would tire a much younger man. Only then was he ready to rest, and it was the only time I was conscious of his age."

Parks was supposed to have said, "I've worked Jolson up to where he is old enough to play himself."

The settlement of his difficulties with Columbia turned out to be a hollow victory. He never did get to make his own movies. It was rumored that the banks turned him down for financing saying he had proved himself only as Al Jolson, but had yet to do so as Larry Parks.

Moreover, to some in Hollywood the actor's early grudging regard for the two Jolson films smacked of ingratitude. After all, The Jolson Story had rescued an obscure "B" movie player named Larry Parks and made him a star. His comments then could be called impolitic, at best. Retentive industry memories may have been another reason no one in the film capital exerted themselves to find work for Parks there during his subsequent fifties blacklisting.

Though Betty Garrett says he mellowed with the years and came to appreciate fully his superlative, once-in-a-lifetime characterization, Parks still seemed to be smarting a bit in 1950 when he and his wife returned from a European tour and were interviewed by The New York Daily News. Betty expressed concern that their infant son, Garrett Christopher, who had remained at home in California, might have forgotten them. "Nonsense," said Parks. "As soon as we reach the house I'll put on a Jolson record and he'll recognize me immediately."

Around 1955, impressionist Jerry Stone was working in a small New York club when he noticed Larry Parks walk in. Recalls Stone, "Off the top of my head, I immediately went into my favorite scene from The Jolson Story, the final one where Larry as Jolson returns to show business. He goes out on the nightclub floor, says 'It's nice to be remembered' and speaks to the audience for a while before going into his song. But it was Larry talking, not Jolson singing, that I was doing. Afterward, Larry came back to see me and said he really enjoyed the bit 'because,' he told me, 'everyone always imitates Jolson, but I've never heard anyone do me before.'"

Seeing Parks through must have been the knowledge that many moviegoers and critics agreed with the reviewer who wrote that Larry Parks and the voice of Al Jolson made a much more agreeable Jolie than Al Jolson and the voice of Al Jolson.

Reference

1. Hal Derwin dubbed Larry Parks' singing in Down to Earth.

■ ACCURACY, SMACURACY! ■

> I was never going to be the world's greatest costume designer, but there was no reason I could not be the smartest. When you can make an actress beautiful or an actor handsome, you can succeed in Hollywood, as long as you know the right people to please. That's why I have always said that I am a better politician than I am a designer. I know who to please.
>
> Edith Head

"Accuracy, smacuracy! I want the broads to look good!," commanded Harry Cohn.

Mary Ann Nyberg, who was then assistant to Jean Louis, the designer of the women's costumes for The Jolson Story (and Jolson Sings Again), had innocently remarked to the studio chief that Jean Louis was striving "for accuracy" in the creation of the wardrobe for each period in the story.

Harry Cohn got his wish, broad Evelyn Keyes looking especially good.

Cohn didn't have Joseph Walker, one of the foremost women's cameramen, under contract for nothing. Unlike most of his fellow moguls who wanted their female stars to appear glamorous at all times, even at the supermarket, Cohn didn't care if they looked like bag ladies off the lot as long as they looked their best on the screen. When Broadway actress Julie Harris came to Columbia to recreate her much-lauded stage

Jean Louis, who designed the women's clothes for The Jolson Story and Jolson Sings Again.

role of the bizarre tomboy in The Member of the Wedding (1952), Cohn was aghast when he visited her set for the first time. "She scares small children," he later commented.

The minor Cohn-Nyberg contretemps aside, difficulties on The Jolson Story did not extend to the designing of the apparel for the film, nor to the creating by Clay Campbell of the make-up or the hair styles by Helen Hunt. All three propinquitous, top-notch departments sailed through their assignments more or less oblivious to any tensions in the vicinity.

Couturier Jean Louis, whose achievements over the decades belie his reticent personality, was at Columbia Pictures about two years when he was set to design the distaff garments for The Jolson Story. A Parisian, he had worked for Hattie Carnegie's maison de couture in New York for seven years. One of Carnegie's regular customers was Harry Cohn's wife, Joan, which, Jean Louis feels, may have been the reason why one day in 1943 he received a phone call from Columbia to come out and work there. He became the studio's first in-house fashion maven--until Jean Louis, Columbia had borrowed designers as they were needed. He remained there until Harry Cohn died in 1958, then moved over to Universal until the late sixties, his fashions having long since become synonymous with, in the best sense, Hollywood glamour. Freelancing, Jean Louis designs a prestigious wholesale line today.

He notes, "If Harry Cohn were still alive, I'd be at Columbia yet. I liked it there very much."

Jean Louis goes on to inform, "Before we started work on the costumes for The Jolson Story, we researched by going through old photos of Al Jolson and Ruby Keeler. Of course, we couldn't put the same kind of dress that Ruby Keeler had worn on Evelyn Keyes; they had different figures, different personalities. Ruby wore simplified things, though, an idea we tried to follow through with on Evelyn's clothes. But it was a long and costly production, and the wardrobe was expensive.

"Technicolor was still rather new at Columbia then. We had a Technicolor adviser present at all times [Morgan Padelford]. He would say things like 'No, you can't use red--it will bleed.' We had trouble with red in films then, which is why you don't see that color on Evelyn in the picture. As I recall, she wore a lot of blues, greens, yellows and golds.

"Jolson was on the lot quite often. No, we didn't discuss the designs with him beforehand. He would look at them and say, 'Fine, fine.' If Harry Cohn said they were all right, Jolson would defer to his judgment. Harry had the final say on everything, an authority he exerted, I might add. And because of his friendship with Jolson, Harry showed a special interest in The Jolson Story."

Jean Louis notes that Jolson Sings Again was "not as

lavish, more contemporary, therefore not as complicated to design for as The Jolson Story."

Evelyn Keyes remembers, shortly after she was set for the film, being ushered into the office of Harry Cohn who told his secretary to hold all calls, he'd be looking at film in his private projection room for the next ten minutes. "The film consisted of wardrobe tests of my clothes for the picture, photographed ahead of time to be sure they looked all right. These, designed by Jean Louis, were smashing. We watched silently, pleased. Harry never praised, only complained when he didn't like something," says Keyes. Afterwards, the mogul's first words to her were, "I'm going to make you a very big star."

As with so many other artists and artisans who worked at Columbia through the forties, Jean Louis mentions Gilda first when asked to name the creme of those films on which he has worked. He won an Academy Award in 1956 for The Solid Gold Cadillac--Oscars for costume design were not established until two years after The Jolson Story (in 1948).

The credit "Gowns by Jean Louis" adorned dozens of films, many earning him Academy nominations. Among his films: A Thousand and One Nights, Tomorrow Is Forever, The Lady from Shanghai, Down to Earth, All the King's Men, Born Yesterday, Affair in Trinidad, From Here to Eternity, It Should Happen to You, A Star Is Born (Judy Garland version), Miss Sadie Thompson, The Caine Mutiny, Queen Bee, My Sister Eileen (Betty Garrett version), The Eddy Duchin Story, Picnic, Pal Joey, Bell, Book and Candle, Imitation of Life (Lana Turner version), Pillow Talk, Judgment at Nuremberg, Back Street (Susan Hayward version), Guess Who's Coming to Dinner?, Thoroughly Modern Millie, Lost Horizon (Peter Finch version), and Forty Carats.

Mary Ann Nyberg, who was an early Jean Louis illustrator-assistant, arrived at Columbia in time to work on The Jolson Story and departed soon after Jolson Sings Again. Just before her sudden death in 1979 of a cerebral hemorrhage, what she remembered, mainly, was the lot as "a beehive of activity, with something going on everywhere. I was very young, and it was valuable experience for me. The workroom people taught me skills that would soon be extinct, such as beading, so that when I became a designer myself I was able to tell my work-

Evelyn Keyes models one of the costumes created for her by Jean Louis in The Jolson Story.

room people how to do it. Jean Louis designed the women principals' clothes for the Jolson pictures, and there was a wardrobe department run by Tommy Dawson that took care of all the men, as well as the lesser female cast members."

After Columbia, Louis B. Mayer, boss of Metro-Goldwyn-

Mayer, hired Nyberg first as "an arbiter of taste. I would watch the rushes of all M-G-M pictures and comment on everything--the music, the sets, etc., saying things like, 'Nobody can dance for forty-five minutes and not be a bit winded!' Eventually, I designed the clothes for Metro's The Bandwagon, starring Fred Astaire and Cyd Charisse, and Lilli, with Leslie Caron. Elsewhere, I also did The Man with the Golden Arm, starring Frank Sinatra, Eleanor Parker and Kim Novak, and about 85 percent of Judy Garland's A Star is Born, among others. I always did both men and women's clothes."

Nyberg's widower is Arthur Knight, the critic, author and teacher.

• • •

Clay Campbell was Columbia's make-up chief from 1940 until 1966, when he retired to Corona del Mar--"Just give Clay a sailboat and a place to sail it and he's happy," says long-time friend Barbara Hale. He calls working on The Jolson Story and Jolson Sings Again two of his happiest work experiences.

He also got to appear briefly in The Jolson Story, typecast as a make-up artist preparing Jolson/Parks for one of his films.

Recalls Campbell, "Larry Parks' performance is still the greatest job of dubbing I've ever seen. There weren't many problems in the way of make-up. Everybody pretty much looked like themselves. We didn't try to make Larry look just like Jolson; that would have been impossible. It was not a picture that required a great deal of complicated make-up, like A Song to Remember, The 5,000 Fingers of Dr. T, and Salome, all of which I did. Or The Story of Louis Pasteur, with Paul Muni at Warner Bros. in 1936. I must have lost two pounds every time I applied Muni's beard: he examined each and every whisker! The one thing on Jolson Story was the gradual aging of several of the characters--Larry; William Demarest, who played Jolson's manager; Ludwig Donath, Jolson's father; and Tamara Shayne, his mother. Also, we had to make Demerest, Donath, and Shayne somewhat younger than they really were for the early parts of The Jolson Story.

"For Larry's middle-age make-up, we used the old high-

Mama Yoelson (Tamara Shayne), second from left, asks Julie (Evelyn Keyes) to get Jolson to sing at the Yoelsons' anniversary dinner, while Papa (Ludwig Donath) and Steve (William Demarest) look doubtful in The Jolson Story.

light and shadow technique, which is not too easy in color but can be used very effectively in black and white. Around the eyes we highlighted the wrinkles by having the actor squint and hold it while we patted the highlight on the high parts. For the grey (white) hair at the temples, we took Larry into the hairdressing department where Helen Hunt bleached the areas we wanted white so that when the whiting (Max Factor's) was applied it did not photograph with a bluish cast. Sometimes we used the hair whiting alone. Sometimes we would add some white pancake for a final touch.

"On Demarest and Donath, hair styles made a great difference in their ages. Hair-pieces (small wigs) were used in both cases. Corrective make-up (highlight and shadow) was also used extensively.

"Almost ten years later I made up Larry's wife, Betty

Garrett, for the musical version of My Sister Eileen. She played a modern young woman, which is what she was, so it was easy."

Barbara Hale, whom he made up for her leading lady assignment in Jolson Sings Again, was--with her husband, actor Bill Williams, and children--Campbell's next-door neighbor in Van Nuys, California, for years until he moved to Corona del Mar in 1963. "She was truly 'the girl next door,'" he jokes.

Campbell goes on, "I first met Al Jolson in 1939 when I was at 20th Century-Fox and he was playing a cameo role in Hollywood Cavalcade there. I remember I borrowed his blackface wig to wear to a Hollywood costume party.

"Jolson was around the sets of The Jolson Story and Jolson Sings Again quite a bit. I wasn't there all the time, you understand. I was the department head and had my executive duties to take care of, too, so I had assistants stand by for the people. Jolson made himself up for 'Swanee,' a blackface number and the only one he actually performed himself (in long-shot) in The Jolson Story. He had 'blacked-up' since he was a kid, so he knew just the way he wanted it. He came to make-up to put it on, though, and used a pail of water to wash it off afterwards."

Although Columbia had not done many Technicolor films prior to The Jolson Story, this presented no special difficulties to Campbell and his make-up department. "I did the make-up for one of the earliest Technicolor pictures while at Warners, God's Country and the Woman, with George Brent and Beverly Roberts, in 1936. And at 20th in 1938 and 1939, I did a number of the big Technicolor Shirley Temple and Alice Faye films. The make-up for color movies was not all that different from black-and-white movies--maybe a little darker," says Campbell.

"I think we knew as we worked on The Jolson Story that it would be a great hit. We certainly thought it the best musical we had seen done at Columbia. And we were very musical in the make-up department there. My staff as well as the actors being worked on would bring in their favorite records early in the morning and we would play them while they were being made up. It sort of soothed the rough edges."

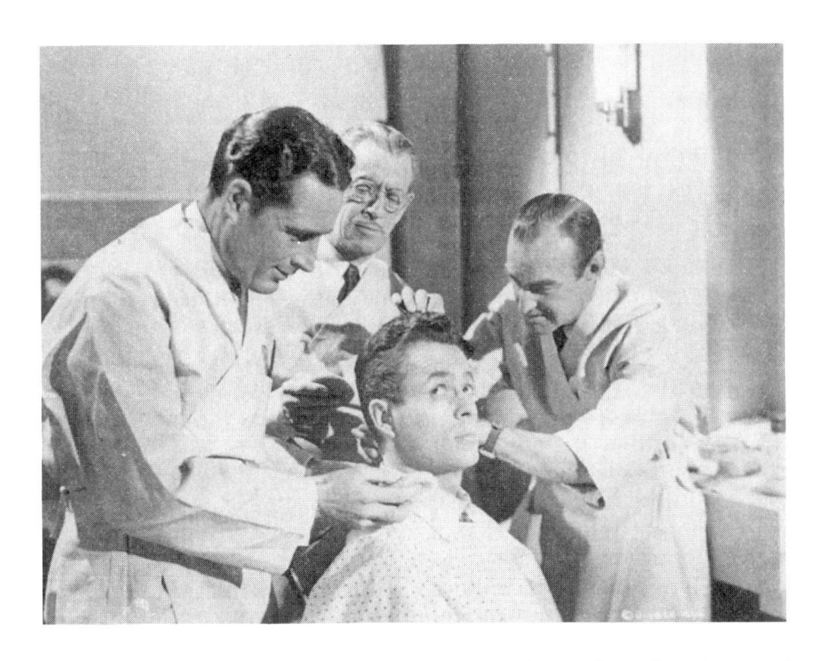

In The Jolson Story, Clay Campbell, left, Columbia Pictures' long-time make-up head, is typecast as a make-up artist preparing Jolson (Larry Parks) for a scene in The Jazz Singer.

He did Rita Hayworth's make-up for Cover Girl (in which, doing just that, he again appeared on screen) and Gilda, rating as two of his other pet films the fanciful The 5,000 Fingers of Dr. T and Born Yesterday. For the latter, Judy Holliday won the best actress Oscar in 1950. "Harry Cohn tested every blonde in Hollywood for the plum star role of Billie Dawn," recounts Campbell, "but wouldn't think of using Judy Holliday, who originated the role on Broadway, because he thought her too fat. Finally, he got me down there to make her up and she got the part. I made her up thereafter for all her Columbia films, sometimes, while I left the department in the hands of assistants, being sent off to New York or Washington, D.C., to do it."

After The Jolson Story was completed, Larry Parks and Evelyn Keyes gave him a photograph he treasures. It was a pose of Al Jolson and Ruby Keeler--autographed to Campbell by their biographical counterparts, Larry Parks and Evelyn Keyes.

• • •

Helen Hunt was top hair stylist at Columbia for almost thirty-five years. At $500 a week, she boasts she was also Hollywood's highest paid one.

"When I left Columbia," she says, "I opened a salon in Beverly Hills, then sold it five years later. Katharine Hepburn asked me to come back to Columbia to work with her on Guess Who's Coming to Dinner?, so I returned for five months. I was sixty-five when that picture was finished in 1967 and retired to Palm Springs."

She can recall no problems on the Jolson film biographies: "There was no research for The Jolson Story to speak of; everyone seemed to know the period." (Though, in truth, the preponderance of that decade's upsweeps and fluffy, shoulder-length hairdos in the pre-forties-set film indicates that those in charge did not want to risk alienating modern audiences with the unstylish coiffures of previous decades--from on high, after all, had come the edict "Accuracy, smacuracy!"

"On the other hand," notes Hunt, "because of its exotic nature a movie like the first version of Lost Horizon, starring Ronald Colman, took weeks and weeks of research. There were sketches made of the hairdresses and costumes. They were tested and photographed, and then all over again after the actors had been cast.

"I guess you could say I reported directly to Harry Cohn. He seemed to have a lot of respect for my work. When I first went to Columbia in 1929 I was in charge of both hairdressing and make-up. Later, when the union was formed they became separate departments but we worked very closely. During my years at Columbia we had three or four designers in the wardrobe department, but Jean Louis was the highest rated one. Clay Campbell, who ran the make-up department, Jean Louis and myself attended all production meetings. We got on well together."

"Besides all women's coiffures, I also had charge of the

Helen Hunt, Columbia Pictures' top hair stylist for almost thirty-five years, created the coiffures for The Jolson Story and Jolson Sings Again.

men's tinting--including toupées and wigs," Hunt affirms. "As you probably know, Jolson worked in some long-shots of The

Jolson Story. Harry Cohn told me to order a minstrel wig for him. He only worked a few days but he loved it. I put his wig on him each morning. He was very proud of the speed with which he could slap on his blackface make-up. I think it only took him about five minutes.

"There were no problems with Technicolor, in spite of its relative newness."

Asked, inevitably, if the stars gossiped under the dryers, and if she remembered anything the Jolson people talked about while so engaged, she deftly fields the question(s) by answering, "In those days the hair dryers were so noisy that the actors couldn't do much talking about anything.

"We were all very close on the Jolson pictures. I was especially fond of Larry Parks, Evelyn Keyes, and Barbara Hale. I loaned Larry and his bride, Betty Garrett, my beach house for their honeymoon."

Helen Hunt's favorite among her films--by now, unsurprisingly--is Gilda, starring Rita Hayworth (born Margarita Cansino). Explains Hunt, "Rita was with Columbia over twenty years. During that time I personally cared for her hair, and, even though it wasn't in color, I think Gilda showed off the beauty of it best." In the earlier Cover Girl, there was a flash of her on-screen doing Hayworth's hair. It was Hunt who not only originally suggested that the young Hayworth's black hair be dyed red but supervised the lengthy electrolysis treatments that gave Hayworth a higher, nobler hairline. The "new" Rita Hayworth quickly attained stardom.

Hunt married a Movietone News correspondent who was with 20th Century-Fox for thirty-five years. She does charity work and paints now. "Some day I will get someone to write a story or book about my own experiences," she promises. "My childhood was unusual. My parents were deaf-mutes. I was born in a sod house on a prairie in Western Kansas. In 1904 my father sold out and moved to Los Angeles. After six months they went by covered wagon to Utah. This saga goes on and on."

"There were real problems then," asserts Helen Hunt, who obviously has taken love goddesses and mere moguls in her stride.

▪ SUCH A TSIMMES![1] ▪

> When a thing ceases to be a subject of controversy, it ceases to be a subject of interest.
>
> William Hazlitt

For a film that, upon initial release, even its rare detractor managed only to call "innocuous," The Jolson Story has proved surprisingly controversial through the years.

J.J. (Jake) and Lee Shubert were the fabled but feisty sibling entrepreneurs and theater-owning monopolists who didn't speak to each other for half a century. When they took over Lew Dockstader's Minstrels briefly in 1909, the package contained an increasingly popular minstrel man named Al Jolson. He soon left the troupe and played vaudeville for a while, but the Shuberts remembered him. Consequently, Jolson was given a small spot in the first production at the Shuberts' luxurious new Broadway theater, the Winter Garden, in Jerome Kern's La Belle Paree (1911). Following praise by critics and public, his part kept growing and growing. Jolson, despite a tempestuous relationship with the Shuberts (one area, at least, in which the entertainer was not exceptional), went on to star in many Winter Garden shows, his name and that of the theater becoming almost synonymous during the halcyon years of both. His last performance there was in 1926.

One writer referred to the playhouse as Jolson's "personal kingdom."

Flash forward several decades. As preparations for The Jolson Story got underway, Harry Cohn got to thinking that it would be a good sentimental idea, as well as a sound publicity move, to première the film at the Winter Garden. This idea was quickly scotched when, just after shooting had begun late in 1945, Columbia Pictures received a letter from the Shubert brothers insisting they be paid for any usage of the Winter Garden in the movie, or they would sue. They wrote that they had been planning a dramatization focusing on the theater themselves. Perhaps remembering that the Shuberts had once billed Eddie Cantor $1900 for glue which they claimed was needed to build the elaborate sets for his show, Cohn snarled to Sidney Skolsky, "They'll do anything to make a dime. The hell with 'em!" The Winter Garden was essential to the Jolson story and remained prominent in the film, sans recompense to the Shuberts. The theater was mentioned in the dialogue, likewise in a chronological montage of Jolson Winter Garden marquee replicas that one critic called the most accurate part of the picture.

Shortly after the film opened in late 1946 at New York's Radio City Music Hall where long lines were forming all day long, the Shubert theatrical organization sued Columbia for $50,000 damages and an injunction to halt further showing of the picture. The Shuberts alleged that Columbia had "misappropriated" the Jolson Story idea from a story called Winter Garden which writer Ward Morehouse had sold to the Shuberts for $750.

However, Supreme Court Justice James B.M. McNally threw the Shuberts' claim out of court, holding that the Jolson film in no way resembled the Morehouse story and that anyway the Shuberts hadn't been hurt. McNally observed that they still had the Morehouse material and could produce it whenever they wished. It was never staged.

In 1954, Columbia planned a large-scale reissue campaign for The Jolson Story, re-recorded in stereophonic sound for the new wide screen. "HEAR Al's whistling actually come from the balcony!," caroled the new ads. Variety reviewed the results: "Dressed up in a wide screen format and directional sound, the eight-year-old Sidney Skolsky Technicolor production retains all of its original powerful impact. The new technical additions only gild the lily. Basically, it's still that inimitable Jolson songalog soundtrack behind the letter-perfect Larry Parks impersonation that carries the sock."

A capacity audience attended the première of the revamped Jolson Story at the Brooklyn Fox Theater.

One of the ads for the 1954 reissue of <u>The Jolson Story</u>.

But it was the McCarthy era. Picket lines of American Legion protesters, irate because Larry Parks recently had admitted he once had been a Communist, quelled the euphoria. The demonstrating Legionnaires were instrumental in having Columbia cancel reissue campaign plans and withdraw the film.

Almost fifteen years later, protests of a different nature were heard.

In the summer of 1968, more than fifty Portland, Oregon, residents--"about half black and half white," a reporter estimated--marched back and forth in front of KPTV studios there opposing the then-airing The Jolson Story. Between choruses of "We Shall Overcome," the assemblage explained it was offended by the blackface make-up in the film and its connotations.

"We are simply very tired of television's distortion of the black image," said protester R.L. Anderson, adding that there was a feeling that "shows like this are pre-planned."

Anderson, who was black, went on. "People certainly can't develop much respect for the black population when blacks are constantly depicted as bumblers who happen to be able to sing and dance."

Beryl Linn, white and co-spokesperson with Anderson for the group, said that one of the most damaging aspects of the film was that "it gives white children an inaccurate stereotype of the Negro.... When race relations are difficult in the first place, the damage television shows like this can cause is multiplied."

Demonstrators noted that for several days phone calls had been made to KPTV requesting the movie be cancelled, but that station management had remained silent. The protest lasted from about 11:30 p.m. to 12:30 a.m. The Jolson Story was shown in its entirety.

A couple of days later The Portland Oregonian took an editorial stand on the matter. The newspaper said, in summation,

> The swift change [in black civil rights] came about because so many Americans, both black and white,

> spoke out strongly to demand it. Some of the demands, such as the ostracism of Little Black Sambo and the bowdlerizing of lyrics in Show Boat songs, seemed unnecessarily extreme at the time. But a drastic alteration of public attitude was indicated, and drastic measures accomplished it. The Al Jolson Story [sic] today is an anachronism, a rather mediocre film biography of one who was a great entertainer in an era now irrevocably past. We cannot un-write history, so there is no point in pretending it didn't happen: not so many decades ago singers and actors did blacken their faces and audiences were amused by it. But the reaction to the re-run of The Al Jolson Story is proof enough that it can't happen in America any more. The owners of the film may as well put it back in the vault to stay.

That same summer, Larry Parks was interviewed during a Chicago play engagement and, with the Portland editorial in hand, commented, "I don't see it that way. The movie was made innocently enough, without any desire to offend. I think if you start suppressing old films for reasons like this, you're cutting off your own past. I thought Bill Cosby's recent special on TV was wonderful, the one tracing the rise and fall of the Negro stereotype in movies. I think that sort of approach to Hollywood's past is the wise one, instead of trying to ignore it or forget it."

Clay Campbell, who headed Columbia's make-up department when The Jolson Story was made, concurs with Parks today. "There was absolutely no thought of the blackface make-up in the picture being offensive to anyone when we did it. We never dreamed about such a thing, or that people would be upset about it one day. After all, it is historically accurate. These objections are ridiculous. There was real reason for whites to object to the TV show Roots, which went on night after night without a sympathetic white person in sight. That was a conscious effort to malign and distort, it seems to me," opines Campbell.

If the studio did not consider that blacks might be insulted by the blackface numbers in The Jolson Story, there was some concern at the top as to how whites in the South would react. Black singer Lena Horne has said that in her M-G-M movies of the forties she was allowed to do little more

Al Jolson.

than come on for a song "pinned to a pillar like a butterfly so that the numbers could be easily cut out in the South." Perhaps because the central figure in The Jolson Story was a white man in blackface, there were no recorded incidents with the film upon release below the Mason-Dixon line.

Few seemed offended by the "blacking up" in the film in 1946. A rare dissenter was the veteran West Coast film critic Edwin Schallert, although his obtuse phrase-turning makes it unclear whether he objected on racial, esthetic, or personal grounds. In his generally favorable Los Angeles Times review, Schallert felt that

> Larry Parks comes off amazingly well.... I don't care for his make-up in blackface in the close-ups, because it is a bit repellent. But that is no issue if you want occularly to blot it out now and then while listening to the numbers. In any case, it is probably actual enough, but it might have been modified as far as the mouth decor is concerned.

It was a different world then. Even some of the film's publicity, which would be considered insensitive if not downright racist today, was naive. In a February, 1947, issue of Screen Stars, columnist Jerry Asher reported that Larry Parks suddenly had left the set of The Jolson Story while still in blackface to "walk" with a friend whose wife was having a baby in the hospital. If true, and "tinsel town" publicity from those years is always suspect today, the incident must have played like a scene from I Love Lucy or All in the Family. Continued Asher, "In the fathers' waiting room was another blackface gentleman. Only his was the real thing! Turning to Larry for sympathy, he moaned, 'If the good Lord don't send that baby heah soon, Ah's goin't turn white!'"

On the eve of his Jolson Story-inspired comeback, in his first movie since 1939, Jolson himself played entirely in blackface in the George Gershwin story, Rhapsody in Blue, produced at Warner Bros. and released in 1945. Tenth-billed in smaller type than the principals, Jolson appeared as Jolson in a few short scenes built around the origin and introduction of the song "Swanee," which he sang in a somewhat hurried production number. Only an old photo on sheet music showed him without black make-up. The decision to have Jolson render his cameo in blackface may have been for camouflage prompted by the fact that in the plot he was supposed to be a quarter of a century younger. Jolson also was recuperating from pneumonia during the shooting of the Gershwin biography, which was begun late in 1943. Nevertheless, there was something faintly degrading about watching Al Jolson--for so long the center of attention and the star whose Jazz Singer at this very studio had popularized sound--being passed backstage without a nod by the film's leading lady, Joan Leslie, who proceeded to play a scene with leading man Robert Alda while Jolson just stood out of focus in the background. The entertainer's reputation aside, a giant ego was not necessary for him to revel in the imminent success of The Jolson Story.

There are two stories told about how Al Jolson actually first came to wear blackface, an event that took place shortly after the turn of this century in Brooklyn and which soon provided Jolson's breakthrough in show business. (Three stories, if one counts the version in The Jolson Story.) Jolson himself once claimed that "a Negro dresser" during teen-age vaudeville years suggested he would be much funnier if he "blacked up." The more popular version has blackface comedian James Francis Dooley, sharing the bill with Jolson, advise the tyro that burnt cork would be the perfect complement to his Southern accent--which, in turn, some said that he leaned on to obscure the Jewish-European traces in his speech. [After marrying the gentile Ruby Keeler, he had his pronounced Semitic nose bobbed and all earlier photos within his control retouched to accommodate the new proboscis.]

In his 1970s biography of Jolson, Michael Freedland wrote that no one believed the minstrels with burnt cork on their faces were actually Negroes. "In a way," he wrote, "they were a race of their own: they were rarely as insulting as non-Jewish actors playing characters like Fagin or Shylock."

Even the regal Ethel Barrymore once donned blackface for a Broadway play. So did the somewhat less majestic Bugs Bunny, who, in a World War II cartoon short promoting the sale of war bonds, wore blackface to impersonate Jolson and sang "My Sammy" (meaning Uncle Sam).

Although Jolson stopped blacking up in 1948, two years before his death, blackface make-up really did not become an issue during his lifetime. Eventually, it mainly seemed

Jolson (Larry Parks) sings "I'm Sitting on Top of the World" in *The Jolson Story*.

simply to fall out of fashion. Consequently, Jolson's feelings on the matter are not recorded. It seems safe to say, however, that, Jolson being Jolson, he would have defended the manner in which he had earned a notable living for most of his adult life.

Ten years after the Oregon ruckus over the blackface in *The Jolson Story*, a stage biography called *Jolson* had its first public performance in New Jersey. Near the end of each show, star Clive Baldwin, onstage at his dressing room table, began applying Jolson's blackface make-up for the first time in his career. When he finished blacking up and stood in full wigged, white-gloved Jolson regalia, audiences invariably burst into applause. Tension, at least in this area, had lessened somewhat.

The Jolson Story is still shown on television around the country, though perhaps not as often as the sequel, *Jolson Sings Again*, which has only brief blackface footage.

• • •

When The Jolson Story was given a major reissue in 1975 in 70mm, it was time for Jews to voice offense.

In a scathing Wall Street Journal critique of the whole picture, Joy Gould Boyum wrote,

> Cantor and Mrs. Yoelson are the film's most unrealistic, tasteless and, in fact, embarrassing inventions. They are Jewish in the way that Stepin Fetchit was Negro, with their ethnic character making for the running bad joke of the film. Horseradish, skull caps, gefilte fish, all become the basis of folksy laughter, and we are treated to an endless series of Yiddish accented two-liners on the order of: "He's in Indianapolis, Mama." "Oy, Papa, he'll come home scalped."

Critic Boyum asked if audiences of 1946 really could have been so primitive in their taste to believe such jokes hilarious or so naïve in their view of character to find these types convincingly human.

Yes and Yes.

To wit:

When The Jolson Story first came out, Dance magazine, which liked the film, viewed the ethnic aspect as "a brave if not entirely successful attempt to treat with some depth and dignity an orthodox Jewish family, a subject from which moviemakers usually shy away." Even more enthusiastic in its overall concensus, Liberty magazine additionally observed, "Jolson's pious parents, in some of the sweetest scenes in many a movie, read his Variety rave notices with Old World confusion and pride." Kate Cameron of The New York Daily News, in her 1946 four-star review, seemed to think that Ludwig Donath and Tamara Shayne, who portrayed Cantor and Mrs. Yoelson (Jolson), "made" the film. "Tamara Shayne and Ludwig Donath play Al's parents with an endearing warmheartedness," cheered Cameron, "that raises the picture out of the class of ordinary back-stage dramas into that of top-ranking film entertainment."

There appears to be no end to the controversy for a

film about a man whose gospel according to Irving Berlin was simply "Let me sing and I'm happy."

As Mama Yoelson might have exclaimed, "Such a tsimmes, Papa!"

Reference

1. Tsimmes, or tsimes, is a common Yiddish word meaning a fuss or mix-up.

▪ JOLSON AS JOLSON AT LAST ▪

> There are two tragedies in life. One is not to get your heart's desire. The other is to get it.
>
> George Bernard Shaw

In 1943, Shelley Winters, an effusive starlet reasonably fresh from Brooklyn, bumped into Al Jolson on the Columbia lot, where she told him that she and her whole family had always been fans of his. Jolson replied, "Gee, kid, I wish you'd tell Harry Cohn about that. They're gonna do my life story here, and I'd sure like to play myself." She noticed that he had dyed black hair, a deep tan to hide his wrinkles and tried to affect a springy, youthful walk.

Al Jolson finally got his wish to portray Al Jolson when he starred in the _Lux Radio Theater_ presentations of _The Jolson Story_ and _Jolson Sings Again_. They were aired live on February 16, 1948, and May 22, 1950; and while Jolson proved not exactly wrong for the part, his performances were ample support for those who felt that in Larry Parks the right man had been chosen to embody him in the Jolson film biographies.

First, a little about _The Lux Radio Theater_, a Monday night tradition during more than twenty years on the air. Its opening fanfare with the announcement "Lux Presents Hollywood" can still send chills up the spines of those old enough to remember its glories. The program, which began on NBC in New York in 1934, originally dramatized stage plays. Moving to CBS for its second year and then, in 1936, to Hollywood, the format was changed permanently to feature only adaptations of movies. It quickly became one of the most popular shows in radio history.

Cecil B. DeMille, noted producer-director of film spectacles, was hired as host and director. He remained in these posts until 1945, when he refused to pay the Los Angeles local of AFRA (American Federation of Radio Artists) one dollar for a fund to oppose a proposition that would have abolished the closed shop method of employment in California. Because he felt that no organization had the right to impose a compulsory political assessment upon any citizen, and rather than pay the one dollar to a cause in which he did not happen to believe, DeMille sacrificed his $100,000-a-year Lux job and was banned by the union from radio and, ultimately, television until he died in 1959.

During these fourteen years, however, he made some of his most successful films, including Samson and Delilah, The Greatest Show on Earth, and The Ten Commandments.

William Keighley, also a respected Hollywood director, who, furthermore, sounded like the authoritative, well-spoken DeMille, gracefully replaced him on radio. He remained with the Lux program until its final show in 1955.

Jolson made many appearances on The Lux Radio Theater, starting with Burlesque, co-starring Ruby Keeler, in 1936. He did The Jazz Singer twice for Lux, once in 1936, another time in 1947 when his Jolson Story mother and father, Ludwig Donath and Tamara Shayne, again played his parents. The second version of Jazz Singer is generally considered Jolson's best acting performance on the radio series, indeed, some feel, his best acting performance anywhere--superior even to his work in the film. He starred in the program's Swanee River in 1945. Jolson Sings Again was his Lux swan song.

In The Old Time Radio Book, Alan G. Barbour wrote that of the incredible array of stars who had appeared on The Lux Radio Theater over the years, to him Al Jolson was the most exciting of all. Barbour explained his choice: "The only real criterion seems to be the intangible feeling a listener gets when a certain magical talent leaps out of the airwaves and touches him. To me, that happened every time the legendary Al Jolson made an appearance. By any standards, he was a terrible actor, but when he began to sing, electricity seemed to fill the air."

William Keighley, who had directed Jolson's last starring

Ludwig Donath, Al Jolson, Evelyn Keyes and William Demarest on The Lux Radio Theater dramatization of The Jolson Story in 1948.

film vehicle, The Singing Kid (1936), was in charge when the Jolson biographies were dramatized for Lux Soap. For the radio Jolson Story, Jolson, of course, played Jolson as an adult, and Evelyn Keyes, William Demarest and Ludwig Donath recreated their original roles. This time, Demarest also acted as narrator, filling in some of the gaps wrought when two hours-plus of movie were compressed into an hour of radio--less, with commercials and other irrelevancies. Different players were cast as youthful Asa Yoelson and Mama Yoelson: a young man with a deeper singing voice, closer to the standard baritone register than that of Rudy Wissler, who dubbed the vocals for the film's Scotty Beckett; and a Teutonic-sounding woman who approached her character--indeed, overtook and passed her--with a gutturalness that must have jarred those remembering the gentle Mama of the film's Tamara Shayne.

Evelyn Keyes, as in the film, made a late entrance, and for a while her abbreviated radio dialogue tended to reduce her to exclamations such as "Oh!" and "Al!," as well as "Oh, Al!" Jolson's acting was on the hammy side, almost completely our of "sync" even with 1948, which, after all, was several decades after his entry in show business. Bringing to life the young and breathless Al was especially troublesome for him. His performance was more of a reading, lacking the proper emotional shadings, although as he moved closer to his own age in the part he gained assurance.

Accompanied for both radio Jolson stories by Louis Silvers and Orchestra (Silvers, with his "Vitaphone Orchestra," had performed similar chores for the 1927 film of The Jazz Singer), Jolson was on surer turf in the musical interludes, giving the expected heartfelt renditions of "Ma Blushin' Rosie," "My Mammy," "Toot, Toot, Tootsie! (Goo'bye)," "You Made Me Love You," "April Showers," "Liza," "The Anniversary Song," and "Swanee." Nevertheless, a certain subdued quality was apparent in these Lux vocals: Jolson evidently felt obliged to "bring down" his Winter Garden style for the intimate medium of radio. He might better have let radio "come up" to him.

• • •

The screen's Jolson Story was superior to the sequel, Jolson Sings Again. As radio fare, though, the follow-up Jolson saga, aired two years later, had the edge on the earlier Lux presentation of the first Jolson saga.

For the airwaves Jolson Sings Again, William Demarest again narrated while Barbara Hale and Ludwig Donath also repeated their screen characters. The unbilled, accented actress who had portrayed Mama Yoelson in the first broadcast performed the part a final time--less aggressively than in the Jolson Story airing, perhaps because of the role's brevity in the sequel. Donath was polished in both radio outings. Interestingly, Demarest was able to put more punch into his Jolson Sings Again radio performance than he had achieved in the film version. Leading lady Hale had opportunities denied earlier to counterpart Keyes, grabbing several laughs with her drawling homespun humor.

Perhaps because he was required to run less of an acting

Barbara Hale, Al Jolson and William Demarest on The Lux Radio Theater dramatization of Jolson Sings Again in 1950.

gamut in Jolson Sings Again, Jolson's enactment was smoother this time around. He was, after all, playing himself in his own age bracket now, which clearly put him more at ease. He had fun with the part, dipping into his Southern accent intentionally every now and then and, in the more freely interpreted songs, slipping in such familiar self-congratulating, spoken Jolsonisms as "It's a gift" or "Oh, dat pretty."

The songs: "Is It True What They Say About Dixie?," "Back in Your Own Back Yard," "Chinatown, My Chinatown," "I'm Just Wild About Harry," "Baby Face," "I Only Have Eyes for You," "Sonny Boy," "Toot, Toot, Tootsie! (Goo'bye)," "Carolina in the Morning" and "Rock-a-Bye Your Baby with a Dixie Melody."

Incidentally, as preparations to make The Jolson Story began in the sequel's radio story, Jolson and Larry Parks did not meet as they had (thanks to trick photography, Parks, meeting Parks) in the film. Their encounter was mentioned on the Lux hour but was accomplished off-mike.

Many incidents in the broadcast of "Jolson I" had to be digested or simply dropped because of the crowded nature of the screenplay. (Columbia did not then know there would be a sequel.) When Jolson Sings Again was aired, however, because of its simpler narrative the producers managed to insert material not in the film. One new scene had Jolson, fidgety during the Santa Barbara preview of The Jolson Story, wander around outside the theater and talk to a newsboy.

Another bit not in the celluloid Jolson Sings Again occurred when the preview theater manager unthinkingly addressed Jolson as "Mr. Parks."

"I hope my wife knows me when I get home!," responded Jolson--to the delight of the program's studio audience (by then perhaps aware that the entertainer harbored at least a smidgen of resentment toward his younger, more visible alter ego).

Jolson's peculiar pill-taking business at this juncture in the film was omitted in the radio version.

Narrator Demarest wrapped up the dramatization of Jolson Sings Again by calling it "The story of a man who came back as no man ever did before."

Jolson came back one more time that evening--for The Lux Radio Theater's closing "informal" stars' chat, this one eventually to prove tragically ironic. When Jolson mentioned that there would probably be a third movie, William Demarest rejoined, "It would have to be called Jolson Sings Again and Again and Again...."

"You mean," asked a faintly incredulous-sounding Barbara Hale, "there would be another movie about your life?"

Replied Jolson with characteristic jauntiness, "I'm still living, honey, I'm still living."

Al Jolson would be dead in six months.

In the fall of 1950, Jolson, aged, tired, and ill, paid his own way to Korea and gave a hundred and sixty shows for our troops. Back home in Palm Springs, California, he visited briefly with wife Erle and small son Asa, Jr. (whom they adopted in 1948),[1] then flew to San Francisco to guest on Bing Crosby's radio show. There on October 23, 1950, in the city where he first gained prominence as a "single" performer, Al Jolson died of heart failure. With him in his hotel room were his long-time manager, Louis ("Eppy") Epstein, and his musician cronies, Harry Akst and Martin Fried. Harry Cohn was at the Friars Club when he heard, and wept openly in front of the members. Jolson was buried in Hollywood's Hillside Memorial Park, where his gravesite features an open-air, pillared mausoleum, a terraced waterfall and a statue of him down on one knee ostensibly singing "My Mammy."

Six months from then, Larry Parks was also virtually buried in Hollywood when he answered the question that began, "Are you now or have you ever been....?"

Reference

1. Al Jolson, Jr. (as he later was called), who received crippling injuries in a car accident in the sixties, was last known to be operating Al Jolson, Jr., Enterprises, including a small recording studio and two publishing companies on Nashville's Music Row.

▪ EPILOGUE ▪

Inspired by the recent successful television sales of old Jolson records, in the mid-1970s Columbia Pictures went to its vaults for the 70mm-stereophonic sound print of The Jolson Story that had been prepared for a 1969 reissue of the film in England. Toward the end of 1975, only months after Larry Parks' sudden death by heart attack, The Jolson Story was given a major re-release in the United States.

This time, unfortunately, moviegoers were so caught up in the strobic sensationalism of contemporary films that they stayed away. Many who did go complained, as did the Hollywood Reporter reviewer, that "The 70mm print crops heads too closely in some of the scenes." This was done to accommodate the wider new screen--even Gone with the Wind suffered the ignominy of sundry cast decapitations in this dubious "improvement" over the old postage stamp-shaped screen. There was also some grousing that blowing up the film to fit the enlarged new screen had caused graininess.

The West Coast première of The Jolson Story '75 was held at the Beverly Theater in Beverly Hills, followed by a buffet supper at the Friars Club which Jolson had helped to found and where the film's producer, Sidney Skolsky, was guest of honor. Among the others attending were Evelyn Keyes, William Demarest, and Parks' widow, Betty Garrett, and their sons, Garrett and Andrew.

Despite the vintage film's commercial failure now, at least show business circles once again became aware of the riches that could be mined from the Jolson story decades after the great entertainer's death.

Late in 1978, the "World Première" of a new musical play entitled Jolson was staged at the Paper Mill Playhouse in Millburn, New Jersey.

English-born Clive Baldwin, who had been making a living for years with both a singing and speaking voice startlingly like Jolson's, starred in the biographical musical comedy that covered the years of Jolson's relationship with Ruby Keeler (this time called Sally Baxter). The hackneyed book by Leslie Eberhard and David Levy stressed Jolson's alleged egomania, compounding the negativism by dramatizing a particularly inauspicious career epoch in the entertainer's life.

Furthermore, the clean-cut Baldwin, physically a more likely candidate for The Snooky Lanson Story, never suggested the electric stage presence with which Jolson mesmerized audiences. Baldwin moved and acted stiffly, and even his natural Jolson-like vocal gifts were undercut by a fatal new score that eschewed the Jolson standards everyone came to hear. Near the start in the Paper Mill run, however, the composers, Irwin Levine and L. Russell Brown, who earlier had written the hit song "Tie a Yellow Ribbon 'Round the Ole Oak Tree," were talking about strategically inserting a few familiar Jolson tunes. "Sonny Boy" and "My Mammy" found no substitutes in such intentionally derivative new numbers as "Little Sammy" and "Give Me a Good Ole Mammy Song."

Then, early in 1979, a musical dramatization of Jolson's entire life called Joley was presented at the North Stage Dinner Theater in Glen Cove, Long Island. [It was initially to be called Jolie, the usual spelling of Jolson's nickname, but then the creators realized that the mother of the Gabor sisters was named Jolie, and, fearing their show would be thought to be a biography of her, changed the spelling of the title.]

Although the veteran comedian-actor Jack Carter, who did Jolson imitations in clubs, originally had been up for the title role, when Joley opened Larry Kert of the New York theater was starred.

"It ran eight weeks," recalls director Jay Harnick. "About half the score was original songs, with lyrics by Herbert Hartig (who also wrote the book) and music by Milton Delugg. It was a no-bullshit story about this great entertainer who was not really a loveable character. Near the beginning, for instance, we had Georgie Jessel's character delivering his flowery Jolson eulogy and then saying privately, 'He was the worst son-of-a-bitch that ever lived.' But audiences, conditioned to love Jolson, wondered, 'Why are you telling

Sherry Rooney and Clive Baldwin in the title role of Jolson, a musical biography presented in 1978 on stage at the Paper Mill Playhouse, Millburn, New Jersey.

us all this?' The new songs were okay; they moved the story along. But the main success of the show was in the old, familiar tunes as performed by the star, Larry Kert--who, incidentally, did not attempt an imitation of Jolson but was more of a synthesis. As far as the story was concerned, there was no struggle-and-fail-struggle-and-fail in Jolson's life; he was clearly marked for stardom from the start. So we had to deal with personal conflicts."

Joley librettist-lyricist Hartig, who researched Jolson for six years, says he had never really been a fan but became fascinated by him "as the first superstar and the typical American hero who turned out to be a heel. But with Joley there

Larry Kert as Al Jolson in *The Parade of Stars* at the Palace Theater, New York, in 1983.

were insurmountable production, money, and time problems, as well as internal wars. Larry Kert began to believe he was the whole show. In the many years he had been in show business, he had never received the personal audience acceptance he received as Joley, so the show that made this possible must have had *something*. The following year, singing only the old Jolson songs, he toured the hinterlands in a production I had nothing to do with called *Al Jolson Tonight!* that was my show written sideways."

The writing of *Al Jolson Tonight!* was credited to Nicholas Dante (co-author of *A Chorus Line*), the direction and choreography to Michael Shawn.

Larry Kert is a good Broadway belter who made his mark as the young lead in the original production of *West Side Story*, and whose sister, songstress Anita Ellis, dubbed Rita Hayworth's singing in *Gilda*. During early stages of *Al Jolson Tonight!*, Kert said, "It's a production about Al Jolson as he really was, not as he was portrayed in the movie *The Jolson Story* ... Jolson made six or seven people unhappy, but about sixty million happy. We're going to tell a couple of the sadness things because we all have a crack in our mirror someplace." When audiences once again rejected the unsympathetic Jolson, though, the portrayal was softened a bit.

On May 22, 1983, television viewers got a look at Larry Kert's somewhat bloodless Jolson when he sang a medley of the man's songs on an ABC network special called The Parade of Stars, produced at the Palace Theater, New York, by Alexander Cohen. Kert also does Jolson selections in his nightclub performances.

In mid-1982, Jeff Britton, who produced the two Kert musicals about Jolson, announced he was starting all over again with a new stage script ("blessed by Ruby Keeler") by Larry Siegel and Walter Blen. This one was to deal with the Jolson-Keeler marriage plus the rivalry between Al Jolson and his brother Harry. Larry Kert was not mentioned for this production, but at various times Bert Convy and Eddie Fisher were.

In 1984, Jack Carter turned up again with new plans to portray Al Jolson. He revealed that he hoped to star in a one-man stage "drama with music" that he and publicist-author Michael Druxman were writing entitled Jolson: The Legend.

Somehow, one can't help doubting the possibility that, decades from now, there will be talk of a show called Prince: The Legend. Or even by the time this book comes out.

▪ FILM CREDITS ▪

THE JOLSON STORY. Columbia Pictures. Released: October 10, 1946. Producer: Sidney Skolsky. Director: Alfred E. Green. Screenplay: Stephen Longstreet. Adaptation: Harry Chandlee, Andrew Solt. Associate producer: Gordon S. Griffith. Cinematographer: Joseph Walker. Dances staged by: Jack Cole. Production numbers directed by: Joseph H. Lewis. Musical director: Morris Stoloff. Gowns: Jean Louis. Film editor: William Lyon. Make-up: Clay Campbell. Hair styles: Helen Hunt. Assistant director: Wilbur McGaugh. Art decoration: Stephen Goosson, Walter Holscher. Set decoration: William Kiernan, Louis Diage. Montage director: Lawrence W. Butler. Sound recording: Hugh McDowell. Vocal arrangements: Saul Chaplin. Orchestral arrangements: Martin Fried. Music recording: Edwin Wetzel. Re-recording: Richard Olson. Technicolor color director: Natalie Kalmus. Technicolor associate: Morgan Padelford. Running time: 128 minutes.

CAST: Larry Parks (Al Jolson), Evelyn Keyes (Julie Benson), William Demarest (Steve Martin), Bill Goodwin (Tom Baron), Ludwig Donath (Cantor Yoelson), Tamara Shayne (Mrs. Yoelson), John Alexander (Lew Dockstader), Jo-Carroll Dennsion (Ann Murray), Ernest Cossart (Father McGee), Scotty Beckett (young Al), William Forrest (Dick Glenn), Ann Todd (young Ann), Edwin Maxwell (Oscar Hammerstein), Emmett Vogan (Jonsey), Eric Wilton (Henry), Coulter Irwin (young priest), Jimmy Lloyd (Roy Anderson), Adele Roberts (ingenue), Bob Stevens, a.k.a Robert Kellard (Henry), Dan Stowell (ticket seller), Charles Marsh (man at theater), Harry Shannon (Riley the policeman), John Tyrrell (man in line), Joseph Palma (brakeman), Ted Stanhope (electrician), P.J. Kelley (doorman), Bud Gorman (call boy), Charles Jordan (assistant stage manager), Edward Kane (Ziegfeld), Pierre Watkin (architect), Fred Howard (man), Lilian Bond (woman), Eugene Borden (headwaiter), Eddie Rio (master of ceremonies), Will Wright (movie crank), Arthur Loft (stage manager), Edward

Keane (director), Eddie Featherstone (assistant stage manager), Bill Brandt (orchestra leader), Pat Lane (cameraman), Ralph Linn (recorder), Mike Lally (lab manager), George Magrill (stage gaffer), Helen O'Hara (dancer-actress), Jessie Arnold (wardrobe woman), Donna Dax (publicist), Clay Campbell (make-up man), "Sonny Boy" (Louis Traeger), Fred Sears (cutter), Elinor Vandiveer (maid), Franklyn Farnum, Bess Flowers (extras in audience), Major Sam Harris (man in nightclub), George and Ethel Martin, Rod Alexander, Virginia Hunter (chorus).

JOLSON SINGS AGAIN. Columbia Pictures. *Released:* August 17, 1949. *Producer:* Sidney Buchman. *Director:* Henry Levin. *Screenplay:* Sidney Buchman. *Cinematographer:* William Snyder. *Songs staged by:* Audrene Brier. *Music:* George Duning. *Musical director:* Morris Stoloff. *Costumes:* Jean Louis. *Film editor:* William Lyon. *Make-up:* Clay Campbell. *Hair styles:* Helen Hunt. *Assistant director:* Milton Feldman. *Art decoration:* Walter Holscher. *Set decoration:* William Kiernan. *Sound recording:* George Cooper, Philip Faulkner. *Music advisor:* Saul Chaplin. *Orchestrator:* Larry Russell. *Production manager:* Jack Fier. Photographed in Technicolor. *Running time:* 96 minutes.

CAST: Larry Parks (Al Jolson) Barbara Hale (Ellen Clark), William Demarest (Steve Martin), Ludwig Donath (Cantor Yoelson), Bill Goodwin (Tom Baron), Myron McCormick (Ralph Bryant), Tamara Shayne (Mrs. Yoelson), Eric Wilton (Henry), Robert Emmett Keane (Charlie), Peter Brocco (captain of waiters) Dick Cogan (soldier), Martin Garralaga (Mr. Estrada), Michael Cisney (writer), Ben Erway (writer), Helen Mowery (script girl), Morris Stoloff (orchestra leader), Philip Faulkner (sound mixer), Virginia Mullen (Mrs. Bryant), Nelson Leigh (theater manager), Margie Stapp (nurse), Milton Delugg (overseas accordionist), Major Sam Harris, Bess Flowers (on-stage extras), Frank McLure, Jock O'Mahoney, Betty Hill, Charles Regan, Charles Perry, Richard Gordon, David Newell, Joe Gilbert, David Horsley, Wanda Perry, Louise Illington, Gertrude Astor, Steve Benton, Eleanor Marvak (bits).

BIBLIOGRAPHY

Agee, James. Agee on Film. New York: McDowell, Obolensky, 1958.

Atkinson, Brooks. Broadway. New York: Macmillan, 1970.

Bacall, Lauren. By Myself. New York: Knopf, 1978.

Best, Marc. Those Endearing Young Charms. Cranbury, N.J.: Barnes, 1971.

Brenman-Gibson, Margaret. Clifford Odets: American Playwright. New York: Atheneum, 1981.

Cahn, Sammy. I Should Care. New York: Arbor House, 1974.

Capra, Frank. The Name Above the Title. New York: Macmillan, 1971.

Carey, Gary. Cukor & Co. New York: Museum of Modern Art, 1971.

Carey, Gary, with Joseph L. Mankiewicz. More About All About Eve. New York: Random House, 1972.

Casper, Joseph Andrew. Stanley Donen. Metuchen, N.J.: Scarecrow, 1983.

Chierichetti, David. Hollywood Costume Design. New York: Harmony, 1976.

Ciment, Michel. Kazan on Kazan. New York: Viking, 1974.

Connor, Jim. Ann Miller: Tops in Taps. New York: Franklin Watts, 1981.

Corliss, Richard, ed. The Hollywood Screenwriters. New York: Avon, 1972.

Crowther, Bosley. The Lion's Share. New York: Dutton, 1957.

DeMille, Cecil B. Autobiography. Englewood Cliffs, N.J.: Prentice-Hall, 1959.

Dick, Bernard F. The Star-Spangled Screen. Lexington: University Press of Kentucky, 1985.

Dickens, Homer. The Films of James Cagney. Secaucus, N.J.: Citadel, 1972.

Dmytryk, Edward. It's a Hell of a Life But Not a Bad Living. New York: Times, 1978.

Eells, George. Hedda and Louella. New York: Putnam, 1972.

Eells, George. The Life That Late He Led. New York: Putnam, 1967.

Ewen, David. Complete Book of the American Musical Theatre. New York: Henry Holt, 1958.

Fordin, Hugh, ed. Film Daily Yearbook of Motion Pictures and Television. New York: Film TV Daily, 1970.

Francisco, Charles. The Radio City Music Hall. New York: Dutton, 1979.

Freedland, Michael. Jolson. New York: Stein and Day, 1972.

Gelman, Howard. The Films of John Garfield. Secaucus, N.J.: Citadel, 1975.

Guiles, Fred Lawrence. Hanging on in Paradise. New York: McGraw-Hill, 1975.

Halliwell, Leslie. Seats in All Parts. New York: Scribner, 1985.

Head, Edith, and Paddy Calistro. Edith Head's Hollywood. New York: Dutton, 1983.

Hirschhorn, Clive. Gene Kelly. Chicago: Regnery, 1974.

Jessel, George, with John Austin. The World I Lived In. Chicago: Regnery, 1975.

Keyes, Evelyn. I Am a Billboard. New York: Lyle Stuart, 1971.

Keyes, Evelyn. Scarlett O'Hara's Younger Sister. Secaucus, N.J.: Lyle Stuart, 1977.

Knight, Arthur, intro. The New York Times Directory of of the Film. New York: Arno, 1971.

Kobal, John. People Will Talk. New York: Knopf, 1986.

Kobal, John. Rita Hayworth: The Time, The Place and the Woman. London: Allen, 1977.

Larkin, Rochelle. Hail, Columbia. New Rochelle, N.Y.: Arlington House, 1975.

Lawrence, Jerome. Actor: The Life and Times of Paul Muni. New York: Putnam, 1974.

Loney, Glenn. Unsung Genius. New York: Franklin Watts, 1984.

Maltin, Leonard, ed. Hollywood Kids. New York: Popular Library, 1978.

Michael, Paul, and James Robert Parish, eds. The American Movies Reference Book. Englewood Cliffs, N.J.: Prentice-Hall, 1969.

Michael, Paul, and James Robert Parish. The Emmy Awards. New York: Crown, 1970.

Moore, Dick. Twinkle, Twinkle, Little Star. New York: Harper & Row, 1984.

Navasky, Victor S. Naming Names. New York: Viking, 1980.

Osborne, Robert. Academy Awards Illustrated. Hollywood: Marvin Miller, 1965.

Parish, James Robert, and Ronald L. Bowers. The M-G-M Stock Company. New Rochelle, N.Y.: Arlington House, 1973.

Parish, James Robert, and Lennard DeCarl. Hollywood Players: The Forties. New Rochelle, N.Y.: Arlington House, 1976.

Parish, James Robert, and Michael R. Pitts. Film Directors: A Guide to Their American Films. Metuchen, N.J.: Scarecrow, 1974.

Parish, James Robert. The RKO Gals. New Rochelle, N.Y.: Arlington House, 1974.

Peary, Danny, ed. Close-Ups. New York: Workman, 1978.

Ragan, David. Who's Who in Hollywood. New Rochelle, N.Y.: Arlington House, 1976.

Sarris, Andrew. The American Cinema. New York: Dutton, 1968.

Schary, Dore. Heyday. Boston: Little, Brown, 1979.

Sennett, Ted, ed. The Old-Time Radio Book. New York: Pyramid, 1976.

Silke, James R. Here's Looking at You, Kid. Boston: Little, Brown, 1976.

Silvers, Phil, with Robert Saffron. This Laugh is on Me. Englewood Cliffs, N.J.: Prentice-Hall, 1973.

Skolsky, Sidney. Don't Get Me Wrong--I Love Hollywood. New York: Putnam, 1975.

Springer, John. All Talking! All Singing! All Dancing! New York: Citadel, 1966.

Swindell, Larry. Body and Soul: The Story of John Garfield. New York: Morrow, 1975.

Taylor, John Russell, and Arthur Jackson. The Hollywood Musical. New York: McGraw-Hill, 1971.

Thomas, Bob. King Cohn. New York: Putnam, 1967.

Thomas, Bob. Winchell. Garden City, N.Y.: Doubleday, 1971.

Tuska, Jon, ed. Close-Up: The Contract Director. Metuchen, N.J.: Scarecrow, 1976.

Twomey, Alfred E., and Arthur F. McClure. The Versatiles. Cranbury, N.J.: Barnes, 1969.

Vallance, Tom. The American Musical. New York: Barnes, 1970.

Vermilye, Jerry, and Mark Ricci. The Films of Elizabeth Taylor. Secaucus, N.J.: Citadel, 1976.

Walker, Joseph, and Juanita Walker. The Light on Her Face. Hollywood: ASC Press, 1984.

Wiley, Mason, and Damien Bona. Inside Oscar. New York: Ballantine, 1986.

Wilk, Max. They're Playing Our Song. New York: Atheneum, 1973.

Winters, Shelley. Shelley, Also Known as Shirley. New York: Morrow, 1980.

Zierold, Norman. The Moguls. New York: Coward-McCann, 1969.

ABOUT THE AUTHOR

Doug McClelland, a freelance writer-lecturer on film, is the author of six previous film-related books:

The Unkindest Cuts: The Scissors and the Cinema

Susan Hayward: The Divine Bitch

Down the Yellow Brick Road: The Making of the Wizard of Oz

The Golden Age of "B" Movies

Hollywood on Ronald Reagan: Friends and Enemies Discuss Our President, The Actor

Hollywood on Hollywood: Tinsel Town Talks

McClelland was an arts editor for The Newark Evening News in the 1950s, and editor of Record World magazine in New York City from 1961-1972. His work has appeared in a number of anthologies, including Hollywood Kids, 500 Best American Films to Buy, Rent or Videotape and The Real Stars (volumes one, two and three). He has also been published in such periodicals as Films in Review, After Dark, Hollywood Studio Magazine, Films and Filming, Quirk's Reviews, Film Fan Monthly and Filmograph.

In addition, Doug McClelland has been a consultant on many books by the prolific James Robert Parish, several of them for Scarecrow Press.